CHINA

BY BIKE™

TAIWAN, HONG KONG, CHINA'S EAST COAST

CHINA
BY BIKE™
TAIWAN, HONG KONG, CHINA'S EAST COAST

Roger Grigsby

THE
MOUNTAINEERS

Published by
The Mountaineers
1011 SW Klickitat Way
Seattle, Washington 98134

8 7 6 5 4
5 4 3 2 1

Published simultaneously in Canada by Douglas & McIntyre, Ltd.,
1615 Venables Street, Vancouver, B.C. V5L 2H1

Published simultaneously in Great Britain by Cordee,
3a DeMontfort Street, Leicester, England, LE1 7HD

Manufactured in the United States of America

Edited by Kris Fulsaas
Maps by Roger Grigsby
All photographs by Roger Grigsby
Cover design by Watson Graphics
Typesetting and layout by The Mountaineers Books

Cover photograph: Badaling Great Wall; *inset:* country road in Shandong
Frontispiece: Hanshan Temple, Suzhou

Library of Congress Cataloging-in-Publication Data
Grigsby, Roger.
   China by bike / Roger Grigsby.
      p.   cm.
   Includes index.
   ISBN 0-89886-410-0
      1. Bicycle touring--China--Guidebooks. 2. Bicycle trails--China--Guide-
   books. 3. China--Guidebooks. I. Title.
   GV1046.C6G75   1994
   796.6'4'0951--dc20   94-17104
                                                              CIP

Printed on recycled paper

ACKNOWLEDGMENTS

Many thanks to the following people for helping make this book possible: The folks at The Mountaineers Books, for their encouragement, expertise, and patience. Mrs. Qingyi Dougherty, the Chinese language teacher who started me down the road to China. Roger and Marcy Sands at the Bicycle Center in Santa Cruz, for technical help acquiring and setting up bicycles and touring gear. Dr. Alex Moulton, whose wonderful Moulton bicycles make China's rough roads a pleasure to tour. Mr. Li and his Kowloon Flying Ball Cycle Shop, for technical help, information, and letters by early "guerrilla cyclists" who braved the wrath of China's public security forces. David Bliss, Kevin Grigsby, and Michael Grigsby, who were co-pilots and photo models on these tours. Carol West and Karl Cook, who kept my business, O'mei Restaurant, running smoothly while I cycled in China. My parents, who infected me with a love of travel, and my wife, April Shen, for tolerating a house full of bikes, books, and maps.

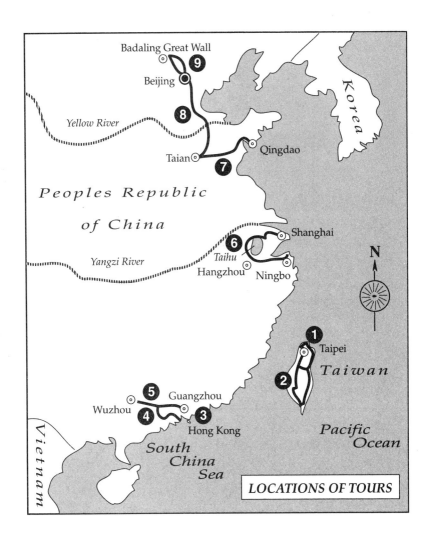

LOCATIONS OF TOURS

CONTENTS

PREFACE

Why has no one published a guidebook for bicycle touring in China until now? Before Deng Xiaoping opened the eastern coastal provinces for economic development, the People's Republic of China (PRC) was not legally open for independent bike travel. When the PRC first permitted independent travel to foreigners in 1981, the only legal way to travel was by conventional transportation—train, bus, or plane—between cities that had been designated as "open areas." If you got off the train and stayed outside of these areas, you were quickly told to get back on and continue to an open area. Under these conditions, it was impossible to legally tour by bicycle.

In the mid-1980s, there were cyclists who rode from Hong Kong to Tibet and from Beijing to Kashgar, but their unauthorized tours involved playing hide-and-seek with the authorities. One such tourist wrote to Mr. Li at the Kowloon Flying Ball Cycle Shop, and said that he had to cycle through larger towns at night to avoid detection and often slept in road workers' huts because hotel workers would report him to authorities. Unless you were connected with a group or paid a hefty fee for official guides, there was no legal way to cycle tour unless you did it "guerrilla-style."

In time, the central government began loosening its economic stranglehold on the eastern coastal provinces, which are situated to engage in foreign trade and generate hard currency. As these areas developed, restrictions on free-form travel were either rescinded or went unenforced. Guangdong Province was open by 1988, and selected areas in Fujian, Zhejiang, and Jiangsu followed. But it was only as recently as 1990 that foreigners were allowed to travel freely throughout the eastern coastal provinces. Although packaged group tours are still an option for cyclists who would rather not deal with trip logistics, commercial tours can never match the freedom and adventure of doing it yourself. Now there is no official barrier to seeing China by bike on your own terms.

Another reason a guidebook has not been published before now is the lack of a method for accurately describing tour routes. A guidebook to cycle touring in China must deal with problems not encountered in western countries: the written language makes signs impossible, most roads lack names and numbers, and detailed maps are only printed in Chinese. But now, the advent of accurate bicycle mileage computers makes it possible to follow routes even if you can't read the signs.

Conventional travel guidebooks focus on destinations and provide important information on transportation, tourist spots, and culture. But the bicycle tourist spends most of the time in between destinations described in conventional guides, passing through small towns and countryside never mentioned in such guidebooks. Because cycle tour-

Opposite: *A modern cycle shop in Shaoxing*

ing focuses on the process of travel, not just the end destination, the cycle tourist also needs:

1. maps and logs to navigate these "in-between" areas;
2. notes on places too small to be in a conventional guidebook;
3. assistance in managing the daily routines of lodging and meals.

China by Bike provides this information. It is a "hand-holding" guidebook for the cyclist who wants to tour China but doesn't know where to start. It is not intended as a comprehensive guidebook to this vast country, and should be used together with a conventional guidebook. This book is not intended as a general introduction to cycle touring, and it assumes that a prospective *China by Bike* tourist has already had some cycle touring experience. Tackling China as a first tour would add cruel new meaning to the term "shakedown tour"!

A NOTE ABOUT SAFETY

Safety is an important concern in all outdoor activities. No guidebook can alert you to every hazard or anticipate the limitations of every reader. Therefore, the descriptions of roads, routes, and natural features in this book are not representations that a particular place or excursion will be safe for your party. When you follow any of the routes described in this book, you assume responsibility for your own safety. Under normal conditions, such excursions require the usual attention to traffic, road conditions, weather, terrain, the capabilities of your party, and other factors. Keeping informed on current conditions and exercising common sense are the keys to a safe, enjoyable outing.

Political conditions may add to the risks of travel in China in ways that this book cannot predict. When you travel, you assume this risk, and should keep informed of political developments that may make safe travel difficult or impossible.

The Mountaineers

Opposite: *Roadsigns in a typical Taiwanese town*

PART I

CHINA BY BIKE

WHY CHOOSE CHINA?

China has long been a favored destination for adventure travelers because its complex culture and history are uniquely outside the domain of western culture. For westerners, travel in China is like visiting another world: everything is new and different. China's isolation over the last 45 years has only heightened this sense of mystery and foreignness.

As China opens to the outside world, its ancient culture is rapidly changing and merging with modern global society. Freeways, high-rise buildings, computers, and satellite television are beginning to invade formerly remote areas. In spite of modernization, China is still an exotic destination: fascinating remnants of old China are waiting to be discovered by tourists who get off the beaten path, especially those who see China by bike.

A cycle tourist in China experiences things that ordinary tourists seldom do. Pedal into a yellow mud village where people are herding pigs and hand-grinding corn on stone mills. After a crowd forms, an old woman curiously feels the hair on your arm and cracks a big toothless grin. It is the first time she has seen a westerner in the flesh.

Ride out of Suzhou through fields of brilliant yellow rapeseed flowers, then stop at the Grand Canal to watch endless trains of barges and junks. Watch a Chinese "cowboy" herd his flock across the road: where else can a thousand white geese cause a traffic jam? Rise before dawn and climb the Great Wall to view the sunrise from the same spot an imperial sentry watched it a thousand years ago.

Leave the steep coast of eastern Taiwan and pump up through a gorge of solid marble. Relax in open-air hot springs before climbing into the clouds and crossing the central mountains. On a rainy day, repair a flat tire on the porch of a Taiwanese farmhouse: grandma serves tea while the whole family grins and offers advice.

In Hebei Province, pass a jangling horsecart with the driver asleep in the back. The driver wakes and gives you a smiling "thumbs up." At a seedy country inn, the owner is proud that you chose his place to spend the night. He paints "friendship is forever" on a scroll and gives it to you to remember the occasion. The cycle tourist gets close enough to everyday life to taste what Chinese call *ren ching wei*, the "flavor of humanness."

Cycle touring also gets you close to the unforgettable tastes and smells of China: the rich taste of braised pork in Wuxi, and the aromatic sweetness of fresh yellow wine in Shaoxing. The sharp taste of raw garlic shoots in Shandong, and the mellow fennel and cumin flavors of Muslim Chinese cuisine. The mysterious smell of incense in temples and the acrid smell of firecrackers. The salty smells of dried fish and fermented shrimp sauce on Hong Kong's islands. The fresh smell of Taiwanese tea gardens and the musty smell of herb shops as you roll through foothill villages.

And then there are the pleasures only a cycle tourist can know: the sharp edge that a long ride puts on your appetite, making even simple food a delight. Wheeling quietly through alleys and lanes where cars

Sampan woman, Lantau Island

can never go. That wonderful feeling of empowerment that comes from propelling yourself thousands of miles along unfamiliar roads in a foreign land.

Everyone has a fantasy of China: inscrutable, mysterious, ancient, and cultured. When people go to China to see that fantasy, they are often overwhelmed and disappointed with the reality. Where is the boy playing a flute on the back of a water buffalo? Where are the poets sipping wine in bamboo groves? How could this place produce the incredible cultural tradition depicted in picture books? The photo-fantasies do exist, but only between long stretches of the real China. This does not mean the real China is not worth experiencing; it just means there is no way you can imagine beforehand what it will be like. Look past the fantasy and you will see some amazing people and places.

Cycle touring in China is not a relaxing "vacation" in the usual sense of the term. Rather than "getting away from it all," you will be in the thick of it all. There will be days when traffic is obnoxious, and times when you want to escape the crowds of people staring at you. Prepare to be exhausted by the mental and physical challenges.

If your touring experience has been in areas of raw natural beauty, be aware that China is different. The tours in this guidebook take the cyclist to few scenes that would qualify as "unspoiled scenery," and that is what you would expect in an area populated for several millennia. Scenery in China almost always includes a human element, from quaint villages to ugly power plants. These tours focus on the culture, the people, and their interaction with the land. Cycle tourists must train their eyes to see the beautiful in the midst of the mundane.

Most westerners think of China as one culture, but at street level the cycle tourist learns that China has many faces. The People's Republic of China (PRC) is considered *the* China, but Taiwan and Hong Kong retain aspects of culture, religion, and scenery that cannot be seen in the PRC. Taiwanese rural scenery is very Chinese, but is distinct from that seen in the PRC. Hong Kong's international flavor and the laid-back life on the outlying islands are different from both Taiwan and the PRC. In the PRC, the southeastern, east-central, and northeastern tours each introduce the cyclist to a different face of the mainland culture: different languages, different architecture, and different foods. The nine tours in this guidebook introduce the cyclist to each of these unique faces of China.

Taiwan

Taiwan, an island off the mainland PRC coastal province of Fujian, has been inhabited by the Chinese and considered a province of China for about 500 years. The original settlers came from Fujian and brought their language (*minan hua*) and culture with them. In 1949 this sleepy island was changed forever when Chiang Kai Shek's Kuomintang (KMT) government fled the mainland as Mao Zedong set up the communist PRC government. The KMT set up shop in Taipei, claiming itself as the legitimate government of the Chinese people. Many soldiers and police loyal to the KMT also fled to Taiwan to save themselves from the slaughter that followed Mao's ascent to power. These people and their descendants are the source of the variety of languages and cuisines in the Taipei area.

The arrival of the KMT was not altogether a benign thing for the native Taiwanese population. While they were all of Chinese descent, the new arrivals were called "outside-born-people," and sometimes considered themselves a cut above the locals. When they first arrived, they had hopes that Mao's government would collapse and they could return to their "real" home and positions of power on the mainland. It did not work out that way.

The Taiwanese, or "native-born-people," suffered confiscation of property and political oppression when the KMT first arrived. Two generations have passed since 1949, and some of the old rifts between "outsiders" and "insiders" have healed. The KMT government has presided over an incredible growth in the island's prosperity, bringing to realization one of the old names for Taiwan: "Prosperity Island." Now some Taiwanese talk of declaring independence as a nation and severing future affiliation with the mainland. The PRC government has strenuously objected to this, confirming that Taiwan is still a part of China, and that the political story of Taiwan is not yet finished.

For cyclists, Taiwan has an abundance of natural beauty and great roads, but some parts of the island are better than others. The economic prosperity of the last two decades has changed the western plains from a predominantly rural rice-farming area into a checkerboard of rice paddies, industrial plants, and high-tech research parks. Although it is flat and easy to cycle, the traffic and large towns make this the least desirable part of Taiwan to tour. The dramatic eastern coast of Taiwan is still relatively undeveloped because it is cut off from the west by the imposing central mountain range. This coast and the cross-island highways that traverse the mountains provide great cycle touring, as does the route along the foothills above the western plain.

In Taiwan, expect an interesting mix of the traditional and the modern. Cities have nightlife and western amenities, but you can be in pastoral countryside after an hour's ride. Every Taiwanese town has at least one colorful temple where incense and prayers are offered and festival days are celebrated with firecrackers and parades. Food is good throughout the island, and Taipei has some of the best Chinese restaurants in the world.

The dark tunnels, cliff-hanger roads, and steep climbs on the Taiwan tours in this guidebook are physically challenging, but they are exhilarating and worth every drop of sweat. The areas explored are not densely populated, so, unlike in the PRC, scenic spots are not overrun by local tourists. For the cycle tourist who wants to see spectacular natural scenery, Taiwan is a must.

Hong Kong and Macao

Great Britain acquired Hong Kong in 1841 as a result of the Opium Wars, and in 1898 added the New Territories. Great Britain's ninety-nine-year lease of Hong Kong will expire in 1997, and control of Hong Kong will revert to the PRC. Currently there is no information on how that will affect visa requirements for entry to Hong Kong.

Hong Kong is small and crowded, with some of the world's highest population densities on the Kowloon Peninsula. Neither the island of Hong Kong nor the tip of Kowloon is a good place to cycle: nonstop traffic, steep hills, and huge crowds. Limit your biking here to getting from the airport to lodgings and to the outlying islands. Plan on exploring Hong Kong itself by foot or tram. The New Territories has village scenery similar to that of the Pearl River Delta in the PRC, but navigating in and out of the urban areas is not worth the results now that the PRC is open to travel.

So why stop in Hong Kong? First, it is a good way to acclimatize yourself to Asia, especially if this is your first visit. You can get over the worst part of jet lag and ease into Chinese culture slowly. The tour of the island of Lantau (Tour No. 3), as well as visits to the small islands of Lamma, Pengchau, and Cheongchau, is very relaxing and offers interesting contrast to the intense cityscape of Hong Kong. These islands, less than an hour from Hong Kong by ferry, offer fishing-village scenery, isolated beaches, and rural countryside. Excellent seafood at a

Temple in the fishing village of Tai O

fraction of the prices found in Hong Kong is another attraction.

Second, because it is convenient to fly to Hong Kong from any part of the world, it is a logical entry point to southern China. Both the Pearl River Delta tour (Tour No. 4) and the Xijiang River tour (Tour No. 5) in this guidebook start with a ferry trip from Hong Kong.

Finally, because most religious sites in the PRC were destroyed during the Cultural Revolution, temples, shrines, and monasteries in Hong Kong are a good place to see living examples of southern Chinese religious practices. Whether you are cycling or not, Hong Kong's status as a world-class international city makes it an exciting place to visit.

Macao is the most convenient cycling entry point into the PRC for those starting their tours from Hong Kong. Macao began life as a Portuguese colony, but is now a melange of colonial architecture and southern Chinese culture that should not be missed.

People's Republic of China

In this book, "People's Republic of China" (PRC) designates the area under the political control of the current government seated in Beijing. It is both a place on the Chinese mainland and a political system. While for most people the PRC is the "Real China," the people of Hong Kong and Taiwan are every bit as Chinese as the people in the PRC: their history and culture come from the same source. The difference is political, not cultural.

The political rulers of the PRC claim that Hong Kong and Taiwan are part of China. The Republic of China (ROC) government in Taiwan largely agrees, except they claim that their government is the legitimate government of China's people, and the PRC government illegitimately occupies China.

One has to admire the pluck of the ROC government and their commitment to a non-communist form of government for the Chinese people, but the reality is that the PRC government has political control of over 1.2 billion people, nearly a quarter of the earth's population. The PRC government and economy is theoretically "socialist," but the reality leans toward a market economy with a heavy dose of political control.

When the PRC was established by Mao Zedong in 1949, his idea was to effect a total revolutionary remake of China: out with the old "man-eating society" and onward to the new "people's paradise." Millions of people lost their lives in the largely unacknowledged holocaust that was the result of Mao's social engineering. The final result: Mao's fantasy didn't work.

Now, the PRC political elite is facing economic reality. They're gradually removing socialist prohibitions against private ownership and enterprise, and the Chinese people are beginning to prosper. But these same politicians still won't admit that they're moving toward "capitalism." They prefer to call it "socialism, Chinese style." Referring to this discrepancy, Deng Xiaoping has said, "Who cares whether you call it a cat, so long as it catches mice...."

What does this mean to the cycle tourist in China? If these changes had not occurred, China would probably still be controlled by xenophobic elites who view foreigners as a cultural pollutant. In short, Deng's economic liberalization is what has made it possible to tour China by bike.

The Pearl River Delta (Tour No. 4) in southern Guangdong Province is a fertile area with rice, sugarcane, and other tropical crops. The language and culture are Cantonese, and the economy is rapidly modernizing.

The prosperous provinces of Jiangsu and Zhejiang in east-central PRC (Tour No. 6) are known as "the land of fish and rice." Cities here were advanced centers of culture even in the thirteenth century, when Marco Polo visited Hangzhou and described it as "without doubt the finest and most splendid city in the world." The languages are related to Mandarin Chinese, but the culture retains a southern flavor.

From Qingdao north to Taian, Beijing, and the Great Wall (Tour Nos. 7, 8, and 9), the culture is northern Chinese and languages are dialects of Mandarin Chinese. Wheat is more common than rice, and the harsher climate has evoked a different architectural response. Shandong Province is considered poor, but has some of the most interesting village scenery of all the tours in this guidebook.

PLANNING YOUR TRIP

Passports and Visas

For most people, a visa is not required to enter Hong Kong or Macao, only a passport. This situation may change when Hong Kong reverts to the PRC in 1997. For more information on visa requirements, check your conventional Hong Kong guidebook.

Taiwan and the PRC both require visas. The Taiwan visa is valid for a period of five years for multiple entries. In the United States, get a Taiwan visa at the Coordination Council for North American Affairs Office. Refer to a good general Taiwan guidebook for addresses.

PRC visas may be obtained in Hong Kong, but why waste time waiting in lines and dealing with officials when you could be riding on the islands? Get a visa in your home country through the PRC consulate. The standard PRC tourist visa is for one entry only and is usually valid for ninety days from issue. Another reason to get a PRC visa in your home country is the possibility of visa policy changes by the PRC. Find out about changes that might affect your itinerary before confirming flight plans, et cetera. Refer to a good general China guidebook for consulate addresses.

It is a good idea to make photocopies of the personal data pages and visa pages of your passport and store them separately in your luggage in case you lose your passport.

Other Documents

Besides your passport and valid visas, no other documents are necessary for travel in China.

There is no need for an International Youth Hostel (IYH) membership card because the hostels in Taiwan and the youth hostel in Guangzhou are not a part of the IYH system. Hong Kong hostels are IYH affiliates, but they are not conveniently located.

These days, student ID cards do not carry much weight in the PRC unless your school has official links with a university in the PRC and you are visiting as part of an exchange program.

Health Insurance

If you have health insurance, check on its applicability to occurrences in foreign countries, and whether your medical expenses while abroad are recompensable. Be prepared to pay for any medical services at the time you receive them, and bill your insurance company later. Don't expect the Chinese clinic or doctor to directly bill your insurance company.

Research

What kind of research should you do before embarking on a cycling tour in China? If your objective is to preplan lodging for every night or plan your budget down to the last dollar—forget it. That kind of precision is both unnecessary and impossible for cycle touring in China. The core information needed for a successful tour is contained in a combination of this guidebook, a conventional tourist guidebook, a phrase book, and the maps listed in the next section.

Plan to supplement *China by Bike* with at least one other conventional guidebook for Taiwan, Hong Kong, and the PRC. *China by Bike* is geared to provide information on the "in-between" places and doesn't attempt to provide information readily available in conventional guides. Use such guides for their major city maps and tourist information, commercial transport information, and further discussion of Chinese culture. Select guides that emphasize detailed city maps and up-to-date lodging options. Guidebooks overladen with color photos and general information about China are not worth their weight in your panniers. The ever-popular Lonely Planet Guides publishes excellent books that cover the PRC, Hong Kong, and Taiwan, but the fast pace of economic change quickly outpaces their price information. Another good guidebook for the PRC is *The China Guidebook* by Fredric Kaplan (New York: Houghton Mifflin, 1991), in the Eurasian Travelguide series.

If you do not speak Chinese, a phrase book is a must-carry item. The compact Lonely Planet *Mandarin Chinese Phrasebook* is excellent, as are phrase books published by Dover, Hugo, and Harrap. Be sure the one you pick has phrases written in Chinese characters as well as romanized text: if you cannot pronounce Chinese properly, the person with whom you are trying to communicate will be able to read the characters in your phrase book. In the back of this guidebook you will find a simple phraseguide oriented to the cycle tourist's needs that can augment any phrase book you choose.

Gear any further research toward making your trip a richer cultural experience by learning more about China's history, geography, culture, and cuisine. The following books are a good place to start. For Chinese history, check out *China—A New History*, by John K. Fairbanks (Boston: Belknap Press of Harvard University Press, 1992). On Chinese culture, consider *Culture Shock! China, a guide to customs and etiquette*, by Kevin Sinclair (Portland, Ore.: Graphic Arts Center Publishing Co., 1990), *Coping with China*, by Richard King and Sandra Schatzky (Oxford: Basil Blackwell Ltd., 1991), and *Swallowing Clouds*, by A. Zee (New York: Simon and Schuster, 1991). The last is a fascinating little book about the interplay of language, culture, and cuisine. Don't overlook books on Chinese cuisine as an insight into the culture.

It has been said that when the Chinese are not eating, they are either talking about food or thinking about it!

Novice bicycle tourists will want more information on bicycle touring techniques, as well as health and safety concerns in third-world conditions. *The Bicycle Touring Manual*, by Rob van der Plas (San Francisco: Bicycle Books, 1993), contains a good listing of secondary sources and is great for learning basic cycle touring skills, bike repairs, and maintenance while on the road. *Bicycle Touring International*, by Kameel Nasr (San Francisco: Bicycle Books, 1992), has information for cycle touring in any country in the world, but the section on China is too general to be of much use. However, it does contain a useful appendix of prevailing winds worldwide, as well as rainfall and temperature tables. On techniques for healthy travel, consider *Staying Healthy: in Asia, Africa and Latin America*, by Dirk G. Schroeder (Chico, Calif.: Moon Publications, 1993), and *The Pocket Doctor*, 2d ed., by Steven Bezruchka (Seattle, Wash.: The Mountaineers, 1993).

Some guidebooks suggest embassies and official tourism agencies as good sources of information, but I found them of little use. The Chinese International Tourism Service (CITS) was set up to coordinate and sell preset tours in China, and to deal with foreigners once they arrive.

Taiwan road signs usually don't have subtitles.

CITS also serves the government's purposes by extracting hard currency from "foreign guests" and by keeping them out of trouble (read: keeping them under control). Another reason CITS has little to offer is it is not accustomed to foreigners traveling by bicycle. The bicycle is used for everyday transportation by the average Chinese; rich people take taxis or have their own car. Because foreigners are considered "rich," many Chinese are surprised that they would tour by bike.

Your travel agent, however, is a useful resource. Don't stop at buying airline tickets; use your agent's services to locate and book a hotel near the airport for your first few days after arrival. Prebooking may save you money, and it will certainly add a sense of security if you know where you will be staying when you step off the plane and ride out of the airport. Make sure your agent has the street address of the hotel and can locate it on a map for you. Do not book a hotel to which it is inconvenient to cycle from the airport.

Maps

In Taiwan and Hong Kong, good Chinese/romanized maps are available in the airports and urban areas. But in the PRC, most maps of a scale small enough to be useful to cyclists are currently available only in Chinese. The best small-scale PRC road maps with romanized place names are the series of four maps by Nelles Maps. Although Nelles Maps don't have Chinese characters, they are informative because topographic shadings give cyclists an idea of the terrain.

Map 1: Northeastern China
Map 2: Northern China
Map 3: Central China
Map 4: Southern China

Buy Map Nos. 2, 3, and 4 for the PRC tours in this guidebook (Tour Nos. 4, 5, 6, 7, 8, and 9). Map No. 1, which covers the far northeastern part of the PRC, is outside the areas covered in this guidebook. Nelles also produces an excellent map of Taiwan.

If you cannot find the Nelles Maps at your local bookshop or map store, try Thomas Bros. Maps, 550 Jackson Street, San Francisco, CA 94133-5188; telephone (415) 981-7520 or (800) 969-3072; fax (415) 981-7529. Otherwise, write directly to Nelles Verlag, Schleissheimer Strasse 371b, D-8000 Munchen 45, Federal Republic of Germany. Nelles Maps were not available in the PRC when I toured there in 1993. Don't wait until you are overseas to obtain them.

In Taiwan, a limited selection of books and maps is available upstairs at the Chiang Kai Shek Airport Departures lounge newsstands. These stands may not be open if you arrive in the evening. In Taipei, look for foreign language bookstores on Chungshan North Road. Once you are on the road in Taiwan, local city and county maps in Chinese are available at magazine stands near train and bus stations.

In Hong Kong, tourist maps of Hong Kong and Macao are available at the tourist information counters in Kai Tak Airport. Look for these counters in the hallway after leaving customs inspection but before entering the Arrivals area. Bookstores in Hong Kong also stock excellent maps of the Pearl River Delta area (Tour No. 4). The "Map of Macao and Zhuhai" and the "Pearl Delta Touring Map" are published in Hong Kong by Universal Publications Ltd.; the "Pearl River Delta Tourist Map" is published by Guangdong Surveying and Mapping Technology Corporation. These maps are also available in some Chinese-language bookstores outside of China. Look for bookstores in Hong Kong's major tourist shopping centers such as the New World Centre at the foot of Nathan Road in Kowloon or in the shopping arcades around major hotels on the Hong Kong side.

Currently in the PRC, small-scale maps with romanized place names are limited to city maps and major tourist destinations, and are designed for people who are using conventional transportation. These maps are usually available at no cost at large tourist hotels, or for a small fee from hawkers near train stations or other transportation hubs.

The best spots in the PRC for maps in Chinese are the New China Bookstores (*Xinhua shudian*) in Guangzhou, Shanghai, or Beijing. Look for them on the city maps of your conventional guidebook. Once you are in the store, find the map section and ask for a *fensheng dituci*, an atlas broken down by province, or a *fensheng gonglu jiaotong dituci*, a transportation atlas by province. In smaller cities—*not* villages—the hotels often have simple town maps available. For Tour No. 9, look for a map of Beijing (*Beijingshichuantu*) that depicts the whole administrative area as far north as the Badaling Great Wall. These maps are available upstairs at the Wangfujing New China Bookstore in Beijing.

Some cyclists may find it easier to use photocopies of map sections or route log segments when they are on the road. Look for photocopying services in the business centers of large hotels, or in photo shops, stationers, and bookstores in larger towns. Ask locals for the nearest *yingyindian*.

Mail and Telephones

To receive mail in Taiwan or Hong Kong, have general delivery items mailed to the central post office in either Taipei or Hong Kong Central. To receive mail in the PRC, tell your friends and family to mail to large cities at the end of your chosen tour(s), and allow at least ten days for the mail to arrive from Europe and the American continents. Receiving mail via general delivery in villages and small cities may be a problem in the PRC.

Sending mail out of China is no problem: write the address in your native language, with the country name written clearly, and it will get there. Stock up on stamps at a major tourist hotel and avoid language problems at a small-town post office. For more information on stamps, packages, et cetera, refer to your conventional guidebook.

Direct-dial international telephone service in Taiwan and Hong Kong is up to international standards in most places. In the PRC, direct-dial international telephone calls and faxes are easily sent or received from any major tourist hotel. These services are rapidly becoming available in more remote areas.

Conditioning

This guidebook assumes that the reader has already done some cycle touring and is used to riding the daily distances of the tour(s) chosen from this book. The best conditioning is to ride often, and to do local tours on terrain similar to the terrain of the China tour(s) you have selected. Begin by doing daily rides with your bike loaded just as it will be when you are touring. Progress to long weekend rides and overnighters if possible. For more detailed information on conditioning for cycle touring, refer to Rob van der Plas's *The Bicycle Touring Manual*.

Once you are in good shape and accustomed to riding a loaded bike, begin mental conditioning for arrival in China. While it is difficult to prepare in advance for a trip into nineteenth-century living conditions, you can at least *imagine* dealing with the frustrations of gawking locals, unusual foods, and unsanitary rest rooms without privacy or running water. For most people, the culture shock will be more challenging than the physical workout. Perhaps the most important ingredient for a successful trip is your attitude.

When to go

In general, the tours in this guidebook are best done in spring or autumn. Summer is possible, but too hot to be pleasurable. Winter tours are possible in Taiwan, Hong Kong, and southeastern PRC, but in east-central and northeastern PRC, it's too cold.

In Taiwan, the typhoon season is late summer and early autumn. There is no predicting just if and when a typhoon will strike, but the east-coast cliff roads on the northern Taiwan tour (Tour No. 1) are *not* where you want to be in a typhoon. Spring rains known as "plum rain" can blanket the island with gray, wet skies for weeks at a time in May and June.

In the PRC, spring tours that begin in the south should be started as early as March; if you are combining several PRC tours, work north as it gets warmer. Fall tours that begin in the south should be started late enough to miss the summer heat. Begin in the south in early September and finish in Beijing just before the serious cold weather sets in. Plum rains in east-central PRC—the Shanghai area—are from mid-June through early July, but it rains on and off throughout spring. In northeastern PRC, Beijing is great in September and October, but is cold from November through mid- to late March.

These time and weather recommendations are based on a south—north direction of travel for combined tours, because that is the direction in which the tours were logged. There is nothing wrong with starting in the north and heading south, but following the route logs in reverse may prove difficult.

Choosing a Tour

Which tour(s) you choose depends on your preference of scenery and terrain, the time required for the tour(s), and the time of year you will go. To get an overview of scenery on any given tour, read the tour introduction and the route log segment descriptions. The terrain on the Taiwan tours (Tour Nos. 1 and 2) and Lantau Island tour (Tour No. 3) is mountainous. The tours in southeastern and east-central PRC (Tour Nos. 4, 5, and 6) are relatively flat, with a few hills. The routes in northeastern PRC (Tour Nos. 7 and 8) are mountainous until you drop onto the Yellow River plain. Tour No. 9 to the Great Wall combines level roads and steep grades.

For the tours in this guidebook, the length of a riding day is based on the pace of an average cyclist who's enjoying the scenery: usually 60 to 100 kilometers a day. Each tour's information block specifies the number of riding days, but the suggested time to allot for a tour is usually longer than the number of riding days, to allow for layovers at tourist attractions along the route.

Cyclists who want to combine the six mainland PRC tours should allow about two months, which includes ship passage, layovers in tourist centers, and a semi-leisurely riding pace.

To combine all the tours in this guidebook into one grand tour, purchase a round-trip ticket with the arrival point in Hong Kong and the homebound departure point in Beijing. Arrange for a four-week layover in Taiwan on the arrival flight. Tour northern and southern Taiwan, then fly to Hong Kong and cycle the outlying islands. Ferry to Macao and do the Pearl River Delta tour, and the Xijiang River tour if desired. Catch a boat from Guangzhou to Shanghai, do the Land of Fish and Rice tour, and ferry back to Shanghai. Then ferry from Shanghai to Qingdao and ride to Taian and Beijing in northeastern China. Do the Great Wall trip, then sightsee in Beijing and fly home. Budget at least three months for this itinerary.

Travel Companions

Solo travel allows freedom and opportunity for adventure, but exposes the tourist to security risks, culture shock, and language isolation. Unless you are experienced at solo travel in foreign countries and/or speak Chinese, one to three touring partners is probably the safest and most rewarding way to tour in China. If you get sick there will be someone there to help, and you will have friends to share the joys and difficulties of your adventure. At mealtimes, a group of two or three people will be able to order more varied and interesting food than a solo tourist.

Keep your touring group small. Large groups can run into problems with lodging space in small towns and will attract more attention from authorities if you wander off the main route. Choose cycling companions carefully. Cycle touring in China is tough enough without avoidable compatibility problems.

Budgeting Your Trip

Taiwan, Hong Kong, Macao, and the PRC are developing rapidly, and guidebook prices are often outdated by the time they are published. Food and transportation prices are uniformly cheaper than in the West, but lodging costs vary widely depending upon the level of comfort you require. The safest budget strategy is to bring funds adequate to cover the cost of average-priced hotels and meals for a similar style of tour in your home country.

Pig going to market on Lantau Island

Eat like the locals and your food expenses will be low, even in cities. Get breakfast at a street stall, have lunch at a small restaurant, and dine at a better restaurant or in your hotel. In 1993, food and beverage costs for all six of this guidebook's PRC tours averaged less than US$5 a day per person. No attempt was made to economize; we ate and drank *very* well. Expensive western-style food is an option only in tourist areas, so there is really no choice but to eat like the locals.

Except for airfare to China, transportation expenses for cycle tourists are minimal for obvious reasons. Those who plan on linking the PRC tours will find ship fares reasonable, considering that the fare includes a room for the night.

The largest and most variable expense is accommodations. In Taipei, Hong Kong, Guangzhou, Shanghai, and Beijing, plan on international price levels at good hotels. Outside these cities, this level of quality is not available even if you can afford it. In fact, lodgings may be cheaper and of lower quality than the "worst" available in your home country. For these "in-between" places, plan on a maximum of one-third to one-half of the big-city prices. If you are willing to stay in rustic inns, lodging costs will be unbelievably low (often less than US$1 per night in 1993).

For security, plan to carry funds in the form of travelers checks (TCs) and exchange them for local currency as described in the Handling Money segment of the Survival Skills section below. Credit cards are useful for tourist hotels, emergencies, and cash advances. Cards issued by major groups such as Visa, Mastercard, and American Express are widely accepted, but don't plan on using them outside of major tourist cities.

Plane Tickets

Once your itinerary is decided, be sure to purchase a round-trip ticket in your home country. One-way tickets purchased in the PRC are expensive and not always easy to get. Intercontinental direct flights to Taipei and Hong Kong are available from most countries. Currently, intercontinental direct flights to the PRC land only in Shanghai and Beijing. Flights to other cities in the PRC are available from Hong Kong. Because of the political situation, there are currently no direct flights between Taiwan and the PRC.

Domestic flights within the PRC are available between all major cities, with more being added as provincial airline companies expand. Although airline equipment and maintenance has improved in the PRC, the safety record of some small provincial airlines does not inspire confidence. Currently there are few uniform service standards in PRC airlines. If your planned itinerary includes inland flight in the PRC with your bike, be warned that some of the provincial airlines may not accept the bike, may charge an excess baggage fee, or may require elaborate packaging to accept it for shipment. Don't rely on the information provided by ticket sellers; the people at the check-in counter may operate by an entirely different set of rules.

Getting Your Bike to China

Before buying plane tickets, be sure your carrier will ship a boxed bike as one piece of luggage without extra charges. Most major airlines do this on international flights, but don't wait until you get to the check-in counter to find out.

Plan carefully when packing your bike and gear for the flight to China. Go to your local bike shop and get a new-bike shipping carton. Some cartons use flimsier cardboard, so pick the largest, sturdiest one available. Also assemble a stack of old newspapers (or plastic bubble wrap), strapping tape, and tools for disassembling your bike.

Don't begin packing until your whole rig is assembled and you are wearing exactly what you'll wear on your tour, including your helmet, shoes, and gloves. When you've rechecked your bike and are satisfied that you have everything, put it all in the middle of the room where you can keep track of things as you dismantle the rig. If there is more than one bike to be shipped, pack them one at a time.

First remove the panniers, handlebar bag, and any other luggage. Remove the tire pump, water bottle, mirror, cycle computer, et cetera, and store them in a pannier. To protect the rear derailleur, tape cardboard over it or unbolt it and tape it inside the chain stay. Next, remove the pedals and wrap them in paper so they won't bang around inside the box. Wrap the chain with newspaper to keep it from smudging other gear.

Remove the seat post and saddle, and loosen the handlebar stem. Turn the handlebars sideways, or remove the stem and tape the handlebars alongside the top tube. Wrap newspaper around the greasy stem to keep it from fouling other luggage.

Remove the front wheel (and the front fender if necessary), then turn the forks so they point toward the bottom bracket. At this point the bike should fit into the box. If the receiver unit for your cycle computer is on a part of the fork that might expose it to damage, remove it or move it out of harm's way. Bring extra plastic cable-ties to reattach it.

Before lowering the bike into the box, make a cardboard tube that will fit crosswise in the box, and position it inside the frame triangle to strengthen the box if luggage is piled onto it.

Put your helmet, tent, sleeping bag, et cetera, in the end of the box where the forks will be. Wrap newspaper around them for protection, then lower the bike into the box. Drop the wrapped pedals in, then work in the front wheel, the front fender, and the spare tire(s). Use a piece of cardboard as a buffer between the front wheel and the frame.

At this point, squeeze in the rest of your luggage as best you can. If it won't all fit, pack the panniers in a cardboard box or a bag before checking them in. Unless all pockets are locked or covered, the panniers may arrive with objects missing.

Look around to be sure you have not left out any tools or other parts. Also check that your tickets, passport, money, et cetera, are *not* in the box. Then use strapping tape to close and seal the box. Write your name and address on the box and you are ready to go.

Once you've landed in China, where should you unbox and assemble your bike? Those who plan on departing China from the same city they entered should plan on taking their boxed bikes to the hotel in a taxi or minivan taxi. Then the box can be saved and stored at the hotel until departure. If you will be departing China from another city, you can unpack and assemble your bike in the airport. If possible, do it before entering the crowded arrivals areas in Hong Kong and PRC airports.

When you are preparing to leave the PRC, keep in mind that bike shipping boxes are not currently available at the Beijing or Shanghai airports. They accept bikes "as is," and you take your chances on their condition after the flight. Protect your bike by boxing it at the hotel with a bike shop box (not all Chinese bike shops have boxes) and taking a minivan taxi to the airport. Another option is to carry loose cardboard and tape to the airport and wrap vulnerable parts before you check it in.

BUYING AND OUTFITTING A BIKE

Since this guidebook assumes that you have already done some cycle touring, it's also assumed that you have a suitable bicycle. If you don't have a bike or are buying a new one, be sure it's durable, reliable, and comfortable. You want to enjoy the tour, not merely survive it, so choose a bike that has a frame and forks designed for touring, not racing. Don't use a new bike that you haven't taken on a shakedown tour.

Techno-gadgets that make your bike 0.01 gram lighter and a hair faster are not suitable on a touring rig if they detract from reliability. What's the benefit of a tiny weight savings on a critical component when you are carrying thirty pounds of baggage? Suspension systems are comfortable, but many aren't field repairable with simple tools. Stick with tried, true, and easily repairable components. When equipping your bike, remember that in China there are few modern bike shops to help when cutting-edge technology fails.

Choose handlebars with more than one riding position (dropped handlebars or all-terrain bike—ATB—extensions), a comfortable handlebar covering, and a firm seat. Leather seats are comfortable once they're broken in, but must be protected from water damage. Keep a small plastic bag handy to protect the seat in the rain. Select a pedal setup that is comfortable and efficient, but does not require special cleat systems that may break down or get out of adjustment. Standard pedals with ATB toe clips and nylon straps are comfortable and will not let you down. Pedals that are removable with a 6-millimeter Allen wrench will eliminate the need for a special pedal wrench when you remove pedals to prepare your bike for shipping.

Use tires that are tough and have semi-smooth tread and a low rolling resistance. Avoid knobby tires, which have a high rolling resistance and clog easily with heavy clay. Puncture-resistant tire liners are a good idea. Don't wait until you need a tire to look for one: carry your own folded spare. In Hong Kong and Taiwan, all popular tire sizes are available. Now that ATB bikes are gaining popularity in the PRC, some form of 26-inch tire is usually available. Outside of larger cities, the sizes listed below may not all be available, but they were available in an average Shanghai bike shop in 1993:

26-inch x 1.95-inch knobby ATB
26-inch x 1⅜-inch narrow ATB, semi-smooth tread
27-inch x 1¼-inch road tire
700 x 38 c road tire
28-inch x 1½-inch tire used on heavy Chinese utility bikes
20-inch x 1¾-inch cruiser tire (for a 20-inch Moulton bicycle)

Be sure your brakes work well and use brake shoes rated well for wet conditions. Replace questionable brake cables before starting your tour, and carry spares. If your bike is equipped with cantilever brakes, bring a spare straddle cable in the correct size.

Your gear range should be wide, with the emphasis on low gears. The lowest gear ratio should be no higher than 30 gear-inches, and a 25–gear-inch low gear is preferable. (Calculate this by dividing the number of teeth on the smallest chain ring by the number of teeth on the largest freewheel cog. Multiply the result by the wheel/tire diameter.) If you link several of the tours into an extended tour, start with a new chain and new freewheel cogs if they are worn.

Unless you enjoy scraping red and yellow mud off of your clothing and gear, don't leave home without fenders. For even better protection, attach a mud flap to the back of the front fender. You can easily make one using a piece of car-tire tube.

Use the strongest bike racks you can get, with appropriate elastic straps and shock cords. Even if you don't use front panniers, a front rack is handy for carrying a folded spare tire.

Carry one "squirting"-type water bottle in your frame-mounted bottle cage and a 1.5-liter heavy plastic backup bottle in your luggage. More than one frame bottle is an easy target for thieves and may leak if packed in your bags.

To lock your bike, use a cable and a sturdy lock. U-locks are too heavy, and don't always fit around what's handy in China. A cable lock can also be used to secure your bags to the bike, or to secure several bikes together.

In the PRC, commonly used bicycle pumps are made to fit a Woods valve; they won't fit Presta or Schrader valves. Bring a reliable pump that can be stored in or attached to your luggage. Do not leave your frame-mounted pump exposed on an unattended bike if you do not want it stolen.

A rear-view mirror is a must if you like to know what is roaring up behind you, or to check whether your co-pilot is caught in a flock of geese crossing the road. Mirrors can be helmet mounted or handlebar mounted. Equip your bike with both a safety flasher and a headlight for safety in tunnels and when you are forced to ride in the dark. Choose a flasher of the flashing-diode type, which will operate for hundreds of hours on a single battery. Choose a headlight that uses commonly available size AA batteries and mounts in a location where the beam will not be blocked by your handlebar bag or other luggage. Lights that slip onto handlebar-mounted clips sometimes present this problem. The most versatile type fastens with a cam-operated strap and can be mounted on the head tube, the handlebar ends, or the top of the forks. It also makes a good off-bike flashlight. In addition to your bike light, carry another small flashlight so you can read your cycle computer if you have to ride in the dark.

Navigation Tools

A reliable cycle computer is essential to following the route logs in this guidebook; you must use one. Choose a cycle computer that is accurate, easy to use, waterproof, and convenient to disconnect. Cycle computers come with a wide choice of functions, but the trip meter is the important one. It should read in increments of 0.1 kilometer or smaller.

Another important feature to look for is ease of reading. The larger the numbers on the display, the easier they will be to read. Check the type of information the computer displays. Although the current trip mileage is the significant number for following the route logs, it is also important to know that your computer is continually registering distance. It is possible for a wire to break or short out, and you might travel some distance before finding out what went wrong. The best way to avoid this is to check the speed display regularly, or to get a cycle computer that displays trip mileage and speed simultaneously. Because most cycle computers do not display trip mileage and speed at the same time, look for a computer that displays a "pace arrow" or other indicator that it is currently registering even when it is in the trip mileage mode. Finally, be sure that the computer can be switched

Road markers, such as this one, are seldom seen in South China.

to display miles or kilometers without having to recalculate wheel size or recalibrate the computer.

Be sure the computer is easily detachable for security reasons, and disconnectable (by sliding it back on its mount) for when you want to interrupt metering to leave the main route. Carry backup batteries and directions for recalibration when you change batteries or to a different tire size. Solo tourists may want to consider carrying a backup computer in case the main one malfunctions: without a computer, it's impossible to use the route logs in this guidebook.

The other required navigation tool is a compass. Use an inexpensive flat plastic compass and slip it in the handlebar-bag map case, where you can refer to it while riding. Do not place a radio, a camera, or any other metal object under it or it will not read correctly. Plastic ball compasses that double as keyrings or zipper pulls are a good backup to your main compass.

Bicycle Luggage

The touring rigs usually pictured in guidebooks have four panniers with outside pockets, a handlebar bag, and a bundle of tents and bedding strapped across the back rack. This setup is fine if you do not have to carry luggage up several flights of stairs each night and if theft is not a factor. But in China these *are* factors. Your luggage system must meet three criteria: it must perform well while riding, it must be easy to manage when it is off the bike, and it must discourage theft.

One set of large panniers provides enough capacity for a touring style suitable to China. If you use two sets of panniers, you are probably taking too much gear and will have difficulty navigating elevators, stairs, and public transportation. Panniers must attach and detach quickly, and be easy to carry up to your hotel room in one trip. Your sleeping pad, tent, and sleeping bag should be stuffed into one large waterproof bag that can be strapped on your rack. Loops of $3/16$-inch shock cord stretched around this bag provide a convenient way to attach wet rain gear or clothes that need drying. Luggage should be connectible and have shoulder straps. The main outside zipper should be lockable with a small padlock.

Suitable luggage has few outside pockets on which pickpockets can test their skills. Rain covers protect against both bad weather and prying fingers in crowded areas. If you do not have rain covers, heavy plastic trash bags and $3/16$-inch shock-cord loops will work, but be sure to work out your rain-cover system before starting to tour.

If you plan to take your bike on a train during your tour, bring a reinforced plastic tarp and some cord to wrap the bike. Practice disassembling and wrapping your bike before leaving, and cut the tarp to the minimum workable size. You may find the folded tarp useful for extra rain protection over your luggage, and as a rain cover for your parked bike.

A handlebar bag serves as a portable office. Keep maps, guidebooks, a camera, and valuables here, and never leave it unattended on your bike. Get one that is easily detachable with some form of quick-release hardware and a shoulder strap so you can carry it with you on trips to the rest room. Be sure it has its own rain cover and a zippered transparent map case on top for route-log copies and a compass.

Maintaining Your Bicycle

In China, you can't rely on the local bike shop to take care of your rig; you must be able to maintain it yourself. On any tour you will very likely have to change and repair tires, patch and replace tubes, adjust derailleurs and brakes, lubricate the chain, and clean gear clusters. You may not need the following skills often, but be sure you also know how to adjust hub bearings, bottom brackets, and headsets; replace broken spokes and true wheels to workable trim; remove the freewheel to change broken spokes; refit broken brake and gear cables; replace a worn chain; and tighten crank and chain ring bolts.

Go over your bike and be sure you have tools that fit all the nuts and bolts, including hidden ones like the bolts inside drop bar brake levers. Group tools and supplies into a daily maintenance kit, major repair tools, and a backup supply kit. Store them in separate resealable plastic bags.

The daily maintenance kit contains hex (or Allen) wrenches, a 6-inch crescent wrench, 7-inch channel-lock pliers, an 8-9-10-millimeter Y-wrench, a screwdriver, a spoke wrench, chain lubricant, a tire pressure gauge, tire irons, a spare tube, and a repair kit with tube patches, patch cement, and tire boots. (Make a tire boot by cutting a 2-inch section out of a discarded tire and trimming off the wire bead. To get more mileage out of a tire with a large puncture or slash, position the boot between the tube and the damaged portion.) Also include a rag and some waterless hand cleaner stored in a 35-millimeter film can. Keep this daily maintenance kit easily accessible.

Major repair tools, which can be stored in a less accessible area, should include a freewheel removal tool, a pocket vise, cone wrenches, a pedal wrench, a chain rivet tool, a compact headset wrench, and a compact crankset wrench and extractor. If your bike has a freehub rather than a freewheel, carry a "cassette cracker" to remove freehub cogs for accessing and replacing broken spokes.

The backup supply kit should contain spare cables, spare brake shoes, spare tubes, extra tube patches, tire boots, and bearing grease stored in a 35-millimeter film can. Tape extra spokes and nipples (sized for your wheels) to a chain stay. Other supplies you may want could include spare batteries for your headlight, safety flasher, and cycle computer; $\frac{3}{16}$-inch shock-cord loops for strapping things onto the bike; duct tape for luggage repair; nylon repair patches for tents and sleeping pads; and a small sewing kit.

If you are concerned about your high-tech steed breaking down in a rural backwater village in the PRC, make arrangements before leaving Hong Kong at the Flying Ball Bike Shop (201 Tung Choi Street, G/F, Kowloon, Hong Kong; telephone 3-813661, 3-815919). The owner, Mr. Li, will ship parts into the PRC, accepts credit cards, and can do the whole business by phone.

WHAT TO TAKE

This section covers the basic equipment needed on any of the tours in this guidebook.

Clothing

Select clothing that is comfortable, durable, and easily maintained. Since space is limited, you probably will not carry a separate set of street clothes: choose clothing that performs well while riding, but looks appropriate when you are off the bike. Chinese tend to dress conservatively, so tight, flashy "bike clothes" are not recommended unless you enjoy huge crowds of people gawking at you. Be sure all clothing is hand washable and in colors that do not show dirt easily.

In hot, humid weather, loose stretch-twill shorts are preferable to tight bike shorts. If you do choose to use padded bike shorts, be sure they breathe well and dry rapidly after washing. For cold days, wear stretch tights that are comfortable but not so tight that they attract unwanted attention. Long pants of thin, quick-drying nylon material make excellent wind pants and off-bike wear. Avoid all-cotton shorts or pants, which are uncomfortable when wet and can take days to dry in humid climates.

Here is my recommended list for basic cycle-touring clothes:

> Shorts (1 pair)
> Long synthetic tights or sweat pants (1 pair)
> Underwear (3 pairs)
> Wool/synthetic blend socks (3 pairs)
> Colored T-shirts (2)
> Long-sleeve loose-fitting cotton or Supplex nylon shirt (1)
> Light wool sweater or light synthetic fleece pullover (1)
> Windbreaker or breathable rain jacket (1)
> Ultralight nylon dark-colored wind pants (1 pair)
> Long-sleeve lightweight polypropylene or capilene top (1)
> Short-sleeve polypropylene or capilene silkweight top (1)
> Bandanna (2)
> Cap or beret (1)
> Light capilene gloves (1 pair)
> Plastic thong sandals, in plastic bag (1 pair)
> Mesh bags for storing clothing in panniers (2 or 3)
> Rain gear

In addition to basic clothing items, you'll need:

> Safety helmet with sun visor
> Cycling gloves
> Touring-style bike shoes

For rain gear, a full suit is the most rainproof, but even the "breathable" kind also does a good job of holding in perspiration. A rain cape is easy to put on, is well ventilated, and covers your hands; but in a wind it blows around and doesn't cover the lower legs. My solution is to carry both—a breathable rain suit for long stretches of heavy rain and a rain cape for occasional showers. The rain-suit jacket can double as a windbreaker.

Rain capes (*yu yi*) are the most common rain gear in China. If you do not already have one, they are sold for about US$5 at department stores (*baihuogongsi*) or stalls selling miscellaneous clothing. Get the largest size available in coated nylon rather than plastic, and check inside to see that the seams are pre-sealed.

Store rain gear in an easily accessible place on your bike. When the rain stops, use shock-cord loops to strap it outside your luggage until it dries completely. Mildew damage is likely if rain gear is rolled up and stored wet.

Camping Gear

Of the tours in this book, only those in Taiwan are suitable for camping. In PRC towns, there are few sites where you would feel safe camp-

A flat-tire repair is guaranteed to draw a crowd.

ing, and in less populated areas, country inns are so cheap there is no need to camp. Besides, staying at cheap inns is much like camping! For the PRC tours, you may want to carry a compact sleeping bag and a bivvy bag or groundsheet in case you get stranded far from a town: even if you never use them, you'll feel less vulnerable. At the very least, carry a bag liner or a sheet-bag for use at inns that don't wash their linen regularly.

In Taiwan, a light sleeping bag is adequate for spring and fall tours. Carry a sheet-bag or a sleeping bag liner for warm nights and inns with dubious sheets. Take a tent that is free-standing, well ventilated, and bug-proof. The best places to camp are often in schoolyards, temples, and roadside shelters on hard surfaces that will not accept tent pegs. A bivvy bag is adequate if it is bug-proof, but it will not be as comfortable as a tent in the humid climate. Those going on to Hong Kong and/or the PRC after touring Taiwan should ship their tent home before entering the PRC.

Cooking gear is not necessary in Hong Kong or the PRC because there is cheap food available everywhere, but the boiled water in hotels is not always hot. If you need freshly boiled water to brew your morning coffee or to cook instant noodles, a compact stove comes in handy. Bring a stove that burns kerosene (*mei yu*), a pot or kettle, and a cup and bowl that fit the pot. Kerosene is available at country dry-goods stores and at "oil stores" (look for the large oil drums and pumps in front). Gas stations do not usually sell kerosene and unleaded gas is not common in the PRC. Go minimal on cooking gear in Taiwan as well. A stove that will burn unleaded gas or kerosene, a pot, a bowl, a cup, a spoon, and chopsticks are all you'll need to boil tea or make quick meals of instant *pao mian* noodles. Do not bring a stove that requires special white gas–type fuels or disposable propane cylinders.

Miscellaneous Items

Laundromats are rare in China. Hotels provide laundry service, but they do not always return clothes when you need them. The simplest way is to wash your own clothes by hand. Carry a 10-inch plastic wash basin, because hotel sinks often have broken stoppers. Laundry soap (*xi yi fen*) is cheap and available at dry-goods stores. Use a length of cord for a clothesline, or just hang clothes on your bike. If clothes do not dry before you leave the hotel, put them in a mesh clothing bag strapped on your luggage with shock-cord loops. The plastic wash basin is also useful for bathing at cheap inns and washing mud from your bike when running water is not available. Stuff it with clothing and it will not take up much space in your luggage.

Carry a simple first-aid kit with an elastic bandage, antiseptic cream, 3-inch sterile bandage pads, adhesive bandages, aspirin, cold medicine, anti-diarrhea drugs, and tweezers. Store it where it is easily accessible if you take a spill. Cold medicines, aspirin, and anti-diarrhea drugs will make life more bearable if you get sick. If you take vitamin supplements, bring an adequate supply. Tinactin or another fungicide for athlete's foot is a must in the moist climates of Taiwan and southeastern PRC. Sunscreen is not readily available in high SPF ratings in the PRC, so bring all you will need. Druggists in Taiwan and Hong Kong offer sunscreens, but usually only in lower SPF ratings. Store all drugs in their original containers and do not even think of bringing illicit drugs. In China, they have been known to execute illegal drug users.

In addition to your toothbrush, comb, et cetera, do not forget to carry a small towel: cheap hotels and inns do not always supply them. Towels, toothpaste, and shampoo are available at stores everywhere, and traveler-size soap is provided in hotel rooms. Chinese razors are the double-edged variety but aren't very sharp; you may want to bring your own. Tampons are not commonly available, but standard sanitary napkins are. Before checking out of a hotel, replenish your supply of toilet paper for use at roadside privies. The small roll of toilet paper, soap, shampoo, comb, toothbrush kit, teabags, and stationery provided by hotels are all part of the service: it is expected that you will take them when you leave.

If you wear glasses, bring a spare set or bring your prescription in case you break or lose them. Contact-lens wearers must pay extra attention to keeping their eyewear clean and must carry enough cleaner and saline solution to cover their needs between major cities. Replenish your supplies at stores or druggists inside major tourist hotels.

In addition, the following items will help make life on the road feel a little more like home:

> Shortwave radio
> Journal and stationery
> Sketchbook and art supplies
> Camera, extra camera battery, and a backup supply of film
> Swiss army knife
> Books

SURVIVAL SKILLS

Handling Money

Successful money handling while on tour requires attention to security and skill at currency exchanges. The goal is to always have enough local currency for your needs, but not so much that a successful thief can wipe you out financially. Exchange techniques and suggested amounts differ for each of the areas covered in this book.

The very fact that you are bicycle touring in China signals locals that you have a lot of money on your person. You are an easily spotted target for a thief. The first security rule is: Only exchange enough TCs to provide cash until the next major city exchange opportunity. Don't cash all your TCs as soon as you arrive. The second security rule is: Don't flash cash. Keep a low profile and don't tempt people with the sight of a wad of cash equal to one year of their wages. Keep a purse for daily expenses separate from your main supply, and replenish it in the privacy of your hotel room. The third security rule is: Don't store all

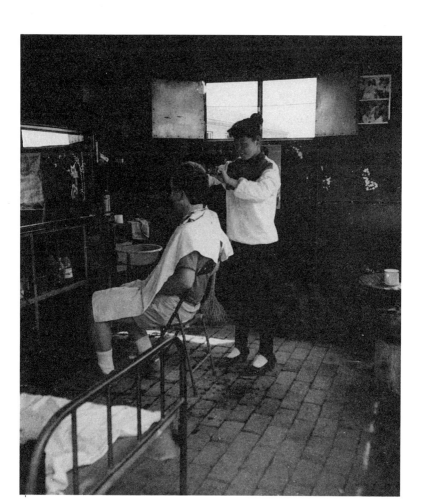

Getting a haircut at a village barbershop in Hebei

funds in one place. Once you've made an exchange, store the currency in several places in your luggage, preferably not with the remaining TCs. In addition to a daily purse in the handlebar bag and a backup supply in other luggage, I store some currency and TCs in a plastic bag stashed in the seat tube, ready to be fished out with a spare spoke if needed.

The currency in Taiwan is the New Taiwan dollar (NT$). Most Bank of Taiwan branches do TC exchanges, but smaller provincial banks may not. In Taiwan, banks are closed on Saturday afternoons, Sundays, and holidays. Unlike the PRC, Taiwan has no widespread informal market in currency.

If you arrive in Taiwan on a day when banks are closed, change money before leaving the airport. Change enough money to last a week, or until you get to the first large city on the tour. Before leaving Keelung, be sure to purchase enough NT$ for the rest of the North Island Loop tour. Those continuing on to the Southern Island Loop can plan to make further exchanges in Hualien, Taitung, Kenting, Pingtung, or Touliu. Although many small towns have Bank of Taiwan branches, the larger branches are better equipped to handle foreign customers. Be sure to save exchange receipts, which are needed to convert extra NT$ back into U.S. dollars.

The official currency in Hong Kong is the Hong Kong dollar (HK$). Because Hong Kong is an international financial center, exchanging TCs and currency is easy. There are banks and private money changers located just about everywhere, even in the subway stations. In the past, Chinese *Renminbi* (RMB) currency was not usable or exchangeable in Hong Kong, but as 1997 approaches, more and more businesses are accepting *Renminbi*. In Macao, the currency is the *pataca* (M$), which is worth a little less than the HK$. Most establishments in Macao accept HK$, but some give you change in *patacas*, making it an interesting exercise to keep track of your change.

When the tours in this guidebook were first logged, there were two kinds of currency in use in the PRC: *Renminbi* and Foreign Exchange Certificates (FEC). FEC was intended for use by tourists and businesses, and to make money for the government by rigging the exchange rates. Bills for hotels, transportation, and tourist attractions had to be paid in FEC. RMB was the "people's money" used by PRC citizens and was not officially available to foreigners. Unofficially, RMB, HK$, and U.S. dollars were all in circulation and commonly used for trade.

Because of the spread between official and informal exchange rates, an underground currency market developed that was anything but underground. Near large banks and tourist hotels, money changers practically tracked down foreigners to change RMB for foreign currency. The foreign tourist "in the know" only used FEC when there was no other option, and certainly did not pay official rates for RMB. Informal exchange of U.S. dollars, HK$, and FEC was the best way to stretch a traveler's budget.

Beginning in 1994, the FEC currency system was abandoned. All foreigners are now allowed to exchange and use RMB. Hotels that formerly would only accept FEC now accept RMB, although at prices that are inflating rapidly. You can get RMB at all banks and at hotel exchange desks, but the official rate is still not as good as the informal rate.

Although FEC is no longer a part of the picture, the recommended money strategy for bicycle tourists in the PRC is basically the same as before 1994: (1) carry TCs for security, (2) change them to U.S. dollars in Hong Kong or at the Bank of China in Guangzhou, Shanghai, or Beijing, then (3) exchange U.S. dollars for local currency either informally on the street or at banks. Those who don't plan to do informal exchanges can skip step two and change their TCs into RMB at banks.

The choice between street exchange or banks depends on the spread between official and informal rates, and your appetite for risk. You must take into account the possibility of being cheated by a fast-change artist, counterfeiter, or thief. Economic changes in the PRC may eventually eliminate the informal market, but until that happens, you will have to decide for yourself whether informal exchange rates make it worth the risk. Street exchanges must be made with cash (usually U.S. dollars), not TCs!

In small towns there is often no market for foreign currency, so plan to make informal exchanges in larger cities. Don't wait until you're in a rural area and nearly out of RMB to begin looking for a place to change money. Stand outside the gates of any large tourist hotel and eventually someone will approach and ask if you want to "changee mah-nee?" Another good spot is outside the main Bank of China branches in Shanghai, Guangzhou, and Beijing. In Guangzhou, you will be approached almost any place around Shamian Island and the White Swan Hotel. If you are staying in a large tourist hotel, porters and baggage handlers are also a good possibility for informal exchanges. When you find someone to exchange with, use the phraseguide to ask him or her the rate. Once the rate and amount are established, be sure to count and inspect the money carefully before giving the person your cash.

In major PRC cities, you can get U.S. dollars and make money exchanges at the Bank of China, open Monday through Saturday, usually from 9:00 A.M. to 5:00 P.M. Hotel cashiers or exchange desks will cash TCs, but will not usually give you U.S. dollars. If there's a profit to be made on the "spread," they want to make it themselves!

Regardless of where you begin your itinerary, exchange some currency at the airport exchange window so you will have local currency as soon as you leave the airport. If you fly directly to the PRC to begin your itinerary, bring a few hundred U.S. dollars in cash for informal exchanges and avoid a trip to the bank on the day you arrive. When your tour is nearing its end, set aside US$20 per person (or its equivalent at official rates) to cover the airport departure tax when you leave the PRC.

Security

Although the Chinese are no more or less dishonest than other people, foreign tourists are perceived as "rich" and provide a powerful attraction for thieves. You are easy to spot because you look different, and one successful theft may net an average worker's annual income.

Places to be especially wary are public transportation centers, ticket halls, and crowded market areas. When sleeping on ferries or ships, keep your cash and papers in a pouch strapped to your body or locked in a locker. Use your tire pump or a stick to secure the sliding windows in riverboat cabins (I was robbed this way once). Stash copies of your passport, TC numbers, credit card numbers, airline tickets, and some spare currency in several places on your bike and person. Then if you are robbed or lose your papers, you'll have backup information for replacing them.

When you stop for a meal, park your bike near a window and select a table where you can keep your eye on the bike. When you are using roadside rest rooms, take turns with your cycling companions and always have someone watch the bikes. Never leave your bike unlocked or unattended with your handlebar bag still attached. Use rain covers on panniers to keep prying fingers out of zippered pockets, and always remove your cycle computer when leaving the bike. Even if it is not stolen, it may be reset by curious locals who inevitably fiddle with the bike. If your bike is not stored in your hotel room, do not leave water bottles, headlights, tire pumps, or other loose gear on the bike.

In hotels, lock your pannier zippers if you leave anything valuable in them. Carry a medium-size padlock to secure lockers on ships, and to lock the doors of cheap inns. When you are paying a dollar a night, you have to provide your own security! Some ship cabin doors and inn doors have neither locks nor hasps for using a padlock. To cover this situation, carry a small adjustable door lock of the type that creates a wedge between the door and the floor.

Soloists must be especially careful because there is nobody to watch their bike while they visit the rest room, buy tickets, or investigate lodging. Plan your luggage packing so all valuables may be taken with you every time you leave the bike. Use a shoulder strap on the handlebar bag to keep it on your person while using public rest rooms.

Police and Security Officers

Taiwan and Hong Kong are open societies and their police and security systems are geared to public safety. There are no "closed areas" except military installations, and the cycle tourist is free to travel nearly everywhere. The PRC, on the other hand, is still not an open society and has many areas that are closed to foreigners. It has a security police system that is used for purposes of political control as well as public safety.

The Gong An, China's Public Security Bureau (PSB), is the PRC's security police force. Depending on how you meet them, they may be friend or foe. Officers drive blue and white cars, vans, or motorcycles with sidecars. Every town has a Gong An office, and one of its responsibilities is keeping track of foreigners who pass through. When you check into a hotel in the PRC, the local Gong An will be notified.

Characters for the Gong An: the Chinese Public Security Bureau

Since the PRC tours in this guidebook are in open areas, you probably will not run into problems with the Gong An. But even in open areas, not all of the Gong An have accepted the idea of foreigners traveling freely without special permits. They may want to see your passport and ask where you are going next.

Cyclists heading offroute west into Guangxi, Anhui, or Hebei provinces can count on a visit from the Gong An. Do not expect them to be polite; they may even barge into your room without knocking. Allow them to inspect your passport, but do not surrender it to them unless they insist. Whatever you do, do not get angry and abusive: the goal is to get them to leave you alone.

Use the phraseguide in the back of this book to tell them you will leave the next day. Tell them where you are headed and say you did not know the area was closed. Then ask if they can suggest the best route back to an open area. They may instruct you to stay inside the hotel compound and not allow you onto the streets. Plan to wake and leave town early before they return to check up on you.

The Gong An will probably be of little assistance if you get ripped off. Do not assume that the presence of police or officials means you are safe. Police aren't well paid in the PRC, and more than a few of them make ends meet by cooperating with thieves. A little paranoia about these matters is not unreasonable.

Road Conditions and Riding Safety

The cycle tourist in China will encounter potentially hazardous situations on the road. Prepare by making sure your bike is safe and ready to handle them. Before heading out each day, check tire pressure, tire condition, and brake adjustment. Also check quick releases, the seat post clamp, and shift levers after any stop where locals may have tampered with them. A loose quick release could cause you to lose your front wheel. The basic safety rules for cyclists are (1) stay aware and (2) wear a helmet.

In Taiwan, with the exception of stretches along the east coast, roads are excellent, with ample shoulders and smooth surfaces. The most hazardous places on the Taiwan tours are cliff roads and east-coast tunnels. On cliff roads beware of falling rocks and mud slides when it rains. Tunnels are often narrow, dark, and dripping with water. Water-filled potholes are difficult to detect until your front wheel drops into one. Be sure to use headlights and safety flashers in the tunnels. Another strategy for long, dark tunnels is to wait at the tunnel mouth until another vehicle approaches, then wave to them to slow down. As they slow, ride into the tunnel ahead of them and let them follow you, lighting the way with their headlights. Each time I tried this the driver understood instinctively that their auto lights were helpful and followed patiently to the end of the tunnel.

In Taiwanese towns, don't let the heavy motorscooter traffic tempt you to ride on the sidewalks. Sidewalks often have dangerous potholes and loose paving tiles. In some parts of Taiwan, guard dogs can be a problem. If you get off the beaten path, you may encounter extremely poisonous snakes, including the *zhuyeqing*, a green snake the color of bamboo leaves. There is no antidote for the venom of some of these snakes: If you get bitten, you die. Drivers in Taiwan are fearless, but generally not reckless. Most are genuinely impressed to see foreigners touring their country by bicycle.

In Hong Kong, traffic is the biggest hazard in the urban area. Cyclists who aren't accustomed to riding on the left side of the road should to be attentive to different traffic and turning patterns. Also pay close attention to streetcar tracks in the Central District of Hong Kong. Riding conditions on Lantau Island are better: automobile access is limited, and traffic consists of an occasional bus.

On PRC tours, the main hazards are road surface conditions, traffic, and weather. PRC riding surfaces vary from smooth cement roads with wide shoulders to rough, narrow sand roads. Unlike more developed countries, PRC's road hazards are not always conveniently marked with flashers or signs. Beware of invisible sand-filled potholes on sand roads and oil spills on paved roads. In the southeastern and east-central PRC the terrain is relatively flat, but the northeastern tours have steep sections where you will need low gears and strong brakes.

In the southeastern and east-central PRC, economic progress has increased the number of vehicles on roads not designed for heavy traffic. Along some sections noisy truck traffic is unavoidable, and when a truck or bus breaks down there are giant traffic jams. Fortunately, cyclists can continue past these jams by carefully weaving through the stalled vehicles.

In urban areas you will ride alongside hundreds of local cyclists. Adapt to their riding style: go slow and go with the flow. Do not stop in traffic lanes, and do not make quick turns or lane changes. A kamikaze "shredder" riding style will get you in trouble. Considering how many people ride together along crowded streets, there are few accidents.

In wet weather, country roads can turn from hard dirt into slippery red or yellow mud, which will clog your fenders, foul your chain, and make braking difficult. Yield right of way to anything that is bigger than you or is honking loudly, including flocks of geese. Also yield to pedicabs, three-wheeled tractors, and horse carts, none of which has good brakes. Because dogs are a culinary delicacy in the PRC, not many are wandering around hassling cyclists!

Health

Most of China is still a third-world country. Hotels and restaurants are not up to international standards and outside of cities sanitation is primitive. It is possible that you will suffer minor infections or illness on an extended tour. If you do get sick, take it easy and do not force your pace.

Small scratches are easily infected because Chinese road dust is polluted with the human waste used to fertilize fields. Wash exposed areas carefully every day, especially if you have open cuts or scratches.

When you drink from your water bottle, squirt water into your mouth without touching the nozzle, which may also be contaminated by this "dust."

In China, diseases like colds and flu are commonly transmitted via unsanitary utensils, but the food itself is usually not a problem. Do not miss out on a significant aspect of Chinese culture by living on crackers and canned goods. Carry your own chopsticks and cup, or sanitize utensils as the locals do: use the phraseguide to ask for a bowl and boiling water, then place the utensils in the bowl and scald them before use.

Serious diseases such as malaria, hepatitis, and tetanus are a potential problem. Malaria exists in southeastern and southwestern China, and hepatitis epidemics occur in all parts of China. Since prevention is the best cure, follow your doctor's advice on innoculation against tetanus, diphtheria, typhoid, cholera, hepatitis, and malaria before your departure.

Dehydration is another potential health problem for cycle tourists. Keep an ample supply of boiled water on hand and stay ahead of dehydration by drinking at regular intervals. Follow the Chinese custom of drinking soup at mealtimes, and do not confuse beer with water. A strict regimen of beer will exacerbate dehydration. If you have diarrhea, pay special attention to replenishing your fluids.

If you are going to get seriously ill or injured on your cycling trip in China, do it in Taiwan or Hong Kong rather than the PRC! One look at rural "hospitals," with dirty walls and floors, and you will be convinced. If you do get *seriously* ill or injured in the PRC, the best strategy is to use your conventional phrase book to get to a clinic or hospital for emergency help in the largest nearby town and then get out of the country, or at least to a major city such as Shanghai or Beijing, for further treatment.

China Shock

Perhaps the most important survival skill is keeping a good attitude to lessen the effect of "China shock." China shock is my term for negative influences that interact to depress the cycle tourist in China. For the first week or two, jet lag will diminish your energy and enthusiasm. At the same time you must confront the rigors of bike touring: exposure to the elements, physical exertion, road hazards, and the mental effort to find and stay on the route.

Add a huge dose of culture shock: poverty, overpopulation, lack of privacy, and alien foods and customs. In China, the cycle tourist is cut off from the cultural supports most people take for granted at home. Outside of major cities, there are no magazines, newspapers, or television in English or other western languages. Solo tourists will not find many people who can speak their language and may experience language isolation. On an extended trip, even seasoned travelers can feel homesick.

Take a deep breath and remind yourself that cycling in China was not meant to be an easy vacation. Remember that you are touring someplace really different, that your tour is an adventure. Keep your mind open and go easy on yourself, and you will not be a victim of "China shock."

Food and Drink

Eating is the Chinese national sport! No matter which routes you choose, China's incredible culinary culture will be a highlight of your tour. It's quite possible to do all the tours in this book and never have the same meal twice, not to mention the variety of snacks, candies, fruits, and beverages unique to each of the provinces visited. Don't be put off by the outward appearance of some roadside restaurants and noodle stalls: the food is nearly always safe and delicious.

In Taiwan, especially in the south, the food is Taiwanese: mild seasoning, lots of seafood, rice, and rice noodles. Japanese influences are evident in restaurants that serve sushi and miso soup alongside Chinese dishes. In larger towns, restaurants offer Sichuan, Beijing, Shanghai, and other regional cuisines.

Breakfast in Taiwan can be soy milk and fried doughsticks, noodles with sesame sauce, crepes with egg, rice porridge with pickles—or even fare from McDonald's. The streetside stalls with fried breads, crepes, and steamed buns are my favorite. Have them with sweet or savory hot soy milk (*doujiang*), and buy extra to go (*daizou*) for a midmorning snack.

For lunch, small cafeterias are easy and have the most choices. They usually open onto the street or market alley, and display cooked food in steam tables. Just point at what you like, then ask for rice (*fan*), rice noodles (*mifun*), or noodles (*mian*). Help yourself to the pot of soup (*tang*). These cafeterias serve tofu, eggplant, egg, and vegetable dishes, which makes them a good choice for vegetarians. Roadside noodle carts have fewer choices, but are quick and cheap.

In larger Taiwanese towns, the most interesting place to have dinner is the night market. These are flea markets, food bazaars, and medicine shows all rolled into one. They all serve local specialties, and most items are snack-size so you can sample everything. Make a pass around the market before choosing. If you order food from a stall and sit down at its tables, the owner will usually help you order drinks and food items from nearby stalls; you don't need to change tables.

Do not forget energy food for the road. Taiwan now has an ample supply of junk-food snacks, but why not try the traditional items? There are excellent candies made of peanuts, black sesame seeds, or puffed rice. Fresh, dried, and candied fruits are available in snack shops and marketplaces. A traditional Chinese road food is *zongzi*, a type of tamale made with sticky rice wrapped in a bamboo leaf. The savory ones (*hsien*) are filled with meat and peanuts, and sweet ones (*tian*) are filled with red-bean paste. Find them in cafeterias and on food carts hanging in bundles over the counter. On hot days, Taiwanese shaved ices with fruit (*shuiguo bing*) are hard to beat. Look for carts or stalls with ice-shaving machines and containers of preserved fruits, beans, and nuts.

A common sight in rural Taiwan is roadside carts selling betel nuts (*bina*), the local stimulant of choice for truckers and cabbies. These nuts come from a variety of palm tree and look like acorns with a bit of red paste smeared on them. Do not confuse these with food!

Outside of Taipei, don't drink tap water unless it has been boiled. Hostels and inns provide boiled water in thermos bottles. Hotels have water fountains with safe water, chilled or hot. Put a pinch of high-grade Taiwan oolong tea in your water bottle and quench your thirst with real Taiwanese flavor.

Although Taiwan has no shortage of eating places, camping cyclists may still want to be prepared to cook simple meals, especially on the stretch across the central mountains. When cooking for yourself in Taiwan, keep it simple. Do not bother with cooking rice or frying foods; that kind of meal is better obtained at a restaurant. Use the excellent instant noodles (*pao mian*) available everywhere. Add a cake of beancurd and some vegetables, and you have a cheap, healthy meal.

Hong Kong is another dining paradise: it is hard to go anywhere in the colony without running into interesting things to eat. All of the regional cuisines of China are represented, as well as excellent East Indian and Southeast Asian cuisines. Western food and fast food are available everywhere. For quick meals, small stands and restaurants that specialize in rice porridge, noodles, and roast meats are a good bet anywhere in Hong Kong.

The tourist who wants a real taste of Hong Kong should not miss the Cantonese tea-breakfast, *yam cha*. Although it is available everywhere in Hong Kong and Kowloon, my favorite place is on the outlying islands. Take an early ferry to Lamma Island and enjoy Cantonese *dim sum* with the locals on the terrace of a harborside restaurant. Then explore island paths and byways until the return ferry arrives.

For dinner, ferry to Cheung Chau Island and walk along the waterfront area. Buy super-fresh seafood from quayside fishmongers and have it cooked to order at the open-air restaurants that come to life at dusk.

In Macao, the food is mostly Chinese but with a sprinkling of Portuguese restaurants and specialties. In alleyways, look for stalls selling delicious barbecued dried meats and cafes with sweet cakes and coffee. As you get closer to the PRC border, Macao feels more "Chinese," and there are many inexpensive food stalls.

Since China has one of the world's great cuisines, you would expect to eat well in the PRC, but until recently that was not the case. Political turmoil during the Cultural Revolution eliminated all but the most basic bland food, and almost killed culinary culture in some areas. Fortunately this has changed in the last few years. Now that the government allows small-scale enterprise, countless restaurants offer tasty, healthy meals at dirt-cheap prices. The surroundings may not always look scrupulously clean, but the food is usually fresh and safe. In fact, much of it is fresher than its counterpart in the West. Pork is butchered the same day it is cooked, and you may see your chicken dinner pecking around the yard as you enter the restaurant.

When eating at a typical roadside restaurant in the PRC, pedal across the parking lot and park your bike where you can keep an eye on it from inside. Take your handlebar bag and cycle computer in with you. Near the entrance there will probably be a glass case with small dishes of cold boiled peanuts, beef, cucumbers, shrimp, et cetera. After getting a table, select the ones you like as a starter.

The menu is on the wall and it is all in Chinese. If you know what you want, turn to the food section of the phraseguide in the back of this book and order. If you do not know what you want, wander into the kitchen and ask the cook to show you what is available. If you see something good on another table, point and use the phraseguide to order that.

Most small restaurants are honest, but some will try to overcharge foreigners who cannot read menu prices. Some even try to charge you for paper napkins and dishes of melon seeds you did not order. From

Interior of a typical country restaurant

the locals' standpoint, you are rich and can afford it if they overcharge you a bit. If you are nervous about this, use the phraseguide to ask for a written total bill in advance. Once you are satisfied with the price, give them the "thumbs up" sign and dig in.

These are *real* Chinese restaurants. Chopsticks are not an amusing alternative to forks; there *are* no forks! Do not wait until you are famished and surrounded by a crowd of curious locals to begin practicing chopsticks skills.

Breakfast in the PRC is the most convenient, economical, and interesting at roadside stalls. In the south, the most common stall breakfasts are rice porridge (*zhou*), steamed rice noodles rolled up with shrimp or pork (*chongfen*), and fried doughsticks (*yutiao*). For a more sumptuous breakfast, try *yam cha* at a teahouse and enjoy a variety of *dim sum* pastries and small dishes with *bonay* tea. Wonton soup, fried doughsticks, steamed buns, soy milk, and pan-fried dumplings are all common along the east-central PRC route (Tour No. 6). On the northeastern tours, try wonton, steamed and fried meat-filled buns, *shaobing* (sesame biscuits stuffed with meat), fried doughnuts filled with date paste, and *jianbing* (savory crepes made to order at streetside carts).

Plan to stop at a roadside restaurant for lunch and a midday break. Lunch is the main meal of the day in many places, and a wide variety of dishes are available. In the south, rice is the starch of choice, but in the north you may choose from noodles, *jiaozi* (meat-filled dumplings), and a variety of steamed and baked breads. Starchy foods, known as the "main food" (*zhushi*), are often served late in the meal, not at the same time as other dishes. Chinese usually have a soup with every meal, a good habit for cyclists who need constant rehydration. Notice that the truck drivers are fueling up on beer and liquor in addition to soup. Another potential road hazard!

For dinner, hotel restaurants are a good choice if you are tired and do not want to ride around hunting for a restaurant. But do not wait until late to eat; hotel dining rooms sometimes close before 8:00 P.M. In country inns, eat at the inn restaurant. Use the phraseguide to ask the cook to prepare local specialties (*feng-wei*). The prices are so cheap that it is worth taking a chance.

Get snacks at roadside stores that sell sweet biscuits, candy, fruits, and canned sodas and juices. For sanitary reasons, purchase snacks that are pre-wrapped rather than the ones in open glass jars. Look for stalls with oil-drum ovens that sell excellent sweet and savory pastries called "cow-tongue cakes" (*niushebing*) because of their shape. In Shandong Province, try *huo shao*, savory muffinlike breads filled with meat and garlic.

In the PRC, do not even think of drinking tap water; drink boiled water (*kaishui*). Fill water bottles at your hotel before heading out, and stop at any restaurant or stall to refill. Even if you are not eating there, locals are happy to give you boiled water. Buy a can of green tea (*lu cha*) and put a few pinches in your water bottle each morning. Bottled spring water is available, but the boiled variety is just fine.

Accommodations

On these tours you will spend most nights in small hotels and inns well outside of tourist areas. Usually there will be few choices, and the service and cleanliness standards will be lower than in the West. Adaptability is a necessary virtue for the cycle tourist in China.

In Taipei lodging is plentiful and expensive. Elsewhere in Taiwan there are clean hotels, inns, and hostels everywhere except the smallest villages. Hotel rooms with a private bath (*tao fang*) are still reasonably priced outside of Taipei. The cheapest inns have bath facilities down the hall, and some even have *tatami* mat rooms left over from the Japanese occupation (1895–1945).

Owners of small inns usually do not mind if you bring your bike into the room, but hotels are not always so obliging. Park the bike outside while you register; then roll the bike into the lobby, smile, and make a dash for the elevator. If that does not work, use the phraseguide to ask where you may safely store your bike.

Informal camping is possible everywhere in Taiwan. School grounds are particularly good because they often have outdoor washing facilities. Wait until school is out to set up your tent on a corner of the sports field, and plan to get out early unless you enjoy being surrounded by a horde of curious kids. Beaches and sandy riverbeds are good informal campsites, but beware of snakes in grassy areas: Taiwan has some of the world's most poisonous varieties. Another bivvy option is small shrines and temples, which usually have shelter, water, and a washing area. Most official campsites in Taiwan were developed by the Youth Movement to accommodate groups of young people. They have barbecue areas, rest rooms, and bathing facilities, but are not always conveniently located on the routes in this guidebook.

In the urban area of Hong Kong, accommodations are plentiful and expensive. You will not be able to bring your bike to your room in the nicer hotels, but they all have luggage rooms where you can store it safely. The Hong Kong YMCA was completely renovated in 1989 and has lost the seedy English charm it once had, but it is reasonably priced and conveniently located at the foot of Nathan Road in Kowloon. It is a popular choice, so reservations should be made well in advance.

In conventional Hong Kong guidebooks, budget travelers are advised to look for rooming houses such as the Chungking Mansions in Kowloon. These are fine if you do not have a bicycle to deal with. The elevators up to these places are often too small to accommodate a bike, not to mention a touring rig with bags. Once you get to the room, there may be no space to put the bike.

On the outlying islands, especially Cheong Chau and Lantau, there are hotels and guest houses that are less expensive than their urban counterparts. These make a good home base in Hong Kong if you do not mind the ferry rides. Lantau also has several roadside campgrounds, which are listed in the route logs for Tour No. 3.

Lodging options in Macao are plentiful, and also quite expensive if you want modern amenities. For budget lodging, look for older Chinese hotels in the streets and alleyways across from the Floating Casino.

Some that were built before there was electric lighting have center-court light wells and colonial-style tall shuttered windows: quite charming if you do not mind the broken sinks and rats. On my last visit, I was advised by the concierge at one such establishment that if I left my luggage on the floor, a rat might chew a hole in it! This "quaint" hotel is listed in the route log for the Pearl River Delta tour (Tour No. 4); refer to your conventional guidebook for other options.

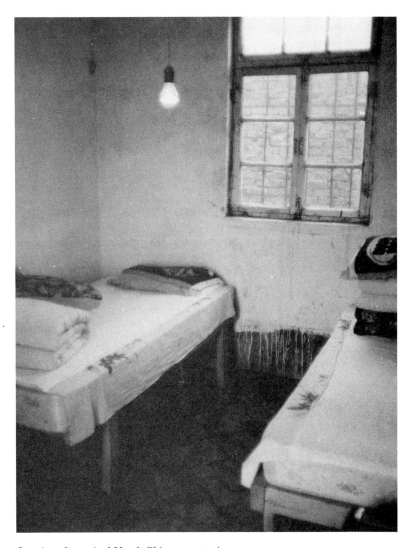

Interior of a typical North China country inn

In the PRC, lodging varies from luxurious city hotels to dirt-floored country inns. Travelers accustomed to western amenities will feel right at home in the expensive tourist hotels of Guangzhou, Shanghai, and Beijing. If your point of entry to the PRC is one of these cities, have your travel agent make advance reservations for the first few days. Shanghai is a hotbed of business and development these days, and the reasonably priced rooms are often all pre-booked.

On the tours in this guidebook, most nights are spent in smaller towns where western-style amenities and service don't exist. Hotels (*fandian*) may have mirrors, marble, and crystal chandeliers in the lobby, but the halls and rooms often have dirty carpets, unwashed walls, and lackluster staff. The first few floors will have rooms with communal bathrooms and hallways that smell like the unclean rest rooms. Upper floors have rooms with a private bath (*biaozhun fang*), chairs, a desk, and some degree of privacy. Even in the better rooms, the hot water is on for only a few hours in the evening. If you arrive before the hot water comes on, get extra bottles of boiled water from the service counter on your floor for washing up. Guesthouses (*binguan*) are like hotels, but often just one or two stories high and spread out with courtyards and gardens. They usually have restaurants and banquet halls for meetings.

Inns (*luguan*) are the ordinary roadhouses of China, and in backward areas they are all that is available. Now that private enterprise is allowed, every highway is lined with signs saying "STOP, EAT, SLEEP" (*Ting-Chi-Zhu*). These inns have a restaurant in front, a muddy courtyard parking lot in back, and a row of tiny brick rooms rented by the room or by the bed. The only hot water comes in thermos bottles, washing facilities consist of (maybe) a chipped enamel basin. The toilet is a brick outhouse across the parking lot, usually with a pigsty next to it. Bring your own towel, sheet-bag, and toilet paper. Inns are dirt cheap, and the floors are sometimes dirt too. Your arrival at an inn will usually cause quite a commotion, attracting neighbors and hordes of kids to see the foreigner. The owner will feel honored that you have chosen his hovel over the neighboring one! There are inns in major cities too, but they usually are not allowed to accept foreigners.

Hostels (*zhaodaisuo*) are operated by Chinese companies or government agencies for their staff, business clients, and unaffiliated travelers. They are very cheap, but most have been instructed by the Gong An to not accept foreigners, especially in cities. Do not confuse *zhaodaisuo* with Youth Hostels, with which they have no affiliation.

At hotels and guesthouses you are required to fill out a form and show your passport. Keys usually are not handed out at the front desk, but at the service counter on each floor. Take your check-in receipt to the service counter, pay *yajin* (see below), and get your key. When service staff bring you hot water in thermos bottles, ask when the hot bath water will be turned on and check to see that they have provided toilet paper in the bathroom.

Outside of Beijing and provincial capitals, hotels don't have set standards for charging foreigners. Room tariffs are listed in RMB, but the clerks may try to make you pay a surcharge because you are a "foreign guest" (some way to treat guests!). This is all negotiable: use the phraseguide in the back of this book to get the best deal possible. In general, negotiate the room price, then pay in advance before management discovers there are foreigners there who can be nicked for a surcharge. Do not let them keep your passport or it may be held hostage for a surcharge. Most places also want *yajin*, a deposit you will forfeit if you steal the keys, the lamp, or the thermos. Pay *yajin* at the main desk or the service desk on your floor, and keep the receipt to get a refund when you leave.

There are no formal check-in procedures for inns: show them your passport, and pay in RMB when you arrive. Ask for a whole room for yourself or your group, or you may have strangers sleeping in the next bed. Bring your bikes inside and use your own lock to padlock the door when you go out.

Camping in PRC? Forget it! In the cities, there is no safe place to camp. In the countryside, lodging is so cheap there is no need to camp. In rustic country inns, you will feel like you are camping anyway.

Language

China's written language and Mandarin Chinese are the common denominator of communication in a country that has hundreds of dialects and subdialects. In Hong Kong and southeastern PRC, Cantonese and its dialects are the most common spoken languages. Moving north along the coast, the language known as *minnanhua* is spoken in Fujian Province and by native-born Taiwanese. In Zhejiang, Jiangsu, and Shanghai provinces, the languages are related to Mandarin Chinese, but you can barely tell it from the way they sound. The languages spoken from Shandong north to Beijing are all fairly recognizable versions of Mandarin. Once you move west into areas where minority peoples live, their languages are not even related to Chinese.

Unless you speak and read Chinese, the largest obstacle to successful cycle touring in China is the language. Most cyclists can navigate road signs and maps in a country that uses the roman alphabet. Hotels, menus, and prices may be difficult, but at least they seem *possible*. This is not the case in China: Chinese has no alphabet, most street signs do not have English subtitles, even numbers may be written several ways.

In Hong Kong, romanization usually allots each Chinese character a single romanized word. In the PRC, characters that are part of a single morpheme (unit of meaning) are generally romanized as one word. The system of romanization in Taiwan is a disorganized combination of the above. For example, a place named South Hill might be romanized *Nan Tang* in Taiwan, *Nam Tong* in Hong Kong, and *Nantang* in the PRC. When doing the Taiwan tours, keep in mind that romanized words on road signs may have spaces or hyphens where those in the logs don't. If you ignore the spaces or hyphens and the word looks the same, it's probably the same word.

A phrase book will help you express yourself, but it won't help you understand the responses you may get. If you use the phrase book to ask a price and the answer is *"liang kuai ban,"* how will you know they just said RMB 2.50? Carry a small notebook and pencil for written answers to questions about times, numbers, prices, et cetera. A notebook is also useful when you take pictures with locals and want to mail copies to your new friends. Use the phraseguide at the back of this book to ask them to write the address clearly in Chinese. When back home, make a photocopy of the address and paste it onto an envelope.

The phraseguide in the back of this book has a section listing common characters on signs for restaurants, inns, guesthouses, and hotels. Learn to recognize these characters so you don't ride past an inn or restaurant when you need one. Make a game of identifying sign characters as you ride and you will soon memorize a basic vocabulary.

No pronunciation guide has been included because the pronunciations and romanizations of Chinese characters vary greatly between the different areas covered by this book. Refer to the pronunciation guides in conventional guidebooks and the phrase books recommended in Research, in the Planning Your Trip section.

Although you do not have to speak Chinese to have a successful tour, learning some basic phrases will make it a richer experience. Basic Chinese is not as difficult as the written language makes it appear. Before your tour, invest some time learning greetings, numbers, and money phrases in Mandarin Chinese. Also learn to recognize Chinese numbers so you can understand prices. Don't be shy; most Chinese respect any attempt by foreigners to speak their language.

Public Transportation

All the tours in this book can be linked with a flight between Taiwan and Hong Kong, and ships and ferries for the rest of the tours. Train transport is not necessary unless you choose an itinerary different than the one suggested. Ship transport was chosen to link the tours because it presents the fewest problems when traveling with bikes.

In Taiwan, if you want to leave before completing the routes, you have a choice of train or bus services to return to Taipei. On trains in Taiwan, bikes aren't allowed as carry-on baggage unless they are dismantled and wrapped. Remove the front wheel and pedals, lower the seat, and pull the handlebars into the frame triangle. Use a cheap plastic tarp and rope to wrap it into a neat package. Once on the train, stow the package in the space between cars.

The public bus system in Taiwan has only one class of service capable of carrying bikes. *Kuokuanghao* buses have two large cargo compartments and each holds two bikes laid on their sides if there isn't much other luggage. If your group is large or other passengers have a lot of luggage, you may run into problems. *Kuokuanghao* service covers western Taiwan from Keelung to Fengkang, and Ilan in the northeast, but doesn't cross the central mountains.

Getting around in Hong Kong is easy: the underground system, trams, buses, and ferries go just about everywhere. But if you want to take your bike along, your choices are limited. Bikes cannot be carried on the underground or on buses, and are only allowed on a few ferries. The Star Ferry does not accept bikes. The Jordan Road Vehicular Ferry is the easiest way to ferry from Kowloon to Hong Kong with your bike. All the Outlying District ferries to the islands accept bikes for a small fee. Full-size ferries to Macao and Guangzhou accept bikes, but not the smaller hydrofoils and jet ferries.

In the PRC, public transportation includes buses, trains, domestic airlines, and ships. Some long-distance buses in the PRC have roof racks for bikes and luggage. For train travel it is customary to ship the bike separately at the shipping department near the passenger terminal. It may not be shipped on the same train as you, and may arrive days later. If you want to try taking your bike on the train with you, you must package it first. Break the bike down, wrap it in a cheap plastic tarp, and tie it with rope. Depending on the size of your rig and where you are trying to board, this *may* get you on board with your bike. If you are traveling solo, you must be able to carry your wrapped bike and luggage on at the same time to avoid ripoffs.

Inland flights are not recommended if you want to take your bike with you. As mentioned earlier, it is currently not acceptable to include your bike as carry-on luggage. You will have to package it carefully for shipping and pay excess baggage fees. With no boarding problems and nominal charges to transport the bike, ships and ferries are the easiest mode for cycle tourists.

Route Finding

Most Chinese signs do not have English subtitles, and route numbers are nonexistent or intermittent. Without signs and route numbers as guideposts, the cyclist who doesn't read Chinese must rely on distances cycled and compass directions. Because of this, the route logs in *China by Bike* are more detailed than those in most guides.

To follow the route logs in this guidebook, you *must* use an accurate cycle computer and a compass to identify turns and reference points in the logs. Begin by calibrating your cycle computer before you leave for your trip.

First, calibrate the computer according to the manufacturer's instructions. Then, to fine tune the calibration, load the bike with gear just as it will be loaded on your tour, check for proper tire pressure, and ride four 0.25-mile laps around a school track (3 to 4 feet out from the inside edge of the track). Adjust calibration so the 1-mile point is as near to your starting point as possible. This is how the bicycles used to log the tours were calibrated.

The goal is to calibrate your computer so that as you tour it registers the same mileages as the route logs, even if the calibration varies somewhat from that recommended by the manufacturer. Once it is calibrated, set the computer to read in kilometers and make a note of the calibration. If you have to change batteries, you will need this number handy.

The route logs in this book were created on actual tours, not extrapolated from maps. While logging the routes, every effort was made to be accurate. Entries were originally recorded in 0.01-kilometer increments, then rounded down to the nearest 0.1 kilometer in the route logs. That means your computer may register the mileage given in the route log a bit before arriving at the turn or intersection (especially if, for example, the original record was 5.19, rounded down to 5.1). Likewise, if your tire pressure is not uniform, or your riding style is more or less wobbly than mine, your readings may vary slightly. Except for a few inner-city segments, log entries are far enough apart that slight variations in metering will not cause you to miss important turns. Use the reference entries—those not in boldface—to ensure you are not drastically off route.

Once you are touring, at the start of each riding day reset the computer trip meter to zero and follow the directions in the route logs. Some long days have several reset points within the log because these spots are logical stopping points for those not wanting to complete the whole riding day. When you leave the route for any reason, even a turn into a parking lot for lunch, disconnect the computer by pushing it back on its mounting bracket so it stops registering. Do not forget to reconnect at the same point when you resume riding!

Once on tour, if your computer is not clicking off the same numbers as the log, the calibration is off or you are lost. Check your tire pressure before adjusting the calibration. Changing the metered tire will also require recalibration if you don't use the same type of tire. The bike used to log the Taiwan tours was different from the bike used on other routes, so a minor calibration adjustment may be necessary between those tour areas.

If you get lost, disconnect your cycle computer, backtrack to the nearest correct log point that you passed, and proceed anew. Once you are back on the correct route, you may have to recalculate the log mileages or rely on the distance between log entries rather than the total accumulated amounts. If you get lost and there are two people in your group using a cycle computer—a good idea—one person should continue metering until his or her computer displays the *next* mileage total in the route log, and then disconnect. Once you have gotten back on track and reach that point in the road, that person can reconnect his or her computer and you will not need to recalculate subsequent mileages.

Even if your computer is calibrated correctly, sometimes roads are under construction, there are detours, or some other factor necessitates a metering adjustment. Re-synchronize your computer with the route logs as follows: If you come up short of an intersection or reference point when the computer displays its mileage, disconnect and ride to that point, then reconnect to continue. If you arrive at an intersection or reference point before the computer displays its mileage, leave the computer connected and backtrack to about one-half the difference, then return to the intersection and the computer should display the correct mileage.

To ask locals for directions, point at the Chinese characters for your destination on the map and use the phraseguide to ask "which way to there?" Be careful with directions from locals: some of them may be lost too!

In China the political subdivisions of the country are province (*sheng*), county (*xian*), city (*shi*), township (*zhen*), rural area (*xiang*), and village (*cun* or *zhuang*). Larger, politically important cities such as Taipei, Shanghai, or Beijing bypass the provincial government and report directly to the national government. In the route logs and on the maps, when a city name is followed by the word "city," it refers to the larger city administrative area, not just the central urban area that goes by that name. Likewise, if a log entry says you've just entered a certain *zhen* or *xiang*, you have entered an administrative area, and may still be some distance from the town that bears the same name. The town name on the map may or may not have *zhen* or *xiang* appended. In the case of villages, if the local sign includes *cun* or *zhuang,* it is included in the name on this book's maps.

Taiwan has a clear system of numbering for national, provincial, and county roads. In the logs they are abbreviated thus:

> NR2 = National Road 2
> PR110 = Provincial Road 110
> CR4 = County Road 4

In Hong Kong, street signs in urban areas have English subtitles, as do road signs on the Outlying District islands. Some roads in the New Territories have signs in Chinese only.

Romanized signage in the PRC is very poor. Outside of major tourist cities, place names on signs are in Chinese characters only. Very few roads have numbers or numbered signs. Along some roads you will see an occasional milestone with a road number, but there is no corresponding number on road maps.

ROUTE LOG LEGEND

X	Intersection, with options to go left, right, or straight ahead; sometimes a traffic circle intersection
T	T-shaped intersection, with options to go left or right
L:T	A side road enters from the left, with options to go left or straight
R:T	A side road enters from the right, with options to go right or straight
Y	Y-shaped intersection, with options to go left or right
L:Y	Y-shaped intersection, with options to go left or straight
R:Y	Y-shaped intersection, with options to go right or straight
Rev	Reversed L:Y or R:Y intersection, with one leg of the Y merging from behind rather than splitting away ahead of you
Disconnect	Disconnect your computer trip meter, but read the rest of the route log to determine whether to reconnect or reset
Reconnect	Reconnect your computer trip meter after having disconnected for side explorations
Reset	Reset your computer trip meter to 0.0
#.#	Log mileage indicates a reference point
#.#	**Log mileage** in boldface indicates an important intersection or change in route
(SE)	Indicates the compass direction you should be traveling *after* making a turn
SE	Indicates a position rather than a direction of travel; i.e., the southeast corner of an intersection
EOD	End point of that day's main route log (End of Day); sometimes referred to as a starting point for the next day

Map Legend

▬▬▬	Main route	●	End-of-day point (EOD)
▬▬▬	Other roads	②	National road
----------	Ferry	172	Provincial road
—·——··	Political boundary	✈	Airport
▬-▬-▬	Railroad	⛰	Mountains
☉	Small town		
◉	City		

Opposite: *Looking through a portal of the Badaling Great Wall*

PART II

9 TOURS GEARED FOR DISCOVERY

TOUR NO. 1: TAIWAN

A NORTHERN ISLAND LOOP
Chiang Kai Shek Airport to Taipei

Distance: Approximately 650 kilometers
Estimated time: 10 riding days
Best time to go: March–June, September–November
Terrain: Mountainous, rugged
Map: Nelles Map of Taiwan
Connecting tour: Tour No. 2

Begin the tour at Chiang Kai Shek International Airport, some 40 kilometers west of Taipei. From the airport follow the coast road around the northern tip of the island, then down the rugged northeastern coast. Head west through Taroko Gorge and cross the central mountains at Tayuling. Coast down through high mountain fruit orchards at Lishan and Kukuan hot-spring resort to the West Taiwan Plain. Near Taichung, head north through the western foothills, and complete the loop at Taoyuan near the airport. If desired, cycle into Taipei for an end-of-tour ride in the city.

CONNECTIONS. International flights to Taiwan arrive at Chiang Kai Shek (CKS) International Airport. The tour begins at the airport, so there is no need to navigate Taipei traffic to get started. Before leaving the airport, do not forget to change money, buy maps if you need them, and store your bike box if you won't be staying at a nearby hotel.

In the upstairs Departures area, there are kiosks that sell maps of Taipei and Taiwan. While in the Departures area, confirm your flight out, or make sure you have the telephone number so you can confirm while on the road.

To connect this tour with Tour No. 2, ride the first four segments to Tailuko, the starting point for Tour No. 2.

When it is time to leave Taiwan, arrive at the airport early enough to get your bike box out of storage, box your bike, and attend to all of the formalities. Don't forget to set aside NT$300 per person for the airport departure tax.

The check-in people at CKS International Airport are not used to handling bikes and may try to charge you excess baggage fees. Just tell them you were allowed the bike as one piece of luggage on the trip to Taiwan and would appreciate the same treatment upon leaving.

INFORMATION. The first day of this tour is a full riding day, so plan on spending the first night near the airport unless you arrive early in the day. The CKS Airport Hotel, telephone (033) 833666, is not inexpensive, but you can store your bike box there if you reserve a room for your final night in Taiwan as well. Get a taxi or shuttle bus

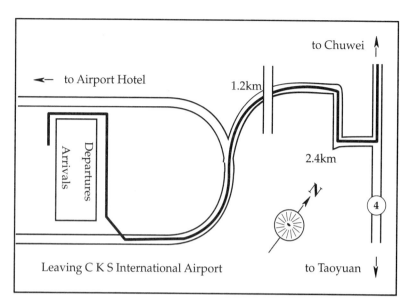

Leaving C K S International Airport

from the airport to the Airport Hotel. Budget travelers who arrive late in the day can spend the night in the airport terminal. (I rolled out my sleeping bag next to the snack bar and discovered one of the cooks sleeping on the other side of the counter!)

If you arrive before dark, you can cycle into Taoyuan for more lodging options. Campers can cycle the first 6 kilometers of the main route to Chuwei Beach and spend the night there.

Taiwan is semi-tropical, with hot muggy summers. Although "plum rains" are likely in spring, and early fall is the typhoon season, these two seasons are still the best time to go.

Budget at least two weeks for this ten–riding-day tour, to allow a rest day in Tienhsiang and a few days to visit Taipei. Remember to cycle on the right in Taiwan.

Also be aware of Taiwan's inconsistent system of romanization: words on road signs may differ slightly from those used in this book's logs and maps.

Side Trip to Taoyuan: 35 km

If you prefer not to stay at the airport and have some daylight hours left when you arrive, you can cycle 17.5 kilometers into Taoyuan for more lodging and dining options. Return to CKS Airport the next day to begin the next segment's route log.

WHERE TO STAY. There are reasonably priced hotels along Fuhsing Road and on side streets near the train station.

WHERE TO EAT. The busy downtown area around the bus station and the train station is a good bet. Noodle shops and food carts set up shop on street corners and alleyways at dusk.

WHAT TO DO. If you spend your first night in Taiwan here, just walking around the downtown area will be a good introduction to the lively evening culture of Taiwanese towns. Join the locals who go out to *sanbu* (stroll) in the parks and shop in street bazaars. Fancy barbershops offer both haircuts and "massages," and young wives accompany their husbands to make sure they do not wander into the wrong kind of barbershop! Evening is every bit as lively as the daytime.

Log:

0.0 Standing in front of the airport Arrivals exit doors, turn right and ride around the building. At the other end of the building, on the Departures side, turn left onto a road and continue until the road begins to loop back to the terminal. At the "CARGO TERMI-NAL" sign, exit to the right and descend into an underpass.

1.2 Ride through the underpass.

2.1 X; turn right at the "NAN KAN" sign.

2.4 X; turn left. There's a gas station on the left.

2.8 T; turn right (E) onto NR4 toward Taoyuan.

8.6 Sign: "NAN KAN."

10.6 Pass under a freeway. NR4 is now co-named Chunri Road.

16.5 The main road ascends an overpass, and a smaller lane stays to the right of the ramp. Stay right in the small lane until the first large intersection. Turn right onto Fuhsing Road at mileage point 16.6.

17.4 EOD; the Taiwan public bus station (Gong Lu Ju) is on the left, with a hotel above the terminal. Other hotels can be found up and down this street.

Chiang Kai Shek Airport to Kinshan: 74.9 km

Leave the airport and head west to the coast at Chuwei. Ride north up the coast through Pali to Bochuantou and explore the 200-year-old Kaitai Tienhou Temple, then ferry across the Tamshui River mouth to Tamshui.

Along the Tamshui quay there are food carts where you can eat barbecued cuttlefish or play pinball for grilled sausages and peanut ice cream. The Taiwanese love to eat and to gamble, and these little carts let you do both. In Tamshui, explore the markets and the temples. If you are inclined to extend your visit in Tamshui, the route log gives the option of staying there overnight and continuing on the rest of the route the next day.

On your way out of Tamshui, stop at Hung Mao Cheng (Red Hair City). This fort was built in 1629 by the Spanish and later taken over by the Dutch. Taiwanese at the time called the Dutch "red hairs," hence the name. Inside the fort are a museum and formal gardens.

Once out of Tamshui, pass Shalun Beach and head north through the countryside to Baishawan Beach, a popular sailboarding spot. Wu

Fishing boats along the Tamshui River

Lung Gong (Five Dragon Palace) has interesting rock formations and Shih Pa Wang Gong (Eighteen Kings Temple) has a celebration on weekends with Taiwanese open-air opera.

End the day in Kinshan, a small fishing town on the northwestern coast. At night there is a hum of boat motors as Kinshan Bay fills with brightly lit cuttlefish boats.

WHERE TO STAY. The Kinshan Youth Activity Center has plenty of campsites, and rooms are inexpensive; telephone 032-982-511, 512, 513. There are also small inns in the downtown area of Kinshan near the bus stop. Those who opt to spend the night in Tamshui will find small hotels in the downtown area. Campers should follow the route log from Tamshui to Shalun Beach at mileage point 4.1.

WHERE TO EAT. Meals are available until 6:00 P.M. in the castlelike main building of the Kinshan Youth Activity Center, and there are drinks, snacks, beer, and barbecued meat at the upstairs snack bar in the hot-spring building. There are also restaurants in the downtown area of Kinshan near the bus stop.

WHAT TO DO. Soak away the kilometers in the hot spring and watch the sun set over the Taiwan Straits. The hot spring is open until 10:00 P.M.

Log:

0.0 In front of the CKS Airport Arrivals exit doors, turn right and ride around the building. At the other end of the building, on the

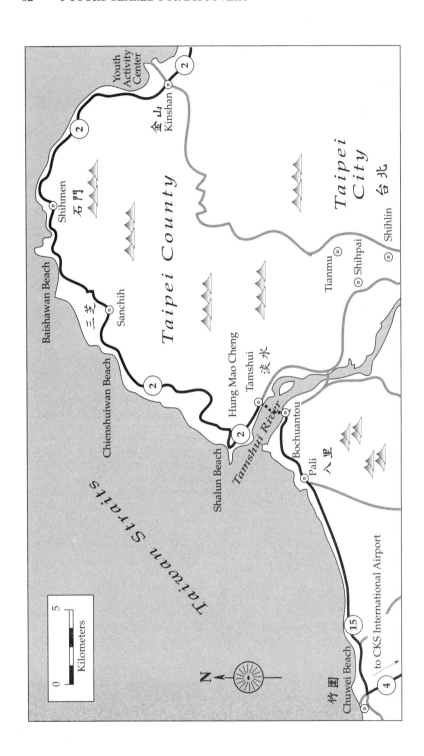

Departures side, turn left and continue until the road begins to loop back to the terminal. At the "CARGO TERMINAL" sign, exit to the right, and descend into an underpass.

1.2 Ride through the underpass.

2.1 X; turn right at the "NAN KAN" sign.

2.4 X; turn left. A gas station is on the left.

2.8 Y; turn left (W) on NR4.

4.9 X; go straight, then left (SW) toward Chuwei Beach.

5.3 R:T, at Chuwei Beach entry arch; turn right (W). Just after the turn are a temple, and small stores selling fruit and snacks. Farther down on the right are old Chinese graveyards.

6.3 Main gate of the beach-recreation area, with a small cafe on the right. Disconnect here to explore further. There are no official camping areas, but the area with tables is covered against rain. If the main gate is closed, slip through the small side gate across from the cafe. When ready to leave Chuwei Beach, reconnect your computer and head back to the entry arch.

7.1 T, at Chuwei Beach entry arch; turn left (N) onto NR15.

7.4 R:T; go straight (NE) on NR15. A right turn here leads back to the airport.

13.2 R:T, just before the Linkou power plant; continue straight ahead.

23.1 Nan Kan Gong Temple is on the right.

24.0 Pa Hsien Le Yuan (Eight Immortals amusement park).

24.3 Enter the village Pali. Continue through town.

29.6 Old Kaitai Tienhou Temple is on the right as you enter Bochuantou. Just past the temple, the first small alley on your left leads to the ferry pier. Go left down the alley, passing stalls selling small blue crabs and donuts filled with red bean paste.

29.8 At the foot of the alley are a cement pier and a ticket kiosk. Purchase ferry tickets to Tamshui. Notice the Taiwanese fishing boats with painted eyes moored along the shore. Disembark on the Tamshui quay and sample barbecued squid, shrimp rolls, and black-colored spiced eggs called "iron-eggs." Disconnect to explore the quay area, then reconnect and push your bike up the alley to Chung Cheng Lu.

29.9 T; head right (E) on Chung Cheng Lu to the main downtown intersection and the bus station. To explore Tamshui, go back (W) along Chung Cheng Lu, and the public market is in an alley on the right. Push up through the narrow stalls to get to the Ancestors Temple and Lung Shan Temple, both worth exploring. To continue the main route, retrace your way to the bus station and the main downtown intersection.

0.0 At the bus station intersection, reset and head west on Chung Cheng Lu, which turns into NR2.

1.5 Hung Mao Cheng is the walled red compound on the right. Disconnect and explore, then reconnect and continue west on NR2.

3.8 NR2 curves sharply to the right.

4.1 X; go straight on NR2 toward Sanchih. A left turn here leads to Shalun Beach, which is suitable for camping if you decide to stay the night in Tamshui.

Roadside dragon on the way to Kinshan

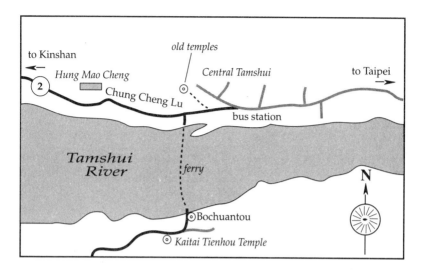

4.8 X; follow NR2 to the left.
8.8 X; follow NR2 left toward Kinshan.
15.2 Pass Chienshuiwan Beach.
16.8 Village of Chih Lan.
24.5 Baishawan Beach.
29.3 Enter Shihmen.
30.4 Pass Wu Lung Gong tourist area.
32.0 Rest stop on the left, Shi Pa Wang Temple on the right.
43.0 Enter Kinshan.
44.0 EOD; Kinshan bus station. There are small inns and restaurants in this area. To get to the Kinshan Youth Activity Center, continue and turn left at the intersection just past the bus station.
44.2 Pass under a red arch into the Kinshan scenic area.
44.4 Y, at Rosa Beach Plaza Hotel Road; go left.
44.7 Y; go up around a hill to the left.
45.0 Entrance gates to the Kinshan Youth Activity Center.

Kinshan to Fulung Beach: 63.6 km

Get up early and breakfast in Kinshan. Find your morning meal by riding down the main street until you see people eating grilled meat-filled buns and hot soy milk in open street stalls. Join them for a traditional Taiwanese breakfast.

Heading out of Kinshan onto the coast, the hilly road passes hibiscus- and azalea-covered cliffs through Feitsuiwan, Yehliu, Wanli, and other upscale beach colonies. Yehliu is famous for its odd shoreside rock formations. Disconnect your cycle computer if you wish to explore these areas, then reset and continue on the route to drop into Keelung, the largest city on the northern coast.

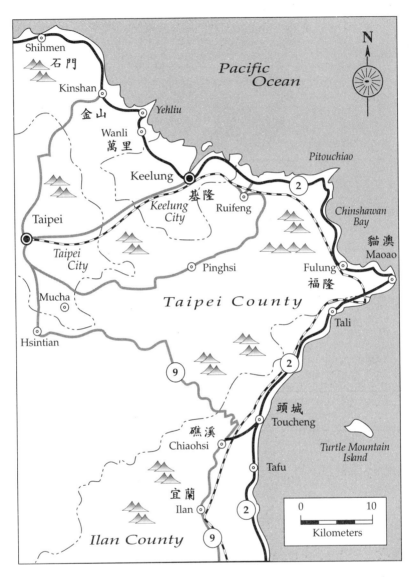

Keelung is the main container-cargo port in northern Taiwan, and is not especially scenic. Still, a cruise on your bike around the harbor, up the hill to the Kuan Yin statue, and around the old downtown area is worthwhile. For local food specialties, ask locals about the Miaokou market area.

After Keelung, the wide northeastern coast road is dotted with fishing villages and an occasional industrial plant. Shuinantong, Aoti, and

Pitouchiao all retain the flavor of traditional Taiwanese fishing-village life. Spend the night at Fulung, considered the best beach in northern Taiwan.

WHERE TO STAY. The Fulung Public Hostel is operated by the Highway Department and has beach campsites and rooms in beach cottages. During the busy summer season, room reservations are necessary; telephone 032-991211-991216, (032) 991509. It's open from June through September. Other lodging is available along the main road in Fulung.

WHERE TO EAT. The main building of the Fulung Public Hostel has snacks, beverages, and meals at reasonable prices. There are other restaurants along the highway in Fulung.

WHAT TO DO. Relax and enjoy the beach scenery. Snorkel gear is available for rent at the Fulung Public Hostel for those who want to see the colorful fish that live in the shallow coastal waters.

Log:

0.0 Retrace from your night's lodging to yesterday's EOD point in Kinshan by the bus station. Reset and head (SE) on NR2.

5.7 Go through a short tunnel and come out near a small harbor.

8.3 Feitsuiwan beach colony.

10.1 Wanli village.

11.1 Y; head left toward Keelung, still on NR2.

13.7 Reach the peak of the grade.

19.2 Y; bear right, heading downhill.

21.1 X, by a police station; turn left.

22.1 Enter Keelung Tunnel. Ride on the pedestrian path.

22.5 Exit the tunnel onto An Le Road.

23.1 X; turn left onto Chung Shan Road, Sec. 1. You are now on the "wrong side of the tracks." Use the overpass to get to the other side.

23.5 Do a U-turn and ascend the overpass over railroad tracks. Then take a right and go down the ramp. Make a hairpin left turn when you are on other side of the tracks and end up at the train station.

24.2 Keelung train station and ferry terminal (Pier 2). Disconnect here to explore the Keelung area. When you are ready to continue, return to the train station and reconnect. Head east from the train station along the busy main street, then turn left at the street just before McDonald's, where a sign says "COAST HIGHWAY."

26.3 Y; bear to the right.

27.2 Y; bear right. Do not take the hard right.

29.0 T; turn right. A sign says "COAST HIGHWAY."

35.0 Pass Shenao coal power plant.

36.1 X; stay straight on NR2.

37.3 Go through the Coastal Tunnel.

40.8 Enter the community of Shuinantong.

43.4 Nanya entrance sign. There is a sign for the start of the "NORTH-EAST COAST."

46.8 Pitouchiao (Nosetip Point), a tourist view spot, is on your left.
47.5 Pass Maopitou Tunnel. There are switchbacks after the tunnel.
54.7 Chinshawan Bay.
57.0 Enter Aoti fishing village.
61.2 Y; stay left on NR2.
63.6 EOD; the village of Fulung. Disconnect and turn left at the Fulung Beach sign to enter the recreation area.

Fulung Beach to Suao: 85.1 km

This segment's ride continues along the northeastern coast to the picturesque fishing village of Maoao, the easternmost place in Taiwan. The next town of any size is Toucheng, which has a beach and a camping area. After Toucheng, leave the main highway for a side trip to Chiaohsi.

Chiaohsi is a resort with hot-spring water piped into hotel rooms. Many guests come here to be rejuvenated by the waters (and by the services of local brothels). The other attraction is Wu Feng Chi Falls.

Back on NR2, continue south through fairly flat terrain passing rice

Roadside noodle stand on Taiwan's northeast coast

paddies, duck farms, and shrimp ponds. End the day in Suao, a small port city handling shipping for the northeastern coast. Suao is also the north end of the Su Hua Highway, the "most dangerous road in Taiwan."

WHERE TO STAY. For inexpensive lodging in Suao, try the Ching Du Hotel just across from the train station; telephone 962586. North of town is the Lung Chuan Luguan, near the cold spring.

WHERE TO EAT. There are small restaurants around the train station and farther west along Chung Shan Road. The market in Suao is north of the main street across from the train station. Be sure to try the local specialty confection: *Suao Yang Keng*, a sweet that goes well with tea. Stock up on road snacks for the next segment's ride; there is not much available until Hoping at mileage point 55.4.

WHAT TO DO. In Chiaohsi, visit Wu Feng Chi Falls. Follow the road past the Happy Happy Hotel to a parking lot. Walk past the gauntlet of souvenir hawkers to a stone path that leads up to the falls. This is a good place to have lunch, but get food before coming up from Chiaohsi. In Suao, if the weather is hot visit Suao Cold Spring (*Suao Lung Chuan*). From the train station, go one block north and turn right (east). After the turn, take the second left (north). Cross the creek, then turn left again to get to the cold spring.

Log:

0.0 At the front gate of Fulung Beach recreation area, reset and turn left onto NR2.

6.4 The fishing village of Maoao is on the left.

11.1 Lailai village.

19.8 Tali village. Tien Gong Temple is on the right.

23.7 Tahsi village.

28.7 Beikuan village.

36.4 Enter Toucheng.

38.1 Sign: "TOU CHENG BEACH."

38.3 L:T; continue straight. To get to Toucheng Beach, disconnect here and go left 0.6 km. When you are through exploring the beach area, return to the intersection and reconnect.

42.5 R:T, at flashing light; turn right (W) off NR2 onto CR4 toward Chiaohsi.

47.7 Cross railroad tracks.

47.7 T; turn right (N). After 0.1 km, take the next left (W) and go up a block to a school.

47.9 T, at the school; turn left (S) onto Chung Cheng Lu.

48.3 X, at the second flashing light; turn right (W) toward the mountains.

49.3 X; go straight through.

50.2 Arrive at the Chiaohsi hot-spring hotel area. The Happy Happy Hotel is on the left. Disconnect and ride about 1 km farther to Wu Feng Chi Falls. Return to the hotel area and reconnect for the return to NR2.

51.2 X; go straight.

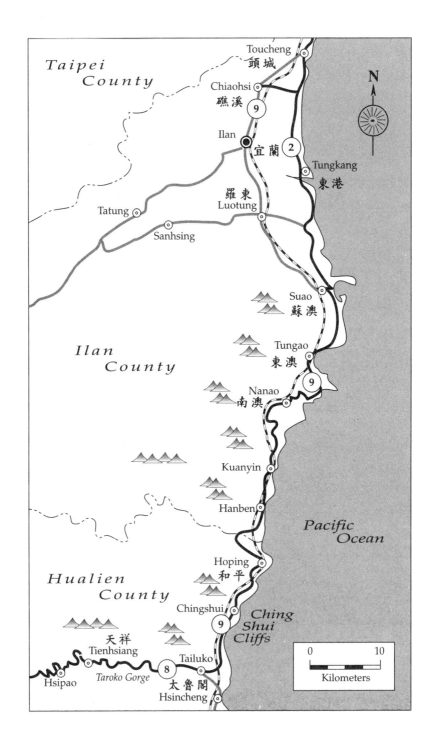

52.2 X; turn left (N) onto Chung Cheng Lu.
52.5 R:T; turn right (E) at the school.
52.6 X; turn right (S) again.
52.7 X; turn left (E), cross railroad tracks, and head back to NR2.
57.9 T, at NR2; turn right (S).
66.8 Y; head left toward Suao.
68.7 Y; go left, up over a bridge.
72.3 X; go straight across the bridge on NR2.
83.1 Enter a 1-km-long tunnel.
84.5 Port of Suao on the left. Turn right (W) onto Chung Shan Road, the main street of Suao.
85.0 L:T; turn left at the town clock and ride one block to the train station traffic circle.
85.1 EOD; Suao train station.

Suao to Tailuko: 83.8 km

The Su Hua Highway frightens Taiwanese because tour buses have a habit of going over the Chingshui Cliffs into the sea. Built in the 1920s, it has been under constant repair to keep mud slides from destroying it. Although in recent years the road has been improved with new tunnels and wider lanes, it is still steep and dangerous. Ride on the ocean side of the road and you will be less likely to get bonked by a rock coming off the mountainside. On the mountain side, you are less likely to be hit by oncoming traffic or go over the cliffs. Whichever side of the road you choose, do not forget to light incense and say your prayers at the roadside shrines!

When leaving Suao, check the sign indicating whether the highway is open. If there is heavy rain or a typhoon, skip this segment and take a train to Hsincheng, then cycle a few kilometers to Tailuko. The Su Hua Highway is no place to be during severe weather.

Tunnels on the Su Hua Highway are often long, not well lit, and full of potholes. Be sure to have headlights and a safety flasher ready. Some of the newer tunnels are lit but have scant room for bikes. In most cases, the old road still skirts the new tunnel along the cliffs, and it is safer to cycle the old road.

Hoping is a possible overnight spot for those who wish to do this segment in two days; it is also a good spot to stock up on road food and snacks. If you do not restock in Hoping, your last chance is in Tailuko before you head over the mountains. Once you are in Taroko Gorge, there is nothing available until Tienhsiang, where selection is meager and prices are high. And from Tienhsiang to Tayuling, stores are infrequent and not always open. If you have room, pack enough for three days when you are in Hoping or Tailuko, and restock in Lishan.

After the Hoping Tunnel, you come out onto the Ching Shui Cliffs. The color of the water below is wonderful, varying from a pale blue-green to a deep steely blue. After this narrow stretch, the road gets better and it is easy pedaling into the town of Tailuko, near the entrance of Taroko Gorge.

If you get to Tailuko before 1:00 P.M., you can continue on to

Cliffs along the Su Hua highway

Tienhsiang instead of stopping for the night in Tailuko. But give your-self plenty of time: the all-uphill ride through the Taroko Gorge takes about three hours, and you don't want to rush this scenic road.

WHERE TO STAY. In Tailuko village, you can stay at Taroko Lodge, on the right as you enter the village commercial strip. For camping, continue through town to the school grounds, or hop boulders down to a gravel shoal along the river.

WHERE TO EAT. In Tailuko, eat at the Lan Lan restaurant a few doors up from Taroko Lodge on the same side of the street, or at other places across the street.

WHAT TO DO. If you choose to spend the night in Hoping, be care-ful about asking about things to do around town. A friend once asked the hotel concierge what was fun to do in Hoping, and she offered her-self! Tailuko is a sleepy little town with not much to do except listen to the wind and river in the gorge above.

Log:

0.0 At the Suao train station, reset and ride a block (N) to the town clock and turn right (E) toward the coast.

0.3 Cross a small bridge and turn right onto NR9 toward Hualien. The road heads up steeply. The sign indicating the open/closed status of the Su Hua Highway is located here.

9.4 Top of the first grade. Watch out for landslides.

12.9 Rest stop and a shrine are on the left. Say prayers and light in-cense for your safe journey on the Su Hua Highway.

15.7 Enter the village of Tungao. Start uphill again.

20.8 Long tunnel. Be careful of water and potholes.

27.0 Enter Nanao.

36.8 Top of the third grade.

42.9 Steep cliffs.

55.4 Hoping. Stock up on road food and snacks. (Lodge here if you cannot make it to Tailuko today; disconnect but *do not* reset your cycle computer.)

60.9 Enter Hoping Tunnel. Beware of potholes.

61.7 Exit Hoping Tunnel onto the infamous Ching Shui Cliffs.

69.8 Pass Chingshui (Green Water).

74.0 New tunnel.

83.8 EOD; entrance gate to Taroko Gorge. Turn left to go into Tailuko village, or reset and turn right to continue on to Tienhsiang on NR8 (see the next segment).

Tailuko to Tienhsiang: 19 km

This short segment ascends through Taroko Gorge, one of the premier scenic spots in Taiwan. The narrow road was cut through solid marble at a cost of many lives and dollars. Along the steady uphill ride, pagodas, temples, and grottoes provide unusual scenes. The Liwu River has many pools suitable for cooling off hot, tired bikers, but there are only a few places where you can get down to them.

Entry gate to Taroko Gorge

In Tienhsiang, enjoy the mountain air, explore Hsiang Te Ssu temple, and enjoy the open-air hot spring at Wenshan.

WHERE TO STAY. The Tienhsiang Guest House at the end-of-day point is good but expensive. Up the road on the left is the Catholic Hostel. Past the hostel on a steep hill is the Youth Activity Center, telephone 038-691111, which has private and dorm-style rooms. Campers can find a spot overlooking the river on the left just after they cross the red steel bridge. The parklike areas around the bus station are also possible informal bivvy spots.

WHERE TO EAT. The Youth Activity Center meals are basic but safe. There is no menu to choose from: you eat what they serve. Food sold in stalls near the bus station is expensive and has usually been sitting there a while. You will be glad you brought snack foods with you.

WHAT TO DO. Enjoy the mountain scenery, Hsiang Te Ssu temple, and Wenshan hot spring. Hsiang Te Ssu is just below Tienhsiang across a suspension footbridge. To get to Wenshan hot spring, go 2 kilometers up the road to the third tunnel. Take the path with a red iron railing down to the right of the tunnel, and lock your bikes there. Cross a suspension footbridge over the gorge and descend to the river on steep steps cut into the side of the gorge. Wade downstream about 30 meters and the hot-spring pool is in a grotto on the left. It's wonderful to go at night, but bring candles and be sure your flashlight is working well. It's customary to wear more than your skin at outdoor public hot springs in Taiwan.

Log:

- 0.0 At the entrance gate to Taroko Gorge, the beginning point of NR8, reset and follow NR8 into the gorge.
- 2.5 L:T, to Chan Guang Zen temple; continue straight.
- 4.6 Silver Belt waterfall.
- 7.5 Hsi Ban Reservoir is on the right.
- 9.3 Begin passing through Swallow's Grotto. Look out to the Liwu River below from holes in the tunnel.
- 15.7 Tzu Mu Bridge, with a rest pavilion on the right.
- 19.0 Cross a red steel bridge into Tienhsiang; EOD, at the bus terminal.

Tienhsiang to Tayuling: 57.7 km

This segment's ride climbs to a pass at more than 2,500 meters elevation on the crest of the central mountain range. The road is steep and narrow with dark craggy tunnels, but the scenery is right out of a Chinese painting: jade green peaks, twisted pines, and wisps of cloud blowing by.

The ride is mostly uphill, with occasional small villages and rest stops. Bring plenty of safe water and stock up on road snacks and food in case you do not make it to Tayuling. The stores mentioned in the route log are not always open.

Tzu Mu Bridge in the Taroko Gorge

WHERE TO STAY. Tayuling Shan Chuang hostel has large *tatami* rooms and is open mid-May through summer. Out of season, it is a good informal camping spot with water and shelter.

WHERE TO EAT. Tayuling Shan Chuang hostel serves basic meals. Also try mountain-food products at the bus-stop food stalls, including soup made with wild mushrooms, lily blossoms, and wild ferns.

WHAT TO DO. Tayuling is definitely not famous for its night life. Enjoy the peace and crisp mountain air while you watch the sun set over the cloud-blown peaks.

Log:

- 0.0 At the bus terminal in Tienhsiang, reset and head uphill toward Wenshan.
- 2.0 Wenshan hot spring is in the gorge to the right.
- 7.8 R:T; continue straight.
- 8.0 Village of Hsipao.
- 9.4 Rest pavilion is on the left, looking down on Tienhsiang.
- 15.3 Village of Losao (elevation 1,117 m).
- 22.1 Hualuhsi Creek.

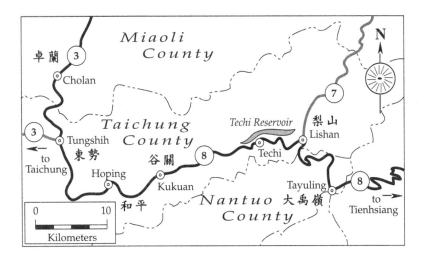

27.1 Hsin Bai Yang rest area. This is a rustic sheltered rest stop with tables, rest rooms, and water. It is a good spot for a lunch break.

36.3 Enter Cien (elevation 1,995 m). Cien Shan Chuang hostel, open from mid-May through summer, is on the hill to the right.

37.0 Go through a half-tunnel with a stream flowing over it, then a second tunnel.

A dark craggy tunnel on the Cross-island Highway

37.4 A food stop is on the right, an apple farm is on the left. Neither may be open.

41.9 Bilu "Spirit Tree" on the left. A snack shop is ahead around the bend. By now you should be riding in the clouds.

47.3 Enter Bilu. Go through two long tunnels after Bilu, then enjoy 4 km of downhill before climbing again.

51.2 Cross Kuanyuan Bridge.

52.8 Enter Kuanyuan.

53.1 Food shops.

57.3 Entry sign for Tayuling (elevation 2,565 m). The small side road heading up to the right leads to the Tayuling Shan Chuang hostel.

57.7 EOD; "downtown Tayuling" has a bus stop and food stalls, but no lodging.

Tayuling to Kukuan: 77 km

Take revenge for the previous segment's uphill grind with a magnificent downhill coast through high mountain pear orchards and hillside villages. This part of Taiwan is famous for snow pears (*hsuehli*), a crisp fruit with the texture of an apple, but the taste of a pear. Out of season, many of the fruits sold at these roadside stands are not local, but imported into Taiwan. After a lunch break in Lishan, continue down the river and end the day at an old-style hot-spring resort located in the Kukuan Gorge.

WHERE TO STAY. In Kukuan, there are the Kukuan Hotel, Ming Chih Hotel, Utopia Holiday Hotel, and more. Most of the seedy old Japanese-style inns have been replaced by expensive western-style hotels. Campers may find a spot on the gravel bars along the Tachia River, but it's not official.

WHERE TO EAT. The resort hotels all have excellent dining rooms. The commercial area around the bus stop has budget restaurants and stores.

WHAT TO DO. Take a hot-spring soak, walk through the Kukuan Gorge, and, if you still have energy, 1 kilometer below Kukuan is the Eight Immortals Mountain recreation area.

Log:

0.0 At the bus parking area in Tayuling, reset and continue to the tunnel entrance on the right. Go through the tunnel, watching for potholes.

8.0 Pass through apple and pear orchards on steep slopes.

12.4 Piluchi, an orchard village, has a snack stand.

20.0 Cross Hohuanhsi Bridge. From here to Lishan, watch out for mean guard dogs near the houses.

28.0 Enter upper Lishan. Eat and restock food supplies at restaurants and stores here. It is cheaper than in the tourist area below.

30.0 Lishan bus station and tourist area. Here there are fruit vendors, restaurants, hotels, and views. Disconnect, explore, and rest. When you are ready to continue, reconnect.

30.6 R:Y; stay left on the main road toward Kukuan.

47.1 Techi Shan Chuang hostel is on the right.

50.0 Enter Techi (elevation 1,400 m).

52.4 Just past the entrance to the Techi Dam tourist area, NR8 splits into two one-way roads; take the one to the right. Watch for bumps where falling rocks have pock-marked the road. There are bad tunnels along this stretch.

60.6 Pass the power station entrance on the right.

63.4 Cross Taren Bridge.

65.3 Pass another dam, then ride uphill.

67.3 Top of the hill; rejoin two-way NR8 and head downhill again.

77.0 EOD; enter Kukuan (elevation 800 m) at R:T above the Kukuan Hotel.

Kukuan to Cholan: 44.7 km

This segment continues down from the mountains through tea gardens, banana plantations, and sugarcane fields. On the edge of the West Taiwan Plain, cut north and take the foothill route to Cholan. Explore the town temple, then have a street-food dinner at the stalls that open around dusk. Cholan is famous throughout Taiwan for its quality fruits, and the local oolong teas are excellent.

WHERE TO STAY. Go 50 meters past this segment's end-of-day point to the next large intersection and turn right. About 250 meters farther on the right is the Liang Bin Lushe (Friendly Guest Hostel), which is seedy but adequate. Campers can continue up the main road until it ends at a school ground.

WHERE TO EAT. There are plenty of food stalls and fruit stands along the main street.

WHAT TO DO. Stroll the main street and explore the town temple across from the end-of-day point. Be sure to step into one of the tea stores and sample the fragrant oolong teas grown in this area. For a really fragrant brew, try the *ching hsiang wulong* brewed in a small teapot and served in miniature cups. The flowery fragrance comes solely from the tea, not from added flowers. A pinch of this tea is great in your water bottle when the weather is hot.

Log:

0.0 At the T intersection above the Kukuan Hotel, reset and head downhill on NR8.

0.3 Bus-stop area with tourist shops and food stalls.

1.0 L:T; go straight on the main road. The Eight Immortals Mountain recreation area is to the left.

3.0 Pass through Yangli.

4.4 Pass through Songke.

9.2 Entrance gate to a Taoist temple is on the right.

High mountain hostel at Tayuling

11.2 Cross Tungli Bridge. You're in the foothills now, passing through banana orchards and bamboo groves.

16.0 Pass the village of Nanshih.

17.8 Pass the village of Hoping.

21.0 Village of Tienlung. The red bridge ahead on the left leads to Puli, near Sun Moon Lake.

21.1 Go through a tunnel and continue straight at L:T after the tunnel.

31.5 Enter the town of Tungshih.

32.5 Y; bear left (NW) on NR8. (A right heads into Tungshih.)

34.4 T; NR8 ends at NR3. Reset here.

 0.0 T; reset and turn right (E). After the turn there is a L:Y; go left (NE) up a hill, winding through farms and orchards.

 8.8 Cross Lanshih Bridge and enter Cholan.

10.3 EOD; X, with NR3 heading left and the town temple across the intersection on the left.

Cholan to Chutung: 80.3 km

Continue north along the foothill route though orchards and strawberry farms, stopping at midday to explore Fa Yun Ssu monastery. When passing through Shihtan and Omei, notice the farmhouse archi-

Gamblers at the Lishan tourist market

tecture: horseshoe-shaped compounds built around a courtyard threshing area. Unlike more industrialized cities on the western plain, these foothill villages retain the feel of traditional Taiwan. Finish the day in Chutung, a larger town with a lively night market along the river.

WHERE TO STAY. The Chutung Talushe hotel is across the river by the large traffic circle. A less expensive choice is the Hsin Tien Ti guesthouse at 15 Tunglin Road, on the left before the river about 1.4 kilometers from the end-of-day point.

WHERE TO EAT. In the downtown area of Chutung there are plenty of restaurants. The night market on streets near the downtown creek is also a good bet.

WHAT TO DO. The best parts of this segment's ride are the Fa Yun Ssu monastery and the countryside scenery. Although it is not a small village, Chutung is another sleeper. The most interesting areas are around the night market.

Log:

0.0 From the intersection in Cholan with the town temple across on the left (previous segment's EOD), reset and head left (NNW) on NR3. Leaving Cholan, pass through vineyards, citrus orchards, and bamboo groves.

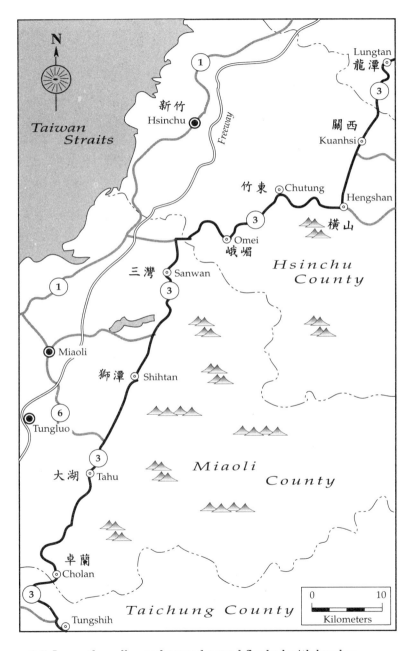

1.5 Leave the valley and ascend a road flanked with bamboo.
6.3 Cross a bridge in the next valley and head uphill again.
7.4 Pass a village.

15.8 Pass through a strawberry-growing area.

16.2 Pass a village and a school off to the left. Stay on the main road.

18.5 Enter Tahu (also called Tsaomei).

19.0 Cross the Houlunghsi River.

23.1 A gate and suspension bridge are on the left. This is the entry to Fa Yun Ssu Zen Buddhist monastery. Disconnect for a side trip to the monastery. Hike the steep moss-covered road through a bamboo forest. There are rest pavilions on the way, and a snack shop in the temple. When your break is over, return to the suspension bridge and gate, reconnect and continue.

23.2 Start across a bridge on NR3.

23.5 On the left is the Yonghe Hostel.

23.7 R:T, with NR6; turn right on NR3 to Shihtan. (Straight leads to Miaoli.) Head uphill into an unspoiled farming area with rice, tea, bamboo, and strawberries.

36.7 Y; bear right into downtown Shihtan.

41.2 Y; bear right, heading down and across a river.

54.4 Cross a bridge into Sanwan.

57.7 Cross Omei Bridge.

59.8 Y; stay right, on NR3.

64.8 L:T; stay straight on NR3 toward Chutung.

67.0 Tea, citrus, and bamboo are growing here as you enter the town of Omei.

69.7 Y; bear left on NR3 toward Chutung.

70.0 A colorful temple is on the left as you leave Omei.

74.1 L:T; continue straight.

74.3 L:T; continue straight.

74.6 A school is on the right.

74.7 Y; bear left on NR3, just past the school.

75.0 T, with bus station nearby; turn left.

79.7 Sign: "ENTERING CHU-TUNG."

80.3 EOD; Y, with a small temple on the left. NR3 heads to the right. To get into downtown Chutung, turn left here and ride about 1.5 km.

Chutung to Chiang Kai Shek Airport: 63.1 km

The final segment of the North Taiwan tour drops out of the foothills onto the coastal plain south of Taipei. This segment's ride is a short one through either downhill or flat terrain. If you plan to leave Taiwan without a visit to Taipei, make your trip back to Taoyuan or the airport a leisurely one by stopping in Lungtan and relaxing at the park where the dragon-boat racers practice. After passing Lungtan, with its lake, temple, and dragon-boats, head into Taoyuan. Dodge traffic through this sprawling western Taiwan city, then head west on NR4 to CKS International Airport.

WHERE TO STAY. In Taoyuan, there are hotels near the bus station. For accommodations near Chiang Kai Shek International Airport, see the Information section at the beginning of this tour.

WHERE TO EAT. In Taoyuan, there are restaurants and food stalls

Traditional Taiwanese farmhouse in the western foothills

near the bus station. On the way out to the airport, there are restaurants in Nankan, and the Airport Hotel has its own restaurant.

WHAT TO DO. Stop in Lungtan and relax at the lakeside park where the dragon-boat racers practice. If you are heading from Taoyuan into Taipei, be sure to get into Taipei well before dark.

Log:

0.0 Return to the Y intersection in Chutung with the small temple on the left (previous segment's EOD); reset and head right (SE) on NR3.

1.1 X; go straight.

5.3 Enter Hengshan, an ugly town with a cement factory.

6.4 Y; bear left toward Kuanhsi on NR3.

8.1 Y; bear left on NR3 and pass through a small village.

16.4 Enter Kuanhsi. The road bypasses downtown. Continue straight toward Lungtan.

27.9 Y; bear right, along Lungtan Lake toward Tahsi.

28.1 L:Y, just past Lungtan Lake; take the main road left, not the hard left or the road going straight.

28.8 X, NR3 intersects with PR113 to Shihmen Reservoir; continue straight on NR3. Now you are out of the foothills on a wide, busy road.

37.1 L:T; continue straight.

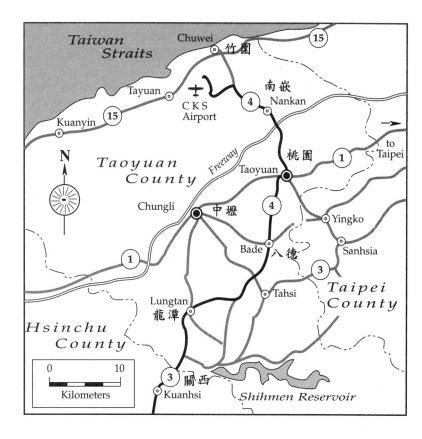

37.5 L:T; bear left. Leave NR3 and begin NR4 to Taoyuan. NR4 is now co-named Chiehshou Road.

46.8 Sign: "ENTERING TAOYUAN."

47.5 Y; bear left (N) on NR4 toward a bridge. Cross Chienkuo Road, then head over a railroad overpass in the slow lane.

48.1 Top of the bridge over the railroad tracks.

48.3 X, bridge ends at Fuhsing Road; turn right (E). You are now on NR1, the main north–south road along the coastal plain.

48.8 The Taoyuan bus station is on the right, at the corner of Minchuan and Fuhsing roads. Reset here to continue to the airport.

0.0 At the Taoyuan bus station, reset and continue (E) on Fuhsing Road.

0.7 X, by a bridge; turn left and follow NR4 (co-named Chunri Road) out of Taoyuan toward Nankan.

6.5 Pass under the freeway.

8.5 Pass through Nankan.

14.3 EOD; L:Y; turn left and ride 2.8 km farther to the airport terminal.

Dragon-boat racers practice at Lungtan.

Side Trip to Taipei: 23 km

For an optional side trip into Taipei, head northeast from Taoyuan rather than west to the airport. In Taipei transportation is almost completely motorized. Unlike large cities in the PRC, few people rely on bicycles for basic transportation. Nevertheless, if you are prepared for thick traffic and polluted air, a bicycle is still an excellent way to explore Taipei. The scope of this book does not include routes in the city of Taipei, but your conventional Taiwan guidebook will have maps of Taipei and its major attractions.

Taipei has many cultural attractions for visitors. There are always exhibits in the art museums and performances of Chinese operas in both Taiwanese and Beijing styles. Your hotel in Taipei will have magazines with up-to-date listings of such events. Cycle north to the suburb of Shihlin and visit the National Palace Museum, where one of the world's greatest collections of Chinese art is displayed. Farther north are Yangmingshan Park, and the hot-spring resort town of Beitou. Southeast of the city is Chihnangong, a hilltop temple with hundreds of stone steps.

Along with Hong Kong, Taipei is one of the world's best places to sample the provincial cuisines of China. It is definitely a food-lover's city. If you are intrigued by Chinese cuisine, you may not want to leave Taipei. Dining in Taipei during a one-year stay in the mid-1970s was the beginning of events that led to this writer owning and operating a Chinese restaurant!

WHERE TO STAY. There are plenty of lodging options in Taipei, and many are in the vicinity of the train station. For more information, refer to your conventional Taiwan guidebook.

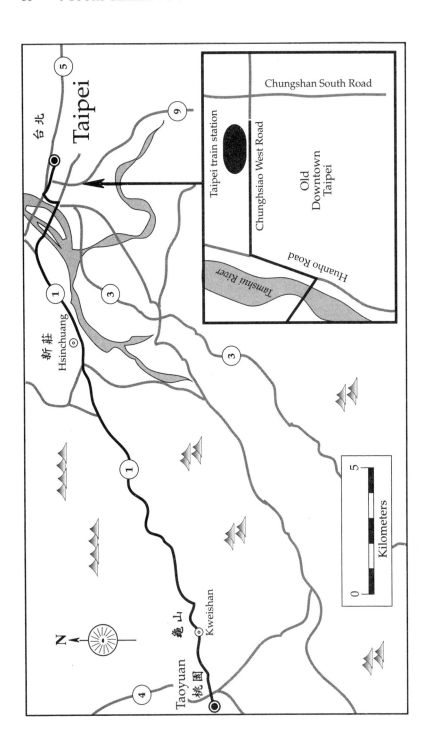

Confucius Temple, Taipei

WHERE TO EAT. Spend at least one evening in the Lungshan Temple night market "food street," where traditional Taiwanese "small eats" are the specialty. Here you can even have freshly killed turtle, or snake's bile in wine, if you like. Another good place for inexpensive and interesting food is the back alleys across Roosevelt Road from Taiwan National University.

WHAT TO DO. In the downtown area, visit the gigantic new Chiang Kai Shek Memorial and the upscale shopping areas along the eastern sections of Chunghsiao Road. Nightlife in Taipei goes on all night long, with bars, clubs, and discos for just about anyone's taste.

Log:

0.0 From the Taoyuan bus station, reset and head (ENE) on Fuhsing Road, which is also NR1. The route to Taipei is largely urban with nonstop truck and scooter traffic. Be careful!

3.0 Town of Kweishan; continue (ENE) on NR1.

12.6 L:Y; continue straight on NR1.

14.5 X, with PR107; continue (ENE) on NR1 through Hsinchuang.

19.3 Y; bear right (ESE) and head across the Chunghsing bridge.

21.8 Roll off the Chunghsing bridge onto Huanho Road. Turn left (NE) on Huanho Road and ride up to Chunghsiao West Road. Then turn right (E) and ride a few blocks to the train station.

23.0 EOD; Taipei train station. City maps are available in bookshops on the second floor of the train station. Use the train station as a bearing point for finding your way around Taipei.

A SOUTHERN ISLAND TOUR
Tailuko to Touliu

Distance: 714.4 kilometers; 130-kilometer side trip to Alishan; 106.3-kilometer link to Tour No. 1

Estimated time: 11 riding days; 2 riding days for side trip to Alishan; 1 riding day to link with Tour No. 1

Best time to go: March–June; September–November

Terrain: Some level, gentle hills, and steep foothills

Map: Nelles Map of Taiwan

Connecting tour: Tour No. 1

The southern Taiwan tour begins on the eastern coast in Tailuko at the entrance to Taroko Gorge, one of Taiwan's most famous scenic destinations. Ride through Taroko Gorge to Tienhsiang and enjoy the mountain scenery and hot spring at Wenshan. From Tienhsiang, backtrack through Taroko Gorge and follow the coast south to Hualien.

Roads south of Hualien are not nearly as dangerous or steep as those to the north, but there are still a few tough grades and switchbacks. Although the whole southern coast is scenic, there are several tourist attractions worth visiting. Hsiaoyehliu has interesting rocks and sea stacks. Pahsientung (Eight Immortals Cave) is an archaeological site/shrine where artifacts of Taiwan's prehistoric inhabitants were discovered. South of Taitung, Chihpen has open-air hot-spring pools, a waterfall, and a forest recreation area with hiking trails.

Farther south, there are roadside farms and tribal villages of Amei *Shandiren*, the native "mountain people" who inhabited Taiwan before the arrival of Han Chinese. At Tawu, cut west across the mountains to Fengkang on the western coast, then continue south to the beaches of Kenting and Oluanpi, the southernmost point of Taiwan. Spend a day or two in Kenting enjoying the beaches and the tropical botanical gardens in the national park, then backtrack past Fengkang and continue north to the medium-size city of Pingtung.

From Pingtung, leave the coastal plain and begin riding the less-developed foothill route on National Route 3. Along this route, roads are narrower, towns are perched on the banks of mountain streams, and suspension footbridges are still in use. From the Chiayi area, take the highly recommended side trip to Alishan, a high mountain resort with forests, temples, lakes, trails, and a sunrise view of the "sea of clouds." You can reach Alishan either by bicycle or the narrow-gauge train. End the tour in Touliu, where you can take a bus or train back to

Two Sisters Pond, Alishan

Taoyuan or Taipei. If you are combining the two Taiwan tours to form a complete *Tour de Taiwan*, go on to Cholan and proceed north to Taipei by following the final segments of Tour No. 1, A Northern Island Loop.

CONNECTIONS. To minimize complicated connections, if you are only doing one of the Taiwan tours, select Tour No. 1. If you prefer the tropical scenery of southern Taiwan and can't do both tours, you will have to take a train to the east-coast village of Hsincheng, then ride to the tour starting point in Tailuko. It will take at least two days and a lot of trouble cycling into Taipei, buying train tickets, wrapping your bike, and riding the train. Why not just add two more days and ride the first four segments of Tour No. 1 to the starting point of this tour?

If you choose not to combine this tour with Tour No. 1, begin at Chiang Kai Shek (CKS) International Airport, some 40 kilometers west of Taipei near Taoyuan. At the airport, change money, buy a city map of Taipei, and confirm your flight out of Taiwan. In the upstairs Departures area, there are kiosks that sell maps of Taipei and Taiwan. From the airport, follow the first and last route logs of Tour No. 1 to get from the airport to Taoyuan, and then from Taoyuan to Taipei, respectively. From Taipei, catch an early train to Hsincheng, a small village north of Hualien on the eastern coast. If you are carrying your bike with you as a wrapped package, get off in Hsincheng, assemble your bike, and ride 4 kilometers west to Tailuko. If you shipped the bike on a separate train, you will have to walk or take a taxi to Tailuko for lodging, and come back to the Hsincheng train station to get your bike later.

If you are not connecting with Tour No. 1, end this tour in Touliu, where there are convenient bus or train connections north to Taoyuan or Taipei. To connect with Tour No. 1, end the tour in Cholan, and then follow the last two or three segments of Tour No. 1 to CKS Airport or Taipei.

It is also possible to shorten this tour to 358 kilometers and five riding days, by ending the tour in Fengkang. Take the Kuokuanghao bus, which can carry bikes in the luggage compartments, from Fengkang to Taoyuan or Taipei. The last Kuokuanghao bus leaves Fengkang at 4:15 P.M. daily.

When it is time to leave Taiwan, arrive at the airport early enough to get your bike box out of storage, box your bike, and attend to all of the formalities. Don't forget to set aside NT$300 per person for the airport departure tax. The check-in people at CKS Airport are not used to handling bikes and may try to charge you excess baggage fees. Just tell them you were allowed the bike as one piece of luggage on the trip to Taiwan and would appreciate the same treatment upon leaving.

INFORMATION. Unless you land at CKS Airport early enough in the day to ride into Taoyuan or Taipei, plan on spending your first night near the airport. The CKS Airport Hotel, telephone (033) 833666, is expensive, but it is conveniently close and you can store your bike box there if you reserve a room for your final night in Taiwan. Budget travelers who arrive after dark can use their sleeping bag and spend the night in the airport terminal.

Budget about three weeks for this eleven–riding-day tour, to allow for sightseeing in Tienhsiang, the side trip to Alishan, and time to visit Taipei. If you combine the two Taiwan tours, you will cycle 451 kilometers of Tour No. 1 in six riding days and 946 kilometers of Tour No. 2 in thirteen riding days (including the side trip to Alishan). Your total mileage will be 1,397 kilometers in nineteen riding days. Allow about four weeks for this combined *Tour de Taiwan*.

Taiwan is tropical, with hot muggy summers. Although "plum rains" are likely in spring, and early fall is the typhoon season, these two seasons are still the best time to go. Remember to cycle on the right in Taiwan.

Hsincheng/Tailuko to Tienhsiang: 23.3 km

From the Hsincheng train station, cycle the short distance to Tailuko, spend the night there, and ride through Taroko Gorge to Tienhsiang the next day.

Along this steady uphill ride, pagodas, temples, and grottoes provide unusual scenes. The Liwu River has many pools suitable for cooling off

A coastal food stall sells "bomb fish."

hot, tired bikers, but there are only a few places where you can get down to them.

WHERE TO STAY. In Tailuko, the Taroko Lodge is on the left as you ride into the village commercial strip from Hsincheng. For camping, there is a school grounds before the commercial area, or you can hop boulders down to a gravel shoal along the river. In Tienhsiang, the Tienhsiang Guest House is good but expensive. Up the road on the left is the Catholic Hostel. Past the hostel on a steep hill is the Youth Activity Center, telephone 038-691111, which has private and dorm-style rooms. Campers can find a spot overlooking the river on the left just after they cross the red steel bridge into Tienhsiang. The parklike areas near the bus terminal are also possible informal bivvy spots.

WHERE TO EAT. In Tailuko, eat at the Lan Lan restaurant a few doors up from Taroko Lodge, or at other places across the street. In Tienhsiang, the Youth Activity Center food is basic but safe. There is no menu to choose from: you eat what they serve. Food sold in stalls near the bus station is expensive and has usually been sitting there a while. Bring snack foods with you from Tailuko.

WHAT TO DO. Tailuko is a sleepy little town with not much to do except listen to the wind and river in the gorge above. Tienhsiang is worth a stopover of at least a day to enjoy the mountain scenery, Hsiang Te Ssu temple, and Wenshan hot spring. Hsiang Te Ssu is just below Tienhsiang across a suspension footbridge. To get to Wenshan hot spring, go 2 kilometers up the road to the third tunnel. Take the path with a red iron railing down to the right of the tunnel, and lock your bikes there. Cross a suspension bridge over the gorge and descend to the river on steep steps cut into the side of the gorge. Wade downstream about 30 meters and the hot-spring pool is in a grotto on the left. It is wonderful to go at night, but bring candles and be sure your flashlight is working well. It is customary to wear more than your skin at outdoor public hot springs in Taiwan.

Log:

0.0 Hsincheng train station; reset and turn left (NE) onto the road across from the large parking lot in front of the train station.

0.6 T, at the main highway, NR9; turn left, toward the mountains.

3.0 School sports field is on the right, a possible campsite.

3.2 Enter Tailuko township.

3.9 Post office is on the right.

4.1 Taroko Lodge is on the left.

4.3 Taroko Gorge entrance gate and the beginning of NR8; reset here.

0.0 Reset and follow NR8 uphill into the gorge.

2.5 L:T, to Chan Guang Zen temple; continue straight.

4.6 Silver Belt waterfall.

7.5 Hsi Ban Reservoir is on the right.

9.3 Begin passing through Swallow's Grotto. Look out to the Liwu River below from holes in the tunnel.

15.7 Tzu Mu Bridge, with a rest pavilion on the right.

19.0 Cross a red steel bridge into Tienhsiang. EOD, at the bus terminal.

Tienhsiang to Fengpin: 99.8 km

Leave Tienhsiang and coast back down through Taroko Gorge. From Tailuko and Hsincheng, the road levels out and passes fields of sugarcane, corn, mangoes, and bananas. This area is also the center of Taiwan's marble industry. Factories here sell everything from ashtrays to tables made of white-and-black *dalishi* marble.

Continue to Hualien, the largest city on the eastern coast. There is a port with rocky beaches, and the busy markets are a good place for a lunch stop. The next large town is Taitung, about three riding days from Hualien.

Leave Hualien through countryside, then cross the Hualien bridge back to the coast, passing piles of black and white pebbles local farmers collect and sell for export. The road ascends steeply into the hills after Shuilien, then pops back out on the coast about 20 kilometers before Fengpin. This segment ends in Fengpin, but if you have made good time, you could go on to Changpin for the night.

WHERE TO STAY. In Fengpin, one place to stay is the Guobin Lushe, telephone 791135. The Guobin is basic, with cement floors, handmade mosaic bathtubs, and the occasional lizard on the walls. There is a good seafood restaurant across the street that also rents rooms. If you decide to continue to Changpin for the night, there are two small hotels and several spartan restaurants. Try the Changpin Lushe, telephone (098) 831111. Campers can find bivvy spots by taking a left at the bus stop and riding down to the high school, which has rest rooms and washing facilities. Take a right around the school to get down to the rocky beach.

WHERE TO EAT. Eat at one of several seafood restaurants along the main highway.

WHAT TO DO. There is not much to do in Fengpin. Have a good seafood dinner and relax.

Log:

0.0 At the Tienhsiang bus terminal, reset and head across the red steel bridge down through the gorge.

19.4 Taroko Gorge entrance gate and end of NR8. Continue through Tailuko on NR9.

22.5 Enter the village of Hsincheng.

24.2 X; follow NR9 right (S) toward Hualien.

28.4 Y; go left, following NR9.

36.0 Y; bear left into Hualien. There is a big gas station at this intersection.

37.8 L:T, turnoff to Hualien airport; continue straight.

40.4 X; continue straight.

41.3 L:Y; continue straight into the urban area. A left turn here leads to the harbor.

42.3 The road goes downhill and curves to the right.

43.2 X; bear right and down a hill. NR9 is co-named Chung Cheng Lu as you enter Hualien.

44.9 X, at Chung Cheng and Chung Shan roads; go straight (SW).

45.3 X; go straight through on NR9 toward Fengpin.

45.5 Pass larger hotels and street stalls serving Taiwanese "small eats."

47.3 Y; make a left turn and begin riding on NR11 heading SE. NR9 heads right to the inland valley paralleling the coast.

51.3 Y, near a large refinery; bear left toward Fengpin.

52.8 Cross Hualien Bridge and leave the coast as you begin a hilly segment.

67.4 Small tunnel; start up a grade when out of the tunnel.

70.0 Reach the top of the grade.

71.5 Enter Shuilien.

72.6 Leave Shuilien and head up into the hills.

79.0 Top of the grade; you are back by the coast again.

99.3 Enter Fengpin.

99.8 EOD; the Guobin Lushe inn is on the left.

Fengpin to Chengkung: 66.5 km

The road from Fengpin to Chengkung continues south, passing fishing villages and beaches with unusual rock formations. Coastal villages here are inhabited by Amei *Shandiren* who live by fishing or farming rice, taro, and sweet potatoes. Their fields sport bright flags on tall poles to scare away birds, and their "tractor," the water buffalo, is treated like a member of the family. When cycling through these villages, you will see Amei people socializing on raised wooden platforms in their courtyards. End the day's ride in Chengkung.

WHERE TO STAY. Chengkung has several small inns along either side of the main road through town.

WHERE TO EAT. Chengkung is a fishing town famous for its lobsters, clams, and small abalonelike shellfish called *Chiukung*. Restaurants along the road through Chengkung have aquariums and re-

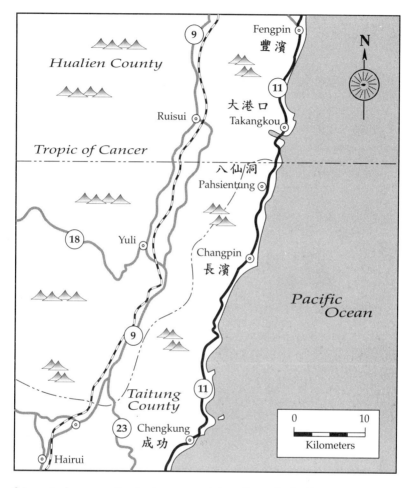

frigerated cases displaying a variety of seafood. Be sure to try *Chiukung* served in their shells with ginger and black vinegar sauce.

WHAT TO DO. Chengkung itself has no tourist attractions, but its fishing port is picturesque. Along this segment's route, plan to stop at the beach parks and view the rock formations and sea stacks. Ten kilometers before Changpin is Pahsientung (Eight Immortals Caves). In 1968 archaeologists found stone and bone implements here, proving human habitation of the caves at least 4,000 years ago. Although it is an archaeological site, it has taken on the trappings of a religious shrine.

Log:

0.0 Guobin Lushe inn in Fengpin; reset and continue south.
0.3 Road veers to the left.

Chengkung fishing-boat harbor

12.2 Enter the small fishing village of Shihtiping.
14.2 The beach park off to the left has interesting rock formations.
16.2 Pass through Takangkou, a native *Shandiren* village.
17.8 Cross Changhung Bridge (Long Rainbow Bridge).
19.2 Enter the village of Chingpu.
23.1 Pass a stone marker on your left as you enter Taitung County.
27.5 Pahsientung (Eight Immortals Cave) is on the right.
32.6 Pass through the village of Sanchien.
36.4 Enter Changpin.
37.2 Changpin bus stop; continue straight. To get to the high school and beach for camping, turn left here.
66.5 EOD; the Chengkung bus stop.

Chengkung to Chihpen: 78 km

Continuing south from Chengkung on National Route 11, the first attraction is Hsiaoyehliu, a seaside park with rock formations jutting up from the surf. Walk your bike down through the food stalls and curio hawkers to get to the rocks. After meditating on the wonders of nature, try some of the fresh papayas or barbecued cuttlefish sold in the stalls.

Next you arrive in Taitung, the second-largest city on the eastern coast. There are plenty of hotels and restaurants if you want to stay in Taitung, but the Chihpen hot-spring district is a better stop. The setting of the open-air pools at the Chihpen Hotel is not as dramatic as Wenshan hot spring in Tienhsiang, but the tropical scenery and colorful lighting at night are delightful.

WHERE TO STAY. In Taitung, there are hotels in the district around the train station. In Chihpen, the Chihpen Hotel, telephone (089) 512220, is a good choice, but rooms are not cheap. There are less expensive inns in the village of Chihpen.

WHERE TO EAT. The Chihpen Hotel restaurant is good if you are staying there, and there are more options in the village of Chihpen. In Taitung, there are snack stalls and restaurants in the vicinity of the train station.

WHAT TO DO. Even if you camp or stay at another hotel, a small

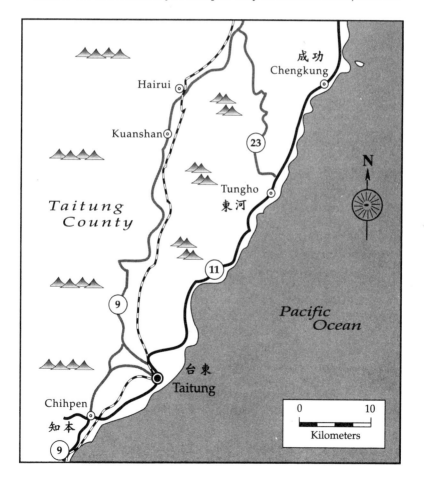

fee will admit you to the Chihpen Hotel's hot-spring pools for a soak. You can also ride about 1 kilometer west from the hotel to see the White Jade Waterfall and Chingchueh temple. Should you decide to linger longer, there are hiking trails farther west in the Chihpen National Forest Recreation Area.

Log:

- **0.0** Chengkung bus stop; reset and continue on the main road.
- **0.5** X, just past Chengkung bus stop; turn right and continue south on NR11.
- **18.8** X; go left on NR11, then cross Tungho bridge into Tungho.
- **29.9** Shanyuanwan beach is on the left.
- **47.2** Hsiaoyehliu parking lot and tourist area is on the left.
- **53.0** Y; go left and continue on NR11 toward Taitung.
- **55.2** Cross a long bridge as you enter Taitung.
- **58.1** X, where NR11 rejoins NR9 coming out of the inland valley; turn left here, heading toward Taitung.
- **59.5** X, with NR9 heading off to the right; go straight through as you enter the Taitung urban area.
- **60.7** X; go straight through.
- **61.2** Signal X, at Nanjing Road; go straight through.
- **61.6** X, at Chungshan Road; turn right (SW) toward the train station.
- **62.3** X circle, at Taitung train station; disconnect here to explore Taitung. **Note**: *Do not reset your computer.* To continue, return to the train station, reconnect, and (with your back to the station) turn right (SE) onto the road fronting the station.

Water buffalo keep the roadside grass trimmed.

62.5 T, at Chunghua Road (Lion Hotel is on the corner); turn right (SW) onto NR11.

62.6 Cross the railroad tracks.

68.7 Cross a bridge. The village in the foothills ahead is Chihpen.

73.0 Cross a large white bridge and drop down into Chihpen.

75.2 Y; bear right and approach a T intersection.

75.5 T; go left, then come to a Y and bear right.

75.7 Leave Chihpen village and head up the valley toward large hotel buildings.

78.0 EOD; cross a bridge into the Chihpen Hotel area.

Chihpen to Fengkang: 90 km

After leaving Chihpen, ride south through Taimali, passing fields of day-lily flowers. The bright orange flowers from this area are considered a superior ingredient for Taiwanese soups and sautés. This southernmost segment of the eastern coast also has many *Shandiren* villages.

At the village of Tajen, leave the coast and head uphill across the southern mountains. This seemingly never-ending grade climbs to 500 meters above sea level at Shouka before descending to Fengkang, a

Rice paddies along Taiwan's southeast coast

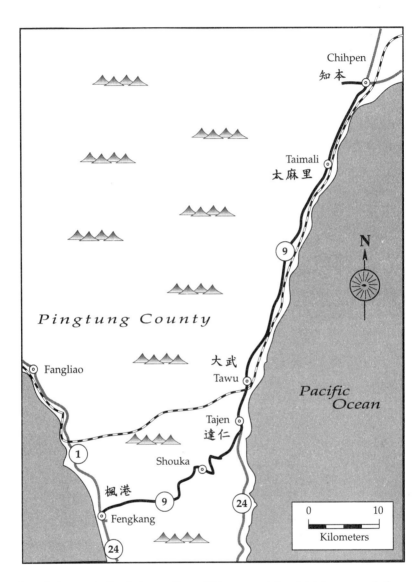

beach town at the intersection of the cross-island highway and the southern end of National Route 1. If you want to end your southern Taiwan cycle tour here, take the Kuokuanghao bus from Fengkang to Taoyuan or Taipei. The last bus leaves at 4:15 P.M.

WHERE TO STAY. Fengkang has no large tourist hotels, but does have reasonably priced inns. Try the Longan Talushe, telephone (08) 8771367, one block north of the end-of-day point on the right side of NR1, across from the beach.

WHERE TO EAT. Local restaurants specialize in barbecued rice sparrows and seafood. Some even serve roast owl, but "normal" Chinese food is also available. There are restaurants across from the bus station and along NR1 north of the bus station.

WHAT TO DO. There are no major tourist attractions here. Relax after the cross-mountain grind and have a cold Taiwan beer with your skewer of barbecued sparrows.

Log:

0.0 Chihpen Hotel; reset and backtrack to Chihpen village.

2.9 Rev Y, in Chihpen village; make a hairpin right turn leading down toward the river.

3.3 Cross the bridge over the Chihpen River and continue south on NR9.

15.5 Enter Taimali.

48.0 Enter Tawu. Have lunch and get snacks here.

69.2 Top of the grade at Shouka. There is a rustic cafe and police station here.

86.0 Hsinlu village. During rainy weather, beware of mud slides between Shouka and Hsinlu.

90.0 EOD; T, at NR1 in Fengkang. The bus station is to the left just before the T.

Fengkang to Kenting: 33.2 km

The nearly level ride from Fengkang to Kenting is a short one, to allow plenty of time for sightseeing in Kenting, another of Taiwan's "must-see" destinations. Once you are in Kenting, make lodging arrangements and then spend the rest of the day exploring this popular beach resort. Follow the road about 8 kilometers past Kenting to the lighthouse and coral gardens at Oluanpi, then return to Kenting and explore the tropical botanical gardens in Kenting National Park.

WHERE TO STAY. As would be expected in a popular resort, there are many lodging options. The pricey Kenting House is on the national park grounds, and Kenting House Beach Annex is on the right as you enter town. The Youth Activity Center, a large facility similar to the ones in Kinshan and Tienhsiang, is on the right, off the main road southeast of the park entry gates. There is also a camping area north of the main road after crossing the creek by the Kenting Hotel. Refer to your conventional Taiwan guidebook for other options.

WHERE TO EAT. Kenting House (both the main lodge in the park and the beach annex) has excellent food, and the main street through Kenting is lined with noodle stalls and small restaurants.

WHAT TO DO. Visit the botanical gardens in Kenting National Park and enjoy the beaches. Snorkeling gear is available for rent at shops along the main street. Ride past Kenting to Oluanpi to see coral formations and the lighthouse. To get to the Maopitou scenic area, backtrack 6 kilometers northwest from Kenting and turn left, heading past the nuclear power plant to the end of the peninsula. North from

Southeast Taiwan coastline

Kenting, visit Ssuchunghsi hot spring by turning inland at Checheng and riding about 6 kilometers.

Log:

- 0.0 T, at NR1 in Fengkang; reset and head left (S) on NR24.
- 12.5 Enter Haikou.
- 14.0 Enter Checheng. A left here leads about 6 km up to Ssuchunghsi hot spring.
- 22.0 Y; stay right on the main road to Kenting. A left turn here leads into Hengchun.
- 32.5 Kenting House Beach Annex is on the right.
- 33.0 Enter Kenting village.
- 33.2 EOD; Kenting National Park entrance gates on the left.

Kenting to Pingtung: 97.8 km

From Kenting, backtrack on National Route 24 to Fengkang, then continue north along the coast, passing shrimp ponds, fruit orchards, and occasional roadside temples. The Fangliao area is famous for its *lienwu*: a crisp red-and-green fruit shaped like a small pear. Don't pass

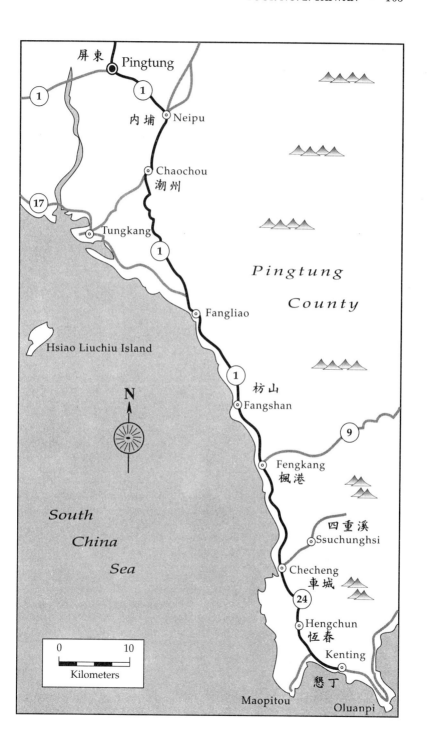

up a chance to try this thirst-quenching treat sold at roadside stalls from late spring through early summer.

Leave the coast at Fangliao on flat, wide roads through fields planted with sugarcane, coconuts, and betel-nut palms. The mountains recede as you head north on the southern coastal plain. End the day in the city of Pingtung and explore its back alleys and thriving night market.

WHERE TO STAY. From the end-of-day point, continue west on Mintsu Lu. There are hotels on the left and right. The Mintsu Hotel is on the right directly across from the bus station.

WHERE TO EAT. Pingtung is a small city with many options. From the train station, head east on Mintsu Lu to get to night-market food stalls. Although Pingtung is not on the coast, the seafood here is excellent. Try boiled freshwater shrimp harvested from the ponds along this segment's route.

WHAT TO DO. If you want real local "color," the road one block south of Mintsu Lu just before the night market is the red-light district and has an interesting old temple. The dark alleys in this area dictate caution.

Log:

    0.0 Entrance gate to Kenting National Park; reset and retrace the previous segment's route back to Fengkang.

  33.2 R:T, in Fengkang near the bus station; reset here.

    0.0 R:T; reset and head straight (N) on NR1.

    7.0 Notice the shrimp ponds with splashing aereator paddles along this stretch.

  16.0 A colorful temple is on the left, surrounded by shrimp ponds. It

Coastal roadside temple near Fangliao

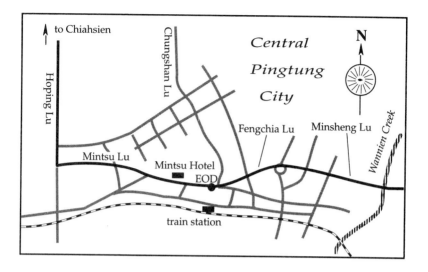

is a good rest stop with rest rooms, a table, benches, water, and shelter.

19.2 Cross a bridge and enter the Fangliao District.

15.0 For the next 5 km there are *lienwu* orchards on the right, a special Fangliao variety called *Heichenchu* (black pearls).

24.8 L:Y; continue straight (NNW) on NR1, now leaving the coast.

34.7 Enter Hsinpi.

43.0 X, at entrance to Chaochou; stay straight (N) on NR1. To go into Chaochou for lodging or food, disconnect and go left here, then reconnect at this intersection to continue.

52.9 Enter Neipu.

53.0 Y; bear left (NW) on NR1.

59.4 Sign: "ENTERING LINLO."

61.6 Y; bear right. Leave NR1, which heads left to Kaohsiung.

63.7 Cross Wannien Creek as you enter Pingtung along Minsheng Lu.

64.3 X circle; bear left (SW) onto Fengchia Lu, the third exit as you go around the circle.

64.6 EOD; X, where Fengchia Lu ends at the intersection of Mintsu Lu and Chungshan Lu. The Pingtung train station is on the left.

Pingtung to Chiahsien: 80.8 km

The wide, flat road out of Pingtung is a mix of rural scenery and light industry. Traffic thins out after Likang and the air is fragrant with *lienwu* blossoms. Roadside buildings and fences are covered with bright red bougainvillea and loofah vines. You will see banana and pineapple plantations around Kaoshu.

After Tachin, the road narrows and follows the Laonung River up

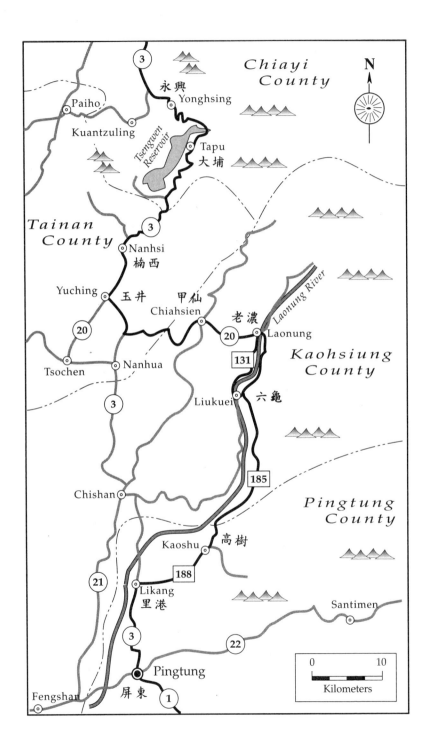

into the mountains. Stop in upper Liukuei for a look at the large Tienhou temple, then roll down into the main part of town across the river. From Liukuei, the route winds through hilly forested areas along a very rural back road. When I rode this segment in 1990, the road was so rough I had to walk the bike at times, and I encountered one of the deadly "green bamboo" snakes. Once back on the main road at Laonung, climb another steep grade and drop into Chiahsien for the evening.

WHERE TO STAY. In Chiahsien there is a hotel across the street from the end-of-day point, or try the Bigong Dalushe at 18 Wenhua Nanlu, telephone (07) 6752352. Go north from the end-of-day point to the first intersection, turn left, and it's a few doors down on the left. If you decide to camp in this area, stay away from grassy areas and beware of snakes!

WHERE TO EAT. Chiahsien is famous for its taro-root products. There are shops up and down the main street that sell taro candy, taro ice cream, and sweet taro soup. In local restaurants, taro is served braised with pork, and as crisp fried chips or soft fried cakes. There are restaurants up and down the main street and side streets near the end-of-day point.

WHAT TO DO. People come here to enjoy the foothill town scenery and sample local products such as the taro confections mentioned above. There are no major tourist attractions.

Log:

0.0 Pingtung train station; reset and, facing north, go left (W) on Mintsu Lu.

0.8 T, at Hoping Lu, with a bridge on the left; turn right (N) toward Likang.

2.7 X; go straight through.

3.2 Signal X; turn left (N) and leave town on NR3.

9.7 Cross a bridge and enter Chiuju.

14.5 Sign: "15 KM TO CHISHAN." You are now entering Likang.

15.3 Y; bear right on NR3.

15.8 X signal; turn right. Leave NR3 and begin cycling on CR188, heading east toward Kaoshu.

17.4 Pass through Chiehtung.

19.0 Begin heading up into the foothills through orchards, bean fields, betel trees, and shrimp ponds.

22.8 Enter Hsinnan.

28.5 Enter Kaoshu.

29.4 End of CR188, beginning of CR185 to Tachin; continue on the main road.

32.9 Y; go left toward Tachin.

36.6 Enter Tachin.

37.3 Bridge after leaving Tachin. Light incense at the temple on the left to keep the "green bamboo" snakes at bay.

37.6 X, after the bridge; turn left and ride along the Laonung River on a narrow one-lane road.

50.0 Enter upper Liukuei.

50.1 X; continue straight. The road on the right goes to a school.

51.1 Liukuei Tienhou Temple and courtyard on the right.

51.2 L:T; go left downhill toward a bridge. The alternate (and possibly better-paved) route to Chiahsien via Laonung continues straight from this intersection. It was under construction at the time this tour was logged, and no mileages are available. If you take it, pick up the route again at the 66.1 mileage point in Laonung.

51.6 Cross a bridge over the Laonung River into Liukuei, with narrow alleys and houses perched on the riverbanks.

52.2 Signal T; turn right onto CR131 toward Laonung. If you turn left, the Hsiuyuehyuan Hotel is 100 m on the right.

54.0 Road pavement ends and a gravel road begins.

54.2 L:T, to Tsaitiehku (Colorful Butterfly Valley); stay straight. This very rural rough road may require you to walk your bike; watch for "green bamboo" snakes.

63.4 T, at larger road; turn left.

66.0 Enter Laonung.

66.1 T; turn left (W) onto NR20 toward Chiahsien. Begin a steep climb.

72.3 Peak of the grade. Coast down into Chiahsien.

80.7 Enter Chiahsien.

80.8 EOD; bus stop on the right, hotel on the left.

Chiahsien to Tapu: 58.6 km

This segment's hilly ride is tough, but the scenic changes from mountain town to tropical valley to lakeside resort make it a rewarding one. Leave Chiahsien and continue along winding foothill roads until you drop into Peiliao in the valley of Houchueh Creek. Follow the level, shaded valley road through fields of sugarcane and pineapple, and orchards of citrus, bananas, and starfruit. You may even see women in small boats harvesting *lingchiao*, a horn-shaped black nut that grows in ponds and tastes a little like a Brazil nut.

After Nanhsi, head into the hills again as you skirt Tsengwen Reservoir on a roller coaster of steep grades. Drop down on bamboo-lined roads to the village of Tapu, where you can spend the night at an inn or camp on the shores of Tsengwen Reservoir. If you have the time to continue on and are equipped for camping, you can follow the next segment's route log to Yonghsing.

WHERE TO STAY. Chiayi Farm (turn left at mileage point 48.1 in the route log below) is a possible overnight stop. In Tapu, there is the Tapu Shan Chuang Hotel, telephone (05) 2521610. There are informal campsite possibilities near the lakeshore, with rest rooms and washing areas near the parking lot. Those who continue to Yonghsing for the night can camp at the school, which has water, wash basins, and sheltered walkways. Teachers who live at the school say that it is not uncommon for campers to spend the night: they may even offer you a classroom to sleep in. Otherwise, use the covered walkway area or the sports field.

Boys playing on a Taiwan temple lion

WHERE TO EAT. Tapu is famous for its dried and fresh edible bamboo. The dining room of the Tapu Shan Chuang serves local mountain produce and freshwater fish from the lake. There are other cheap noodle shops and restaurants in the village area. Campers who choose to stay in Yonghsing should bring food with them from Tapu.

WHAT TO DO. In Tapu, enjoy the lakeside scenery and poke around the old town and its temple.

Log:

0.0 Flashing light at the upper entrance to Chiahsien; reset there and head downhill out of town.

0.4 Cross a bridge and leave Chiahsien, passing rice paddies, taro fields, and banana orchards.

2.8 Y, where NR21 goes left and NR20 goes right; go right, heading uphill.

4.7 Crest of the grade.

9.6 Go through Nanhua Tunnel.

10.7 The newer tunnel road meets the old road again. Swoop down through Maopu and begin another climb.

11.8 Crest of the grade.

12.1 Enter Yushan, still on NR20.

16.0 Enter Peiliao.

16.1 X; go right. The road is now both NR20 and NR3.

21.5 Enter Yuching.

21.6 X; turn right (NNE) on NR3. A left turn leads to Tainan.

22.3 T; go right, heading toward Nanhsi.

27.8 Cross Nanhsi bridge.

28.0 Y; stay right. The left at this Y heads into Nanhsi.

28.6 X, at CR188; continue straight on NR3.

29.7 X; turn right and begin a series of steep roller-coaster hills. This is the south end of Tsengwen Reservoir.

41.7 L:T, at "windy crest," the top of the steep grade; continue straight. The left heads back down to the dam and the east entrance to the lake.

48.1 L:T, leading to Chiayi Farm; continue straight. Chiayi Farm has camping, lodging, and recreation facilities.

58.4 Sign: "TAPU TO LEFT 150 M."

58.6 EOD; L:T, on NR3 above Tapu; turn left. Tapu is the last lodging option before crossing the mountains.

Tapu to Touliu: 86.1 km

From Tapu, the route climbs to the ridgetop village of Yonghsing, then coasts down steep stretches into the valley below. A few kilometers after Chungpu, reach the intersection of National Routes 3 and 18, where you have the option of continuing on the main route to Touliu or taking a side trip to Alishan.

Begin the side trip to Alishan at this intersection or ride into Chiayi, where you can start the trip the next day or ride the narrow-gauge train to Alishan and take a break from cycling. The side trip to Alishan

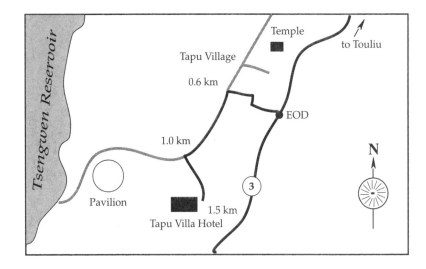

On the narrow-gauge train to Alishan

is all uphill and lodgings along the route are scarce: don't start late in the day unless you are prepared to camp. To get to Chiayi, turn left off of NR3 at the 26.2 mileage point and cycle west on National Route 18 for about 7 kilometers until you merge with National Route 1. Go north on Route 1 another 5 kilometers into Chiayi.

The main route continues through Chuchi to the foothill town of Meishan, famous for its *longan* (dragon eyes). You may see people sorting bags of this leather-skinned dried fruit along the roadside. Leave Meishan on the rolling foothill road, then level out through sugarcane fields as you approach Touliu. The small railroad tracks that cross the road near Touliu are used to transport sugarcane from these fields to nearby refineries.

End the tour in Touliu, where you will find modern amenities and a great night market. From Touliu, take a bus or train to Taoyuan or Taipei to return to CKS Airport. To get to the Touliu train station, go northwest from the end-of-day point. The bus station is a block southwest of the train station.

Cyclists who plan to link up with Tour No. 1, A Northern Island Loop, should continue on the optional link segment to Cholan. From Cholan, follow the final two or three segments of Tour No. 1 to return to Taoyuan or Taipei.

WHERE TO STAY. There are many lodging options near the train station in Chiayi; consult your conventional Taiwan guidebook. At the end-of-day point in Touliu, the KD Hotel is on the left, and the Hsin Du Hotel is on the right. Go along any of the large streets from this traffic circle to find more options.

WHERE TO EAT. Chiayi is a large city with hundreds of restaurants and a night market. Touliu is a medium-large city with plenty of

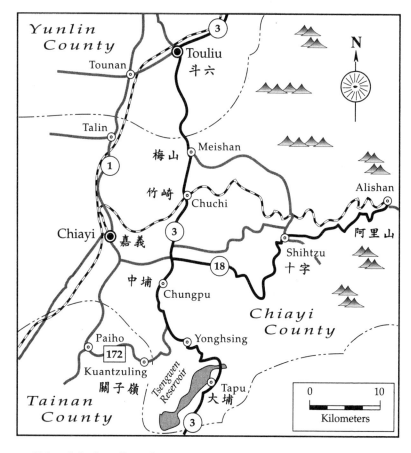

traditional food stalls and modern fast-food restaurants. There is also an extensive night market near the end-of-day point. Go around the traffic circle and take the second street heading due south. If you turned onto Wenhua Road heading east, you went too far around the circle. It's a walk from the end-of-day point, so leave your bike at your hotel.

WHAT TO DO. In either Chiayi or Touliu, enjoy the night market and check out the lively evening shopping scene of a larger Taiwanese city.

Log:

0.0 L:T, on NR3 above Tapu; reset and continue on NR3.

0.9 Gas station and restaurant; continue straight.

5.4 Cross Tapu bridge over the gorge of Tsengwen Creek and begin a steep uphill climb.

23.7 L:Y, in Yonghsing. Reset; the left goes 100 m to Yonghsing school.

0.0 L:Y, in Yonghsing; reset and continue on NR3.
13.4 Pass through Chunglun on a steep downhill stretch.
18.1 Rev L:Y, CR172 at Yunshui; continue straight. A left turn here leads to Kuantzuling hot-spring resort.
23.0 Cross Chungpu bridge.
23.9 Enter Chungpu.
24.1 T; turn left, leaving Chungpu through rice-paddy scenery.
26.2 X, where NR3 intersects NR18; reset and continue straight toward Chuchi. Turn left here to get to Chiayi, or right to begin the Alishan side trip.
0.0 X, where NR3 intersects NR18; reset and go straight.
3.9 X, with flashing light; continue straight.
6.7 X, with flashing light; continue straight.
9.3 Sign: "ENTERING CHUCHI."
9.9 L:Y; bear left on NR3. Chuchi is to the right.
10.3 Y; bear left and continue on NR3.
18.3 Enter Meishan.
18.7 Meishan bus station is on the right.
19.0 Meishan town temple is on the right.
21.4 Y; go right and leave Meishan on NR3.
26.1 X; go left on NR3 toward Touliu.
26.5 X; continue straight.
35.5 Cross the Touliu bridge and come to a large intersection with Yongfu Temple on the left; continue straight (NE).
35.9 L:T; continue straight.
36.0 X; continue straight (NE).
36.2 EOD; large X circle, with the Touliu train station a block NW.

Side Trip to Alishan: 129.6 km

Alishan is one of Taiwan's most famous mountain areas, offering scenic ponds, a Zen temple, forest trails, and a sunrise vista of the "sea of clouds." The 65-kilometer uphill ride through tea gardens and bamboo forests ascends from the hot subtropical valley to the crisp alpine air. The route gains more than 2,000 meters of altitude and cannot be rushed.

Along the route to Alishan there are tea gardens and tasting rooms where you can try *Kaoshancha* (high mountain tea). This tea is high in caffeine and has a special fragrance prized by tea lovers. Tea stores brew successive batches of their tea in small pots for you to taste before buying. Be careful, though; some stores will let you taste a high grade of tea, then sell you a prepacked tin of low-grade tea at a high price. If you want to buy high-grade tea, make note of the container from which the attendant gets the tea to brew your sample, then buy loose tea out of that container. Don't buy expensive tea in cans unless they let you sample the tea in that can first.

Alishan may also be reached by narrow-gauge train out of Chiayi. Follow instructions in the previous segment to get from National Route 3 into Chiayi and find lodging, then buy round-trip tickets to Alishan at the special "Alishan" window in the Chiayi train station. Arrange to

Roadside shrine on the road to Alishan

store bikes at your hotel in Chiayi until your return. In the past, there was an early "local train" with benches and a luggage car: you could take your bike with you on the train and then coast back down. Now there is only one daily tourist train, and it doesn't carry bikes.

If you decide to take the narrow-gauge train to Alishan, don't feel like you are "copping out" on bike touring: it is a special trip unlike ordinary trains. This train route was originally built to haul timber out of the high mountains. You will get good views of all the climatic zones from subtropical to alpine, and the upper stretches are so steep that the train must change directions on switchbacks to reach the top. As the train nears Alishan, you will see shady hillside gardens of *wasabi* (the spicy horseradish used in Japanese cuisine) and an ancient "spirit tree."

To cycle to Alishan from Chiayi, retrace your path from Chiayi to mileage point 26.2 on the previous segment's route log, and then follow the route log below. Once you arrive at the Alishan bus parking lot, navigate with your conventional Taiwan guidebook (most have maps of the Alishan area). There are also tourist maps available at Alishan House.

To rejoin the main route, follow the route log in reverse and enjoy a great downhill ride. At the intersection of National Road 18 and National Road 3, reset and follow the previous route log to Touliu.

WHERE TO STAY. At Alishan, an excellent but expensive choice is Alishan House, telephone (05) 2679811. There are many other mountain hostels and small hotels in Alishan village. Refer to your conventional Taiwan guidebook for more information.

WHERE TO EAT. In Alishan, the tourist area around the bus parking lot has food stalls, and small restaurants line the narrow alleys of the village. Since you are in the mountains, try "mountain specialties" made with wild mushrooms, ferns, or Alishan's huge crisp cabbages. The Buddhist nuns at Tzuyun Zen Temple produce wind-cured cabbage that is excellent when braised with belly-pork. At tourist stalls, try the traditional cakes and confections made with millet and millet sugar.

WHAT TO DO. On the way up to Alishan, taste the high mountain tea. At Alishan, hike the trails to Two Sisters Pond and Tzuyun Zen Temple. Get up at 4:00 A.M. and join other tourists hiking to Celebration Mountain (Chushan) for the sunrise and "sea of clouds."

Log:

0.0 X, where NR18 intersects NR3 (26.2 mileage point in the previous log); reset and turn right (E) on NR18.

3.2 L:T, to Fanlu; stay straight (E) on NR18.

8.7 Chukou, elevation 250 m.

9.1 Changtien bridge, a suspension footbridge.

24.7 Town of Leitou, elevation 1,070 m.

30.5 Hsiting, elevation 1,250 m. Look for roadside barns where tea is fermented and roasted in machines that look like large clothes dryers.

32.3 Meiyuan Hostel.

32.5 Lungtou tea-tasting rooms on the right.

33.1 Lungtou village, elevation 1,280 m.

37.8 Pass Alishan Road toll station.

40.7 Pass hillside tea gardens on the left.

52.0 Pass through the village of Shihtzu.

64.3 Bus station on the right.

64.4 Alishan entrance pavilion; continue straight.

64.8 EOD; Alishan bus parking lot.

Touliu to Cholan (optional link): 106.3 km

This segment continues from Touliu to link this tour with Tour No. 1. If you are not combining the two Taiwan tours, do not take this segment; instead, stop with the previous segment and take a bus or train back to Taoyuan or Taipei.

To connect this tour with Tour No. 1, ride northeast from Touliu through Nantuo County on the foothill route. Chushan is famous for its bamboo handicrafts. You will see piles of bamboo chopsticks and back scratchers drying in roadside courtyards. The road from Chushan to Nantuo is wide and gently downhill through bamboo groves, tea gardens, and sweet-potato fields.

Near Wufeng, leave National Route 3 and cut east to avoid the metropolitan sprawl of Taichung. Ride through mixed light industry and farms, then head north through the Takeng district and one more steep climb. Rejoin National Route 3 and cross the Fengyuan Bridge to meet up with the central cross-island highway.

End the day in Cholan, where you can explore the town temple, then have a street-food dinner at the stalls that open around dusk. Cholan is famous throughout Taiwan for its quality fruits and oolong teas. Try the *ching hsiang wulong*, a really fragrant brew served in miniature cups from a small teapot. This tea is different from the oolong usually sold outside of Taiwan: its flowery scent comes solely from the tea, not from added flowers. A pinch of this tea in your water bottle is great when the weather is hot.

From Cholan, link up with Tour No. 1, A Northern Island Loop, to complete your *Tour de Taiwan*. Follow the last two or three segments of Tour No. 1 to return to Taoyuan and Taipei.

WHERE TO STAY. Go 50 meters past the end-of-day point in Cholan to the next large intersection and turn right. About 250 meters farther on the right is the Liang Bin Lushe (Friendly Guest Hostel), which is seedy, but adequate. Campers can continue up the main road until it ends at a school ground.

WHERE TO EAT. Cholan has plenty of food stalls and fruit stands along the main street.

WHAT TO DO. Stroll Cholan's main street and explore the town temple where this segment's ride ends. Be sure to step into one of the tea stores and sample the oolong teas grown in this area.

Log:

0.0 Large X circle, with Touliu train station one block to the NW; reset and head around the circle. At Wenhua Road there is a sign: "SUN MOON LAKE." Turn right (E) onto Wenhua Road.

1.4 X; continue straight. Sign: "CHUSHAN 17 KM."

8.5 Enter Linnei.

8.9 L:Y; continue straight.

9.5 L:T; continue straight through downtown Linnei.

11.8 L:Y; continue straight on NR3.

14.5 Cross the Nanyun Bridge.

17.3 Enter Chushan.

17.7 Y; curve to the left on NR3.

18.7 Cross the Chushan Bridge.

21.0 Y; bear left on NR3 toward Nantuo.

25.6 Y; bear left on NR3. A right here leads 41 km to Sun Moon Lake.

28.4 Y; bear right (ENE).

29.2 T; turn left, toward Nantuo.

29.5 Enter Mingchien.

36.4 Enter Nantuo on Changnan Road.

37.5 X; go straight through onto Nangang Road.

42.0 X; turn right toward Tsaotun on NR3 (co-named Chunghua Road here). Head downhill just after the turn.

42.4 X, at the bottom of the hill; go straight through.

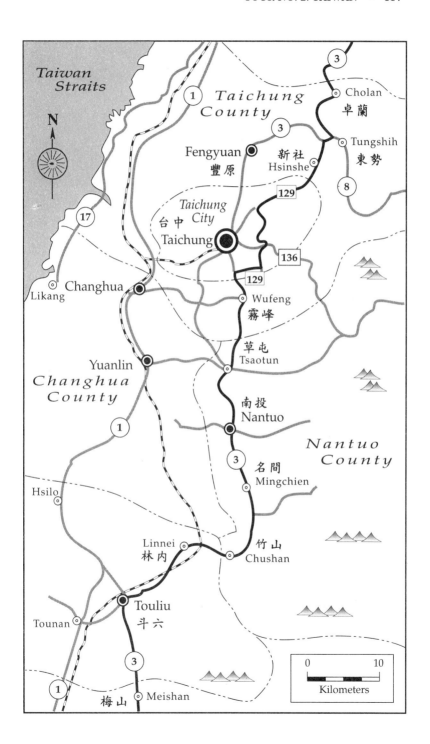

44.0 X; bear left onto a busy semi-country road through rice paddies and banana farms.

45.0 R:T; stay straight.

46.6 Enter Tsaotun.

47.4 Tsaotun temple is on the left.

48.0 Y; stay to the right on NR3 (co-named Chungcheng Road).

48.4 X, at Boai Road (and NR14 coming down from Puli and Sun Moon Lake); continue straight toward Taichung.

55.5 Sign: "ENTERING WUFENG."

56.6 L:Y, with larger road heading left; continue straight, not left. The Taiwan Provincial Assembly buildings are off to the right.

59.5 Cross a long bridge into Tsaohu.

61.1 X, with NR3 going straight; turn right (E) onto CR129 toward Taiping. Continue a few km through a heavily populated area, then break out into open fields. Ride east until you come to a T with a flashing light (no mileage point for this intersection, but you can't miss it); turn left (N) and ride to the village of Shanchiao near Yichiang Bridge.

70.1 T, with flashing light at CR136; turn left (NW) and immediately cross the Yichiang Bridge. After the bridge there is a small amusement park on the left.

70.8 Signal R:T; turn right (N) onto CR129 toward Takeng.

72.8 Signal R:T; go right (N). Straight leads to Taichung.

74.6 Cross a bridge over Putzu Creek, still on CR129.

77.7 Cross the bridge into Takeng and continue (NNE) into the foothills.

79.6 Sky Star Hot Spring Hotel is on the left, and Kaduoli Amusement Park is on a hill on the right. The road gets steeper here.

86.4 Enter Chunghsingling, with the Peak Hotel (Lingshan Lushe) on your left; continue on CR129.

86.7 Peak of the grade.

88.0 Y; go right along a road lined with *pipa* (loquat) orchards.

88.8 T, with police box nearby; turn left (N).

91.1 Y; bear left on the main road through Hsinshe.

92.4 Signal Rev R:Y; bear left and merge with the other road.

95.3 T, where CR129 ends at NR3; turn right (E) and cross the Fengyuan bridge.

96.0 R:T, just across the Fengyuan bridge where the central cross-island highway (NR8) comes in from the south; reset here.

0.0 R:T, just across Fengyuan bridge; reset and continue (E) on NR3. Just after this intersection is a L:Y; bear left (NE) up a hill toward Cholan.

5.0 Start up a grade.

6.1 Top of the grade.

8.8 Cross the Lanshi Bridge into Cholan.

10.3 EOD; X, with NR3 heading left and the Cholan town temple across the intersection on the left.

A TRIP TO THE OUTLYING ISLANDS

Hong Kong to Lantau Island and back

Distance:	57 kilometers
Estimated time:	2 riding days
Best time to go:	September–May; anytime but summer
Terrain:	Mountainous
Maps:	Nelles Map of Hong Kong; tourist maps available in the airport
Connecting tours:	Tour Nos. 4 and 5

After you arrive at the airport in Hong Kong, stay overnight in the Tsim Sha Tsui District before ferrying to the outlying islands and visiting fishing villages and a Buddhist monastery. This tour is best in late fall and early spring. Summer months in the Hong Kong area are too hot for enjoyable touring. Those combining this tour with all of the

Lamma Island waterfront teahouse

PRC tours should either do this tour in March and work north or, for a fall tour, start in early September to arrive in Beijing before it gets too cold.

Lantau Island is the largest and most suitable of the outlying islands for a short tour near Hong Kong. Beautiful beaches, old fishing villages, and a quiet laid-back atmosphere make Lantau a welcome break from Hong Kong.

Begin by cycling to the Tsim Sha Tsui District for an overnight stop. Then ferry to the Hong Kong Outlying District Pier and from there to Mui Wo on Silvermine Bay. Before riding from Mui Wo, explore the small shops and restaurants in Mui Wo back streets, then pedal a roller coaster of steep hills along the southern coast. If you catch an early ferry out of Hong Kong, you should have time to visit Po Lin Monastery in the afternoon, then drop into Tai O for the night.

In Tai O, eat seafood and vegetables seasoned with locally produced fermented shrimp paste. The next day, retrace your route to Silvermine Bay and ferry back to Hong Kong's Outlying District Pier. Retrace your route to return to Kai Tak Airport, or connect with the PRC tours at the Macao Ferry Terminal or the China Ferry Building.

CONNECTIONS. Hong Kong Kai Tak Airport is in Kowloon, about 6 kilometers from the Tsim Sha Tsui District, where the YMCA and major hotels are located. To get your bike to the hotel, your options are to: ride from the airport, take the boxed bike in a taxi, or if it is dark, store the boxed bike at the airport and return to ride it in the morning. Do not try to navigate Hong Kong traffic at night.

Airport buses will not accept bikes, but taxis will if the box is not too large. One new-bike shipping box will fit across the back seat of a taxi, but the huge boxes provided by airlines will not.

In the airport, the best place to unpack and reassemble your rig is the area by the luggage carousels. After customs inspection, change money and get Hong Kong tourist maps at tourist offices in the hallway before entering the crowded Arrivals lobby.

To connect this tour with Tour No. 4, take the high-speed ferry to Macao from the Macao Ferry Terminal, which is located near the Outlying District Pier. The Macao ferry may require booking a day in advance. To connect with Tour No. 5, take the overnight ferry to Guangzhou from the China Ferry Building on Canton Road in Kowloon.

INFORMATION. It is advisable to book lodging for your first night in the Tsim Sha Tsui District on the Kowloon side. Conventional guidebooks suggest cheap hostels and guesthouses such as the Chungking Mansions, though these are not the best choice for cycle tourists. They are inexpensive, but you may have trouble getting your touring rig into the tiny elevators. Do not leave your bike locked outside overnight in Hong Kong.

Later you can relocate to a guesthouse on the bike-friendly outlying islands of Cheung Chau or Lantau. Make them your home base in Hong Kong and ferry in to explore the city. Remember to ride on the left in Hong Kong.

Kai Tak Airport to Tsim Sha Tsui District: 6 km

The ride from Kai Tak Airport into Tsim Sha Tsui is along very busy city streets. Watch out for double-decker buses and old Chinese women pushing vegetable carts. Night life, shopping, and tourism is what this part of Kowloon is all about. Stroll the harbor promenade in front of the Hong Kong Regent and the park area near the new performing-arts complex by the Star Ferry. One of the best times to be out is in the early morning before the crowds hit the streets.

WHERE TO STAY. The YMCA, the New World, and countless other hotels are in the Tsim Sha Tsui area.

WHERE TO EAT. Up and down Nathan Road and along side streets in either direction are literally thousands of bars, restaurants, and nightclubs. There is a lively night market on Temple Street where whole restaurants are set up on the street. If you are tired from the flight and want something more relaxing, your hotel will probably have at least one restaurant.

WHAT TO DO. Get up early and work your way back up to Shanghai Street and Reclamation Road in the Yau Ma Ti District. This area is the scene of lively produce markets and wholesale fruit markets in the morning. Noodle shops and *dim sum* parlors here are filled with local merchants and dock workers: better local color than the other tourists in your hotel! Other interesting Kowloon sights are the bird market in Mongkok, the jade market, and the night market along Temple Street.

High-rise housing estates in Hong Kong

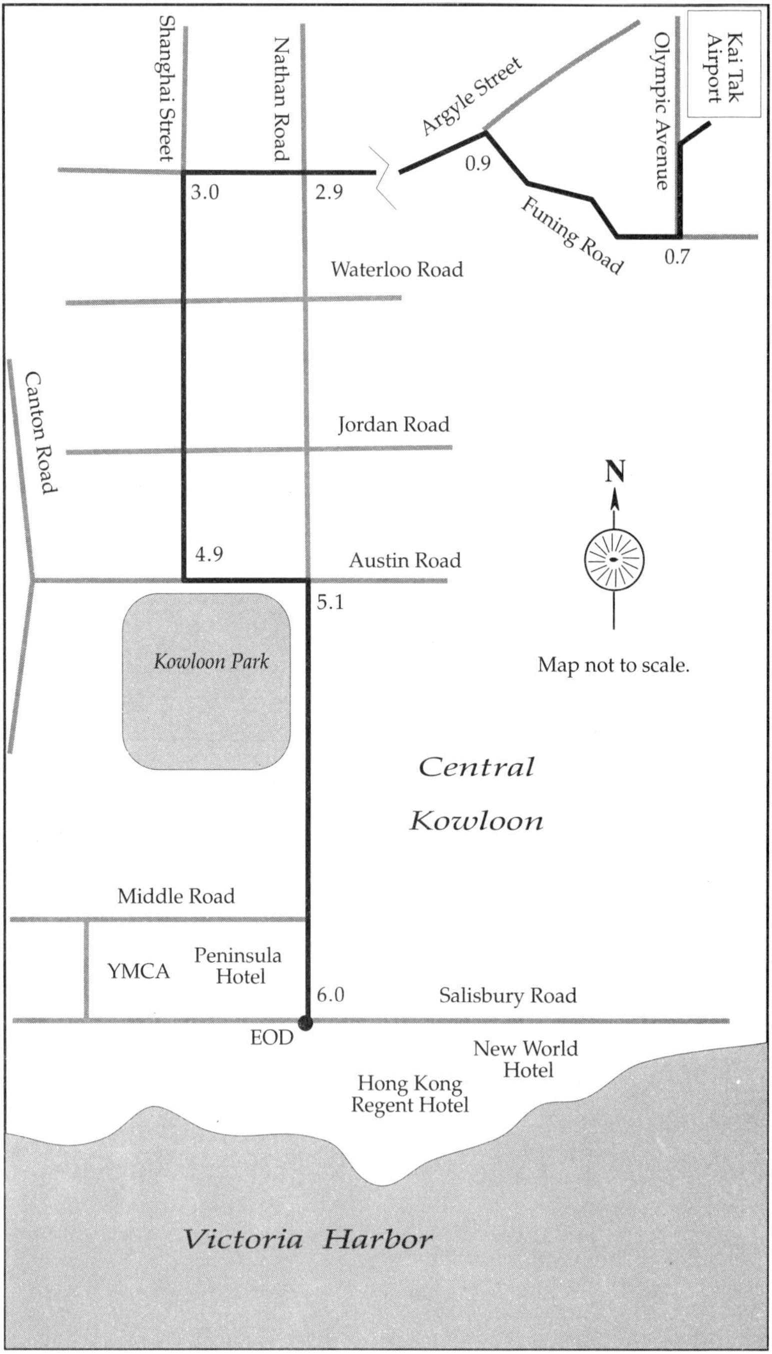

Shanghai Street

Nathan Road

Argyle Street

Olympic Avenue

Kai Tak Airport

0.9

3.0

2.9

Funing Road

0.7

Waterloo Road

Canton Road

Jordan Road

4.9

Austin Road

5.1

N

Map not to scale.

Kowloon Park

Central

Kowloon

Middle Road

YMCA

Peninsula Hotel

6.0

Salisbury Road

EOD

New World Hotel

Hong Kong Regent Hotel

Victoria Harbor

Log:

0.0 As you leave the airport Arrivals area, the bus stop is on your left and Olympic Avenue is on the right. Push your bike to Olympic Avenue and reset to begin the ride.

0.0 At Olympic Avenue, reset and then head left (SSW) on Olympic Avenue.

0.5 X, with Sung Wong Toi park on the right; continue straight.

0.7 X, at Sung Wong Toi Road; turn right (WNW) at the upper end of the park onto Funing Road.

0.9 Funing Road merges into Argyle Street; bear left (WSW).

2.9 X, at Nathan Road; go two more blocks to Shanghai Street.

3.0 Turn left (S) onto Shanghai Street.

3.7 Cross Waterloo Road.

4.9 T, at Austin Road, with Kowloon Park straight ahead; to get to Tsim Sha Tsui, turn left (E). (This is the point to which you will return to get to the Jordan Road ferry for the next segment.)

5.1 Turn right (S) onto Nathan Road and continue.

6.0 EOD; Nathan Road ends at Salisbury Road.

Tsim Sha Tsui District to Tai O, Lantau Island: 22.4 km

To get to the Hong Kong side from the Kowloon side of Victoria Harbor, you must use the Jordan Road vehicular ferry; bikes are not allowed on the Star Ferry. Once you are on the Hong Kong side, get off the Jordan Road ferry and go right to the Outlying District Pier. Passengers with bikes must enter from gangways on the sides of the piers, not the turnstile entry by the ticket booths. Park your bike outside the ticket-line area, get a ticket, then enter from the side ramp onto the lowest deck of the ferry. Ferries to all islands depart here, so be careful that you enter the correct ramp.

Ferries make several stops before their final destination, e.g., the Lantau ferry stops at Cheung Chau first. Be sure to disembark at the right island. Once you're off the Lantau ferry, ride around Silvermine Bay and explore Mui Wo village before heading to Tai O.

To get to "downtown Tai O" from the Tai O bus stop at the end of the route log below, continue past the bus stop and turn right at the town-map display case. Head back along a narrow alley one block, then look left and you will see the *sampan* ferry powered by local women; *sampans* are the shallow Chinese boats that are poled around in canals. This is a wobbly little *sampan*: balance your bike carefully! Take the *sampan* ferry (HK$0.50 for you and your bike) about 30 meters across the harbor mouth to explore the village stores, boatlike shacks, and narrow old streets.

WHERE TO STAY. In Pui O, there is the Seabreeze Hotel; at Tong Fuk beach, there is the Fairview Inn. There is a dormitory at Po Lin Monastery, telephone 5-985-5113. In Tai O, you can find lodging at the Pine Hill Villa. Campgrounds are located at Nam Shan, Pui O, and Lo Kai Wan. Nam Shan and Pui O campgrounds are close enough to the

Tai O sampan *ferry*

ferry pier to be a home base for super-budget travelers who do not want to stay at high-priced Hong Kong accommodations.

WHERE TO EAT. Stock up in Mui Wo near the Lantau ferry landing. There are seafood restaurants in Pui O and at Tong Fuk beach. At Po Lin Monastery, a family-style Buddhist vegetarian lunch is served for a reasonable price. In Tai O, there is a good teahouse restaurant at the top of the market lane after you cross on the *sampan* ferry. Go there for *dim sum* in the morning. The dining room at the Pine Hill Villa serves simple, well-cooked meals.

WHAT TO DO. Explore Mui Wo, visit beaches, visit Po Lin Monastery, and explore Tai O.

Log:

0.0 To get to the Jordan Road ferry, retrace your route from your lodgings in the Tsim Sha Tsui District to mileage point 4.9 in the previous segment's route log, and continue W on Austin Road. Two blocks farther, turn right (N) onto Canton Road. The ferry terminal is 0.2 km farther on the left. Use the gangway near the ticket booth on the north end of the building.

0.4 Take the Jordan Road ferry to the Hong Kong side, get off the ferry, and go right (NW) about 0.2 km along the waterfront. Pass the Central Harbor Ferry Pier and come to the Outlying District Pier.

0.6 Take the Lantau ferry, disembark on Lantau Island, and roll (W) about 0.1 km past the bus parking area to the circle by the Chow Kee Store, and reset. Tourist food stalls are on the right and Mui Wo village is straight ahead.

0.0 X circle by the Chow Kee Store; reset and head left (S) up a steep hill.

0.5 Top of the first grade.

1.0 Begin climbing again. The road is narrow; watch for buses.

2.1 Top of the hill; a park is on the left, then a steep downhill stretch.

2.7 Entrance to Nam Shan campground is on the left.

4.1 Enter the village of Pui O, with the Seabreeze Hotel, seafood restaurants, and tourist facilities.

4.3 L:T, at Chi Ma Wan Road; continue straight. A left turn here leads to the Pui O campground on the beach.

6.2 Top of a steep grade.

9.2 Access to Cheong Sha upper beach.

9.8 Tong Fuk beach on the left, with restaurants and Fairview Inn.

10.6 Prison on the hill to the right.

12.5 Pass through Shui Kou village.

12.6 Lo Kai Wan campsite turnoff is on the left. It is 1 km to the campsite.

13.9 Top of the grade. There is a small park just past here.

14.3 Shek Pik Reservoir is off to the right.

14.6 Start across the dam. There is a prison below the dam on the left.

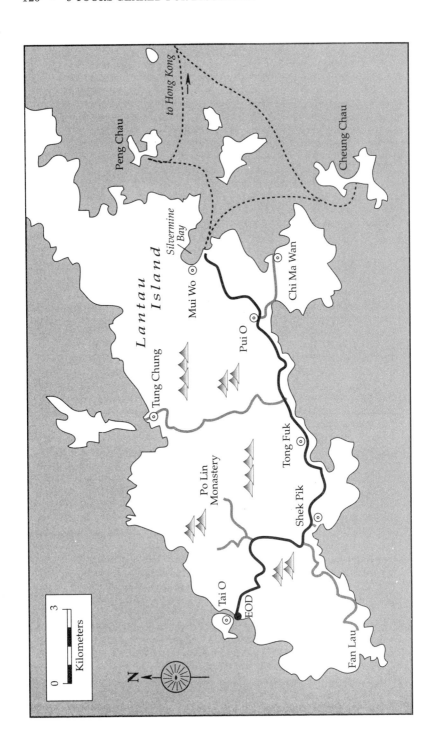

Fishing shacks and sampans *in Tai O harbor*

15.2 Once you are off the dam, begin climbing the steep grade up Ginger Mountain.

17.5 R:T, at the top; continue straight down to Tai O. To get to Po Lin Monastery, turn right here and ride 2 km up a steep grade.

20.0 R:T; continue straight. The road to the right leads to Ling Yen Temple.

21.3 Enter Tai O.

21.6 L:T; continue straight. The lane to the left leads to the Pine Hill Villa hotel, the white building at the foot of the hills on your left.

21.8 EOD; Tai O bus stop.

Lantau Island to Kai Tak Airport: 27.1 km

To return to Kai Tai Airport, simply retrace the two previous segments' route logs. If you are connecting this tour with Tour Nos. 4 or 5, refer to the Connections information for each of those tours.

THE PEARL RIVER DELTA
Hong Kong to Guangzhou

Distance: 433 kilometers
Estimated time: 7 riding days
Best time to go: September–December; March–May
Terrain: Mostly level, with some hills
Maps: Map of Macao and Zhuhai, Pearl
Delta Touring Map, Pearl River
Delta Tourist Map
Connecting tours: Tour Nos. 3, 5, and 6

The Pearl River Delta is the huge drainage of the Pearl River and the Xijiang River in southern Guangdong Province. With rich soil and a year-round growing season, this region has long been a prosperous part of China. Guangzhou (Canton) was one of the earliest Chinese cities to trade with the West, and was historically more open to outside influence than other provinces. As China modernizes, Guangdong continues to be in the forefront of development.

Although the real cycling on this tour begins from Macao, the starting point is the airport in Hong Kong. Spend a few days getting acclimatized and exploring Hong Kong, then ferry to Macao. Take at least a day to enjoy Macao's Portuguese colonial atmosphere before crossing the border into the Peoples Republic of China (PRC) at Gongbei.

As you leave the PRC border area, the developed westernized world fades into a mix of red-brick villages, sugarcage fields, truck farms, and small factories. Head west across the Pearl River Delta through Taishan County, the ancestral home of the earliest Chinese immigrants to the United States. The terrain is predominantly flat, with rice paddies, duck farms, and backward towns. Cut northwest through steeper terrain to Zhaoqing and explore the limestone karst hills and lake scenery in Qixingyan Park. The final riding day bears east on a busy flat highway to Guangzhou, the capital of Guangdong Province. Finish the tour near the Guangzhou Hostel on Shamian Island, where there are still western-style buildings left over from opium-trading days.

This tour can easily be combined with Tour No. 5 to Wuzhou in neighboring Guangxi Province, either from Zhaoqing or Guangzhou. And at the conclusion of this tour in Guangzhou, you can either return to Hong Kong by ferry, or boat north to Shanghai and do Tour No. 6.

CONNECTIONS. Begin this tour at the Hong Kong Kai Tak Airport on the Kowloon peninsula. In the airport, the best place to unpack and reassemble your rig is the area by the luggage carousels. After customs inspection, change money and get Hong Kong and Macao tour-

Ruins of Sao Paolo church in Macao

ist maps at tourist offices in the hallway before entering the crowded
Arrivals lobby. From the airport, ride through Kowloon to the Tsim
Sha Tsui District for lodgings. To get to Macao, take the Jordan Road
ferry to the Hong Kong side of Victoria Harbor. Buy High-Speed Ferry
(HSF) tickets the day before departure at the nearby Macao Ferry Terminal on Connaught Road in the Shun Tak Centre. Jetfoil and hydro-
foil ferries are quicker but do not accept bikes. Tour No. 3, which takes
you around Hong Kong and its outlying islands, can easily be combined
with the beginning of this tour.

On the day of departure, arrive early enough to attend to immigration and customs formalities for departing Hong Kong and entering
Macao. The trip takes about two hours. In addition to food and beverages, the ferry has slot machines to get you primed for Macao's casinos.
After Macao immigration in Macao Outer Harbor terminal, pick up local maps and tourist information if needed, then exit on the northwest
side of the building.

At the end of this tour, when you leave Guangzhou, those returning
to Hong Kong should take the overnight ferry back to Hong Kong from
the Zhoutouzui wharf. Cross the Renmin Bridge, then take the second

right onto Houde Lu and follow the signs to the ferry buildings. Arrange for tickets at any larger hotel in Guangzhou. This ferry arrives in Kowloon at the China Ferry terminal on Canton Road, a few blocks north of the Star Ferry terminal.

Those going north for Tour No. 6, which begins in Shanghai, will find the easiest way to get to Shanghai is by sea. Get tickets at Dashatou terminal (window No. 6, on the right side of the hall) or through your hotel in Guangzhou. Buy tickets well in advance of departure. Boats leave on days of the month divisible by five (the fifth, tenth, et cetera) and depart at 7:30 A.M. Allow at least thirty minutes to ride to Dashatou Wharf from the Shamian Island Youth Hostel area.

Get the best tickets available, because even the "special-class" cabins are pretty bleak. Meals are served three times daily for about an hour, and the selection and quality are not great. Be sure to bring instant noodles, snacks, and fruit, which are not available on the boat. The trip is boring, so you will be glad you have that shortwave radio and some reading material.

Depart from the Dashatou terminal on a riverboat, then transfer to a larger ship in Huangpu Harbor. On the riverboat, board last and stay near the gangway to ease disembarkation. When you board the larger ship, pay a RMB 48 shipping fee for the bike. Once you are on the ship, pay a RMB 15 "storage and handling fee." You will arrive in Shanghai on the third day and disembark at around 10:30 A.M.

INFORMATION. While in Hong Kong and Macao, remember to ride on the left; once you enter the People's Republic of China, ride on the right. Entry and exit procedures for Hong Kong and Macao (still a Portuguese colony) are perfunctory. Entry into the PRC from Macao requires more time. You must fill out health questionnaires and they may check your luggage more carefully.

The Pearl River Delta tour is best in fall through spring. Summer months in southeastern PRC are too hot for enjoyable touring. Even in the winter, it is not really cold in this area. Dress for warm weather and be prepared for rain. Those doing all of the PRC tours in the spring should start this tour in March and work north. For a fall tour, start in early September to arrive in Beijing before it gets too cold.

Allow about two weeks to do the main part of the tour at a leisurely pace, with layover time in Hong Kong, Macao, Zhaoqing, and Guangzhou. (If you are combining this tour with Tour Nos. 3 and 5, add another week to tour Lantau Island and do the side trip to Wuzhou.)

Guangzhou, the end point of this tour, has been open to tourists for a long time, and seems to have drawn more low-life types than other Chinese cities. Foreign tourists here attract thieves like a magnet. Do not leave luggage or any valuables unattended in this city. If you are coming into Guangzhou on a riverboat from Wuzhou or Zhaoqing, be especially careful on the boat. If you get a cabin on the boat, use your padlock to lock *all* valuables in the small locker provided, or keep them strapped to your body. Secure the sliding cabin windows with your bicycle pump or other object.

Pedicab in Macao's downtown plaza

Kai Tak Airport to the Floating Casino, Macao: 11.2 km

After the journey from the Hong Kong airport to Macao Outer Harbor, you will ride around to the peninsula's western side near the Floating Casino. Avoid cycling on the Avenida de Almeida Ribeiro, the main cross-peninsula street. It is narrow and shoulderless, and the locals use it like a freeway.

Plan to spend more than one day exploring Macao. Nowhere else will you get the combination of Portuguese colonial architecture with Chinese markets, narrow alleys, and a port-city atmosphere. The downtown areas are best explored by foot.

WHERE TO STAY. In the alleyways across from the Floating Casino, there are several less expensive hotels. The Hou Kong Hotel, located on the Travessa das Virtudes, is listed as a budget hotel in other guidebooks, but it has been "upgraded" with carpets and crystal chandeliers in the lobby. Although no longer a truly cheap lodging, it is still more reasonable than the big hotels. The hotel with the most "color" for the money, and probably the most rundown in Macao, is the Wu Yang at No. 27-29 Rua de Bocage. Use a current Hong Kong/Macao guidebook to locate other lodgings.

WHERE TO EAT. The alleys near the Floating Casino are filled with restaurants, teahouses, and stalls selling sheets of barbecued dried pork and beef. Along Rua da Felicidade there are good Chinese restaurants, and do not leave Macao without trying the local Portuguese cuisine at La Lorcha, at mileage point 4.4 in the route log below.

WHAT TO DO. Stroll the Rua da Felicidade, the old "pleasure quarter," then climb to the Fortaleza do Monte. Ride north on the peninsula to Lou Lim Loc Gardens and Kun Iam Temple. Go south to Amah Temple and the Maritime Museum.

Log:

- 0.0 At the Kai Tak Airport terminal Arrivals area, as you leave, the airport bus stop is on your left and Olympic Avenue is on the right. Push your bike to Olympic Avenue and reset.
- 0.0 Reset and head left (SSW) onto Olympic Avenue. Remember to ride on the left in Hong Kong.
- 0.5 X, with Sung Wong Toi Park on the right; continue straight.
- 0.7 X, at Sung Wong Toi Road; turn right (WNW) at the upper end of the park onto Funing Road.

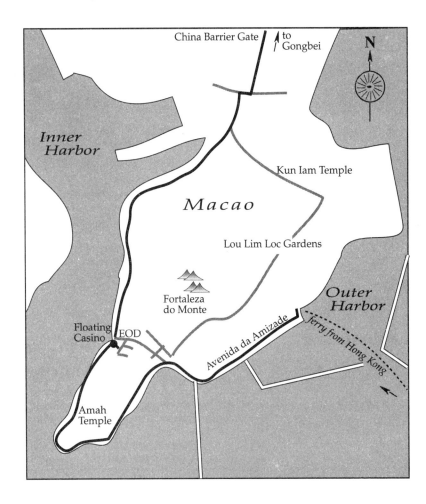

0.9 Funing Road merges into Argyle Street. Bear left (WSW).

2.9 X, at Nathan Road; go two more blocks to Shanghai Street.

3.0 Turn left (S) onto Shanghai Street.

3.7 Cross Waterloo Road.

4.9 T, at Austin Road, with Kowloon Park straight ahead; turn right (W). Two blocks farther, turn right (N) onto Canton Road.

5.3 The Jordan Road ferry terminal is on the left. Use the bike gangway near the ticket booth on the north end of the building. This ferry takes you from the Kowloon side to the Hong Kong side. Once you have made the ferry crossing, get off the ferry and reset.

0.0 Reset and go right (NW) along the waterfront.

0.4 The terminal for the ferry to Macao is a few hundred meters west of the Hong Kong Outlying District Pier, on Connaught Road in the Shun Tak Centre. From the Macao ferry terminal, take the High-Speed Ferry (HSF), which docks at Macao Outer Harbor. Exit on the NW side of the building and reset.

0.0 At the Outer Harbor terminal exit, reset and go left (SW) to the SW end of the building and come to a T. Turn right (S) onto the Avenida da Amizade. Remember to ride on the left-hand side in Macao.

0.5 Pass the Mandarin Oriental Hotel on your left. Arched bridges to Taipa and Coloane Island are off to the left.

1.5 X circle, with a bridgehead on the left and a casino on the right; go around the circle, staying close to the waterfront.

1.9 Hotel Sintra is on the right.

2.0 Y; bear left and continue (SW) along tree-lined Rua da Praia Grande.

2.6 Colegio Ricci is on the right, a buff yellow and white building.

3.8 Round the tip of the peninsula on Avenida da Republica as it curves to the north.

4.3 Red-colored Amah Temple complex is on the right. Continue past old warehouses and arcaded shopfronts. The Maritime Museum is on the left just past the Amah Temple.

4.4 Restaurant La Lorcha, which serves excellent Portuguese food, is on the right. Continue (NE).

5.5 EOD; on the left is the Floating Casino.

Macao to Jingan: 55.9 km

This segment's ride out of Macao is not long, but when you arrive in Jingan you will feel like you have landed on another planet. The whole atmosphere changes after you cross the border: wider streets and fewer tourists, and even the people look different, with plainer clothes of a more rural style.

Formalities at the PRC entry point include the usual health forms, immigration forms, customs declarations, and putting your bike luggage through X-ray machines. After customs, there is a bank on the right where you can change money. Unload your Macanese currency here, but keep a supply of U.S. dollars for street exchanges later. There

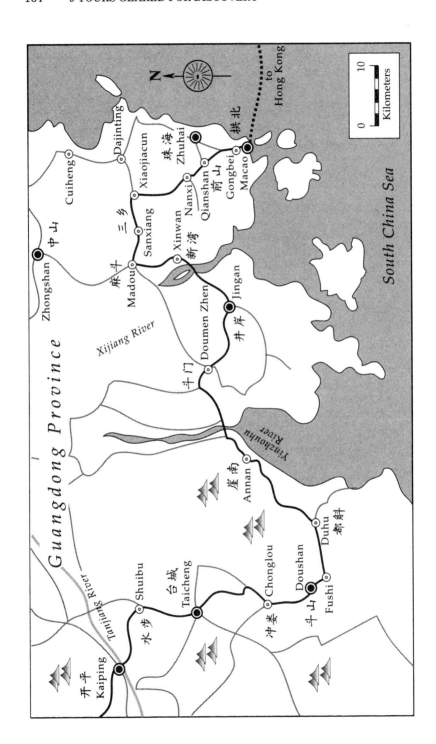

are few places to exchange money in the first two overnight stops at Jingan and Doushan. Exchange at least enough money at the border to last until Kaiping. Even better, exchange enough to last until Zhaoqing, where money is easily exchanged at tourist hotels.

After a dozen kilometers you'll be in the countryside, passing duck ponds, banana trees, and rice paddies. Farmers sell sugarcane along the wide, flat roads.

Turn off of the main road to Guangzhou and pass through the farm town of Xinwan, then cross the Jingan bridge and end the day in Jingan, the Doumen County seat.

WHERE TO STAY. There are not many lodging choices in Jingan. Stay at the seedy Jingan Daxia. Store your bike in your room, not the lobby or courtyard.

WHERE TO EAT. There are small places down the side streets from the hotel. More are along the street one block southwest of the main road.

WHAT TO DO. There are no tourist attractions in Jingan. Once you have checked into the Jingan Daxia, explore stores and markets along the main road and the road a block to the southwest. You will probably be tired and wiped out by culture shock. Just relax!

Log:

0.0 At the Floating Casino in Macao, reset and head (N) on Rua Visconde Paco de Arcos, on the west side of the peninsula.

2.8 Entrance to the Macao border exit point. Walk into the large building and do Macao exit paperwork, then push your bike down a long breezeway to the PRC entry point and proceed with PRC entry formalities.

3.6 Customs exit, which faces N onto the streets of Gongbei. Roll down to the street and reset. You are now in the People's Republic of China!

0.0 At the E–W cross street, reset and go left (W). Remember to ride on the right side of the road in the PRC.

0.2 X, at the first traffic circle; turn right (N) onto Yinbin Dadao.

1.0 X circle; go around and exit left. Bank of China is on the NE corner.

1.3 Exit X circle; head (W) on Yuehai Donglu.

1.7 R:Y, with larger main road to the left; bear left (WNW), staying on the larger road.

3.4 X circle, with a left to Qianshan harbor; don't go left, stay to the right.

3.6 Exit X circle; head (WNW).

3.8 Rev R:Y; stay straight. Watch for merging traffic.

5.0 Y circle; bear right (NNW) toward Guangzhou.

5.7 L:T; stay straight (NNW).

7.7 X circle; exit left (NW) out of the circle onto a divided road, heading into the countryside. (A right exit leads to Xiangzhou.)

9.7 Pass through the blue-tiled Zhuhai city limits checkpoint.

19.2 R:Y, at Xiaojiacun; stay straight (NNW) on the main road. (A right turn goes to Dajinting and Cuiheng, Sun Yat-sen's home.)

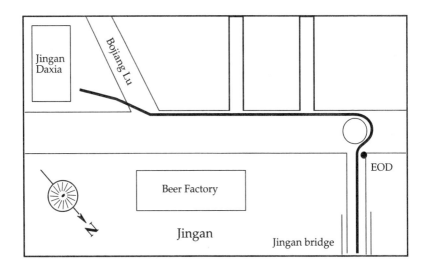

22.0 R:T, leading to Zhongshan hot spring, with a gas station on the left; stay straight on the main road.

24.0 You are now heading (WSW).

25.0 Enter Sanxiang downtown streets. Continue (WSW) through town on the main road.

27.0 Leave Sanxiang, heading up a gentle grade.

29.9 Enter another small town, Madou.

32.7 L:Y; turn left (SW), leaving the main road to Guangzhou. There are restaurants on the left at this intersection. Ahead are stretches of newer road and good rice-paddy scenery.

39.0 Farm town of Xinwan, with countryside and village scenery.

42.3 R:Y; stay straight (W). Then, at the large bridge ahead, turn right and cross Doumen bridge over the Xijiang.

43.6 Top of Doumen bridge. When you're off the bridge, continue (WSW).

44.9 Start across a smaller bridge.

51.3 X circle; go straight and cross the Jingan bridge.

52.3 EOD; X circle at the foot of the Jingan bridge. To get to the Jingan Daxia hotel, turn left (SE) and ride 250 m, passing two side streets on the right. At the third side street, Bojiang Lu, you will see the gates of the hotel on the far right corner.

Jingan to Doushan: 69.6 km

As southern PRC modernizes, many larger towns are changing and losing their character, but along this segment's route, you will see typical old-style southern villages.

After a street-stall breakfast of pastry, noodles, or porridge in Jingan, return to the Jingan bridge and continue through delta countryside to the backward town of Doumen. Pass Doumen, then ferry across a river to the village of Meige, with duck ponds, canals, and *sampans*. After a longer ferry across the mouth of the Yinzhouhu River, enter the shaded downtown streets of Annan, a good place for a rest stop or lunch. From Annan to Doushan, the road varies between cement and sand surfaces, passing through red-brick villages with rice paddies, sugarcane, and bananas.

Doushan is rather decrepit and mildewed, with paint peeling off the colonnaded buildings in the old business district. Turn-of-the-century southern Chinese town architecture is being torn down and replaced all over this part of the PRC, but Doushan still has this style of high-arcaded town architecture. The liveliest areas in Doushan are the traffic circle where the route log ends and along the lakeside park behind the Huaqiao Hotel. Stalls and hawkers in the circle have local snack foods and some will change money.

WHERE TO STAY. The Doushan Hotel or the Huaqiao Hotel are your best bets. If these are filled, there are other small guesthouses along the lake behind the Huaqiao Hotel.

WHERE TO EAT. Get your meals in the Huaqiao or the Doushan, or at street stalls. Stalls around the traffic circle have a good assortment of pastries for breakfast.

WHAT TO DO. Ride around the downtown streets and the park behind the Huaqiao Hotel.

Pondside village in the Pearl River Delta

Log:

0.0   At the traffic circle at the foot of the Jingan bridge, reset and turn right, heading (NNE).

0.6   L:Y circle; go around and exit on the left, heading (SW).

2.6   You are out in the countryside now.

4.5   Earthfill dam is on the left.

9.8   Y; bear right (NNW) toward Doumen.

12.1   Rev L:Y; stay straight, then curve around to (N), entering the backward town of Doumen Zhen.

12.4   Y, in the center of the Doumen marketplace; bear left (NW). Continue through the countryside until the road ends at a ferry dock.

15.7   Ferry dock; take the smaller ferry straight ahead, not the large car ferry on the left. Fare is RMB 1 per person.

15.8   Disembark and exit the ferry compound. At the gate, turn right (N) toward Meige.

16.7   T; turn left (W).

21.4   L:T, with a large bridge to the left; continue straight (W) and climb up along cliffs overlooking the Yinzhouhu River.

25.3   Enter a village after descending from the cliffside road.

27.2   L:T, just after a sandy hill; turn left, roll down to the pier, and take the ferry. While on the ferry, look back at the east banks and notice the old Song Dynasty fort set into the cliffs.

27.5   Get off the ferry and come to a tollgate. Pay RMB 1 per person for tickets, and turn in the tickets at the second gate. Continue (W).

28.0   T; turn left (SW), then the road curves to the (S).

33.1   Enter the town of Annan, with shaded streets, small food shops, and low-end inns.

33.5   T, just past the bus station on the right; turn right (W).

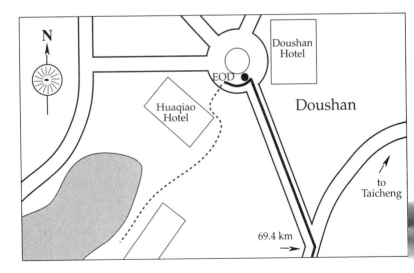

37.8 Old village of Tianbian Cun, with quiet countryside scenery.

43.0 Cross a narrow cement bridge. Just before the bridge, on the right, is a small restaurant that shows soft-porn videos at lunchtime to attract business!

54.1 Village of Yuanshantou.

55.9 Enter the town of Duhu.

56.0 R:T; turn right (W), heading toward Doushan.

57.3 T; turn right (SW). It is open and windy here, and there are seafood restaurants. You are off of the sand road and on a cement road again.

67.0 L:T, to Guanghai; continue straight (WNW) on the main road.

69.4 Y, at entrance to Doushan; bear left into the town center.

69.6 EOD; X circle. The Doushan Hotel is on the right. Entry gates to the Huaqiao Hotel are around the circle to the left.

Doushan to Kaiping: 50.2 km

This segment's ride crosses the heart of the Pearl River Delta through Taishan County, the ancestral home of many Chinese immigrants to the United States. On the way to Taicheng, the Taishan county seat, ride a hill road lined with citronella, orchards, bamboos, and scrubby pine forests. Stop for lunch in Taicheng, explore the market plaza and old streets, then continue through the newer northwestern side of town toward Kaiping.

On the map, the size of Kaiping is depicted the same as Taicheng and Xinxing, but it is much larger and more urban. Greater Kaiping is called Sanbu Zhen, and consists of the three towns of Xinchong, Changsha, and Dihai clustered around the Tanjiang River. The new spirit of enterprise has really taken hold in Kaiping: there are even stalls that specialize in refilling disposable lighters!

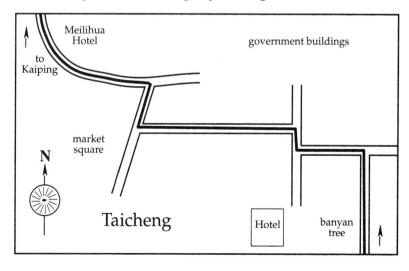

WHERE TO STAY. Find lodging at the Kaiping Daxia Hotel or the Huaqiao Hotel. If these are full, there are others on the south side of the Tanjiang bridge.

WHERE TO EAT. There are lots of restaurant choices in Kaiping. Try the teahouse near Changsha Park or the coffeehouse behind the Huaqiao Hotel. A stall outside the coffeehouse sells a selection of pastries, and it is a hangout for the local "smart set."

WHAT TO DO. The attractions in Kaiping are the street market scenes and the river. Changsha Park is near the Kaiping Daxia Hotel, and there is a lively teahouse in front of the park. Stroll the waterfront for a glimpse of riverboat life. Get city maps at the Kaiping Daxia or the Huaqiao Hotel.

Log:

0.0 In Doushan in front of the Huaqiao Hotel gates at the town center's X circle, reset and ride 0.2 km (SE) back to the Y at the entrance to Doushan (mileage point 69.4 on the previous segment's route log).

0.2 Rev L:Y; do a hairpin left turn and head (NW) out of town.

0.5 Road curves to the right (NW).

8.4 Y; stay left on the main road and enter Chonglou.

8.7 Cross a bridge over a canal.

11.6 Y, with both roads leading to Taicheng; turn left (N) and take the shorter hill route along a road lined with citronella.

18.1 Crest of a grade; coast down (NW).

23.8 X; go straight (NW).

24.1 Cross a bridge and enter the outskirts of Taicheng.

24.4 Bank of China is on the right.

24.7 Large banyan tree is on the left of the town square. Continue straight (N) through narrow streets.

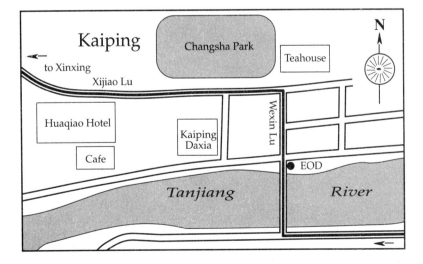

Farmers in paddies near Xinxing

25.2 T; turn left (W).
25.4 T; turn right (N), then—after 12 m—turn left (W) at the next L:T.
25.5 Pass under a pedestrian bridge at the "Bridge Department Store."
26.0 Roll onto a square with a stone pavilion and market area to the left, and a T up to the right. Turn right (E) and head 30 m up to the signal T, then turn left (NW) onto the larger road, which curves to the right after the turn.
26.3 Meilihua Hotel is on the right.
26.5 You are now heading (N) along a wider road with newer buildings and commercial areas.
26.7 Bank of China is on the right.
35.2 Enter Shuibu.
35.4 L:Y; turn left (NNW) onto a smaller road toward Kaiping.
47.8 Head up onto a bridge.
48.1 Exit the bridge, heading (WNW).
48.3 L:Y; stay straight, not left.
48.8 Road narrows and passes under high-tension wires.
49.0 R:Y; bear right onto Tanjiang Donglu.

49.8 Bridgehead on the south end of the Tanjiang bridge; turn right and cross the bridge.

50.2 EOD; the north end of the Tanjiang bridge. To get to the Kaiping Daxia Hotel, go straight one block, bear left at Changsha Park, and turn left again at the next block.

Kaiping to Xinxing: 77.1 km

As you leave Kaiping, the scenery shifts back to rural mode after a few kilometers. Road surfaces vary from marginally paved to hard-packed sand. The route is level for the first half of the day, then it gets hilly, ascending through sparsely populated areas along farm roads. The feeling is that you are riding deeper into the "old" China.

As you ascend the sandy hill into Renhe village, be prepared for a crowd of curious villagers: one old woman even wanted to feel the hair on my arm! Leaving Renhe, watch for pigs on the road, and take note of the farm pond surrounded by terraces of old-style houses on the left. After another climb, this time out of Dongcheng, coast down into a valley and end the day in Xinxing.

WHERE TO STAY. The Xinxing Huaqiao Hotel is comfortable, with clean, modern rooms in the newer wings.

WHERE TO EAT. There is no need to leave the hotel compound for food; the Huaqiao Hotel dining room is excellent. A local specialty is the sweet pickled plum appetizer dish. Also try the local dried fruits available in the hotel gift shop.

WHAT TO DO. There are no major tourist attractions here, just typical southern PRC life. The Huaqiao Hotel and restaurant are a welcome respite after a medium-difficult ride.

Log:

0.0 At the north end of the Tanjiang bridge in Kaiping, reset and head (N) on Wexin Lu.

0.1 Road doglegs left (W).

0.3 L:T, with Changsha Park on the right; continue straight. The left turn leads to the Kaiping Daxia Hotel.

0.4 Huaqiao Hotel is on the left. The road is now Xijiao Lu.

0.7 X circle, with a bus station across the circle; bear right (N) onto Musha Lu.

1.2 X; go straight, then cross the Musha bridge (N).

2.2 Y; go left (NW). (The right fork leads to Guangzhou.)

2.6 Y, with a gas station; go left (W) on Yaogu Gonglu.

5.0 Pass through a village, then head out into the countryside.

18.6 Enter the town of Shatang. Head (NW) through town.

19.5 Leave Shatang.

23.6 Enter Cangcheng, a good lunch stop with lots of restaurants.

23.7 Cross a canal bridge.

23.9 X; continue straight (W).

30.6 Village of Zhangqiao.

37.0 Village of Lungsheng.

37.9 Leave Lungsheng.

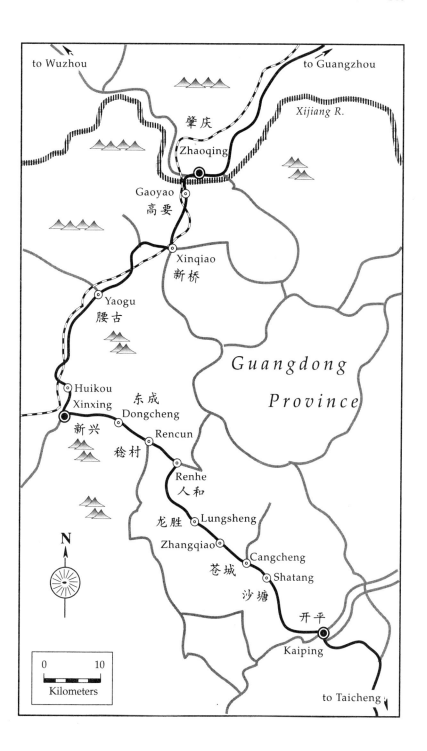

39.3 L:Y; stay straight (NW).

40.0 For the next 1 km, head up into the hills on sandy roads.

44.0 Y; bear right (N).

51.9 Y, as you enter Renhe village at the crest of the hill; bear left (NW). The village is old and backward, with pigs in the road.

59.4 Curve right through the village of Rencun, a more prosperous village with newly painted doors on all the houses.

63.9 Dongcheng school is on the left.

65.8 Village of Dongcheng. Here you will start climbing uphill again.

76.0 Come over a mountain pass and enter Xinxing.

76.4 Start across a bridge, heading (WNW).

76.6 X circle, on the other side of the bridge; go straight (W). (Note that this is the next segment's starting point.)

77.1 EOD; alley on the left leads to the Xinxing Huaqiao Hotel. Go left and uphill 60 m to the hotel gates.

Xinxing to Zhaoqing: 59.6 km

As you leave Xinxing, the road ascends a river valley with terraced rice paddies, red-brick villages, and an occasional whistle from the steam locomotives still in use here. Sand production sites line the riverbanks, and barges and *sampans* ply the river. After the village of Yaogu, the road descends to the Xijiang River. Cross the Xijiang bridge at Gaoyao and enter Zhaoqing.

Zhaoqing has a long history as a tourist destination, the main attractions being Qixingyan (Seven Star Crags) and Dinghu. Visitors arrive by bus and riverboat from Guangzhou, and by jetboat direct from Hong Kong. Not many arrive by bicycle!

Refer to your conventional guidebook for more information on Zhaoqing. If you need to change money, try the exchange counter or cashier at the Huaqiao Hotel or the Xinghu Hotel. For "informal" exchanges, a good place is the lottery-ticket tables on the sidewalk in front of the Huaqiao Hotel. Stand near the tables and someone will eventually approach you.

WHERE TO STAY. If you want luxury, the Xinghu is the biggest and the newest. It is one block east of the end-of-day point on the main road. The Huaqiao, across from the end-of-day point, caters to Hong Kong and foreign tourists, but is not cheap. The Duanzhou, next to the Huaqiao, does not accept foreigners. The Bohai, on the north end of the lake, is old, classic, and cheap. The hot water may not be reliable, but you can count on the service staff of this government-run lodging to be surly and unaccommodating. I like the Heguang, built on pilings over the water right at the entrance to Qixingyan Park. It is reasonable, has a good *dim sum* breakfast, and is near other restaurants and attractions on the main street.

WHERE TO EAT. The hotels all have restaurants, but some of the best food is at street restaurants just east of the Qixingyan Park main gate. Freshness is guaranteed: the fish or animal of your choice is displayed alive in tanks and cages on the sidewalk.

WHAT TO DO. Plan to spend more than a day exploring the lake and craggy islands of Qixingyan Park. Bike along the pathways that cross the lake, then explore the old downtown areas. See the Duanzhou inkstone factory, which makes some of the finest inkstones in China, and visit nearby Dinghushan (at mileage point 17.5 in the next segment's route log).

Log:

0.0 At the Xinxing Huaqiao Hotel gates, reset and ride 60 m down the alley to the main road, then turn right (E).

0.6 X circle; reset on the east side of the intersection.

0.0 X circle; reset and head (NE) from the bridgehead along a road lined with scraggly pine trees. The Xinxing River is on your right.

2.9 Village of Huikou.

5.0 Tollgate (no toll for bikes). Continue (N). A train station is off to the left. Steam locomotives pass through here!

9.9 Cross under a railroad trestle and enter a river valley with rice paddies and great rural scenery.

Hanging houses along the lake in Qixingyan Park

18.2 Cross a bridge and come to a R:Y; stay to the right (NE). The road narrows and follows the railroad tracks.

24.3 Enter Yaogu.

29.5 Crest of the grade.

30.7 Gaudy gas station and tourist stores are on the left. There are lots of good four-table truck-stop eateries along this stretch.

38.0 Stay right on the old route through town, with railroad tracks to the left.

42.6 Y, entering Xinqiao; bear left on the main road, do not go right, down to the market area. The road curves (N) after the turn.

43.3 Leave Xinqiao.

51.0 Gaoyao train station is off to the right.

52.9 X circle; continue straight (N).

53.0 Bank of China is on the right.

53.2 X circle; go straight but stay to the left, heading up the ramp onto the Xijiang Daqiao bridge.

54.1 Tollbooths (no toll for bikes).

54.5 Start across the bridge.

56.2 Exit the bridge. Ride on the sidewalk, not the car lanes.

56.5 Large X circle; turn right (E) onto the busy main road.

57.0 X circle; continue straight.

58.1 X circle, with elevated walkways; go straight (E).

58.9 X circle; dismount and carefully cross the busy intersection to the left, to the gaudy entrance gates to Qixingyan Park. The Huaqiao Hotel is to the right, along with a lot of other hotels and restaurants.

59.0 EOD; gates to Qixingyan Park. The Heguang Hotel is straight ahead, "floating" in the lake; to get to the Heguang, turn right. To get to the Bohai Guesthouse, turn left and follow the lakeside road 3.7 km to the north end of the lake.

Zhaoqing to Guangzhou: 104.8 km

Heading east from Zhaoqing, you get a closer glimpse of the future that awaits Guangdong Province. This road was once quiet and not unpleasant for cycling. Now it is crowded with noisy truck and bus traffic. In traffic jams, country bumpkins lean out of the bus windows to test you with the one word of English they know: "hah-rooowe." But along the way, wander off the road a bit and rural China is still there. Small truck-stop restaurants en route are friendly and will offer you tea at no charge if you stop for a rest. Finish the day at the Guangzhou Youth Hostel on Shamian Island, across from the White Swan Hotel. The Chinese have a saying, "Eat in Guangzhou," and they are not kidding! Guangzhou cuisine has a deserved reputation for being some of the best in China.

WHERE TO STAY. The Guangzhou Youth Hostel is convenient and has showers, although the staff can be surly. Use your conventional guidebook to select other lodgings in this well-touristed city.

WHERE TO EAT. If you are staying in the youth hostel, there are some excellent restaurants just a block from the hostel back along the

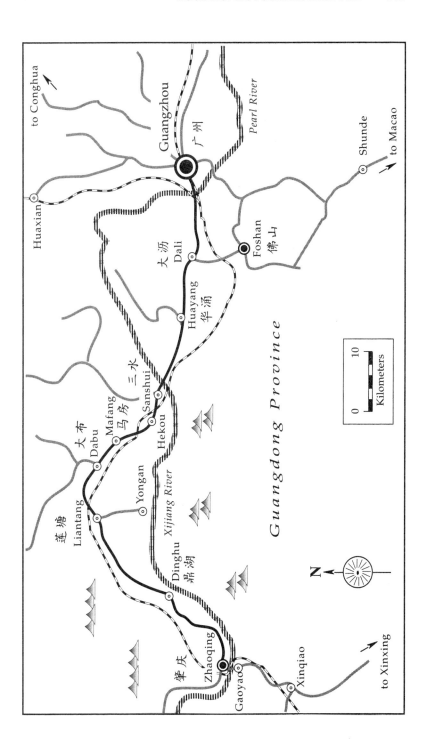

road you came in on. Once off Shamian Island, a fifteen-minute walk east along Liuersan Lu leads to many other eating establishments.

WHAT TO DO. Since Guangzhou is the major city in this part of the PRC, as well as the capital of Guangdong Province, there is plenty to do. Famous restaurants, temples, pagodas, parks, markets, and memorials are too numerous to list. Refer to your conventional guidebook for more information. It is great just to pedal around and soak up the street life in this lively city.

Log:

0.0 At the SE corner of the X circle in front of the gate to Qixingyan Park, across from the Huaqiao Hotel, reset and head (E).

0.2 Xinghu Hotel is on the right.

0.4 X circle; continue straight. There are lots of food stalls on the right.

1.0 X circle; continue straight.

3.0 Leave the city area, but there is still lots of traffic.

10.4 Old road merges into the new highway, which bypasses Zhaoqing north of Qixingyan Park.

10.7 Tollgate (no toll for bikes).

17.5 X; go straight. (A left here leads 0.5 km to Dinghu.)

22.0 Large X; continue straight on the main road as it bears to the left (NE).

36.2 R:T, to Yongan; stay straight (NE).

38.5 Town of Liantang. There are many restaurants along this stretch.

45.0 Cross the Dasha bridge.

45.6 Enter the village of Dasha.

46.8 Rev L:Y; continue straight.

49.5 X; continue straight.

50.5 Tollgate for the Beijiang bridge (no toll for bikes).

51.0 Start over the Beijiang bridge.

52.0 Leave the bridge.

55.2 R:T, to Hekou; continue straight.

60.1 Enter Sanshui.

62.9 Large X circle, with Jianlibao beverage factory on the right; continue straight (E).

64.0 Cross a bridge and leave Sanshui.

71.4 X; continue straight toward Guangzhou.

78.0 R:T; stay straight.

87.4 X; stay straight (ESE). (A right turn leads to Foshan.)

89.7 L:T, onto an expressway; don't turn, stay straight. Now you are well into outlying business districts and heavy traffic.

91.1 R:Y, heading (S) to Jiangmen; stay straight (E).

95.0 X; stay straight.

99.2 Cross under railroad tracks and prepare to turn left just after, to head up onto the Pearl River bridge.

99.4 Turn left (NE) across a wide road onto the bridge approach.

100.2 Exit the first span of the Pearl River bridge; coast down.

100.8 Cross under a toll crossing (no toll for bikes) and start up over the second span of the bridge.

101.6 Exit the second span and head down to X circle.

101.9 Large X circle; start around to the right.

102.0 Exit X circle at the first exit on the right; head (S) onto Huangsha Dadao.

103.6 Stay to the right in the bike lane; do not ascend the ramps on the left.

103.9 Nanzhan railroad station is on the right; continue straight (E) under the elevated roadway through heavy city traffic.

104.5 R:T; turn right (S) and cross a polluted canal onto Shamian Island. You will notice old western-style buildings from opium trade days.

104.8 EOD; T, with a cafe and the White Swan Hotel straight ahead. On the left, a few doors back from the corner, is the Guangzhou Youth Hostel.

Guangzhou Youth Hostel to Dashatou Terminal: 4.5 km

This segment takes you from Shamian Island to the boat terminal for the boat ride to Shanghai, starting point for Tour No. 6. Allow at least 30 minutes to get to Dashatou Terminal from Shamian Island. It is possible to take a domestic flight from Guangzhou to Shanghai,

Leaving one of Guangzhou's many historic temples

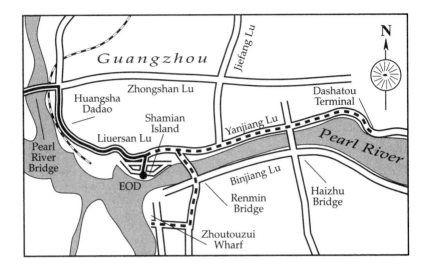

but it is not recommended because of the difficulty of shipping your bike by air.

If you are instead returning to Hong Kong, you will need to go to Zhoutouzui Wharf. From the eastern end of Shamian Island, cross the Renmin Bridge over the Pearl River. Once you are off the bridge, take the second right onto Houde Lu and follow the signs west to the pier complex.

Log:

0.0 At the Guangzhou Youth Hostel, reset and head (N) toward Liuersan Lu.

0.2 T; turn right (E) onto Liuersan Lu.

0.7 Keep to the right, riding under the overhead automobile overpass.

0.8 Stay to the right; do not go up the ramp. You are now on Yanjiang Lu. (The bridge on the right is the Renmin Bridge, which takes you to Zhoutouzui Wharf and the ferry to Hong Kong.)

1.0 At the east tip of Shamian Island, continue (E).

1.4 Nanfang Department Store is on the left.

1.8 Aiqun Hotel is on the left.

2.9 Pass under the Haizhu bridgehead. There is a large park on the left.

4.4 X circle; continue straight through.

4.5 R:T, entry to Dashatou Terminal; turn right (S). At the car circle ahead, the ticketing hall is on the left and the terminal where you board is straight ahead. Stock up on food for your boat trip to Shanghai at the small stores along the main street.

TOUR NO. 5: SOUTHEASTERN PRC

ALONG THE XIJIANG RIVER
Guangzhou to Wuzhou and back

Distance:	204 kilometers
Estimated time:	3 riding days
Best time to go:	September–December; March–May
Terrain:	Mostly level, with some steep grades
Maps:	Pearl Delta Touring Map, city map of Wuzhou
Connecting tours:	Tour Nos. 4 and 6

Ride west from Zhaoqing along the Xijiang River, then leave the river and cross a series of ridges and narrow valleys with yellow-brick villages. Return to the river at Deqing, and continue along relatively level roads to Wuzhou, just over the border in Guangxi Province. Unlike Guangdong, Guangxi is not yet open to free-form bicycle travel; you cannot *legally* ride beyond Wuzhou. Hotel staff report foreign cy-

Riding a sand road in the rural south

clists to the Gong An, who will probably prevent you from continuing farther into Guangxi by bike. But this tour *is* in open areas.

The tour begins in Guangzhou, but the route log begins in Zhaoqing. Get to the starting point in Zhaoqing by cycling the final segment of Tour No. 4 in reverse from Guangzhou, or by taking a riverboat to Zhaoqing. Finish the tour with a ferry trip from Wuzhou back to Guangzhou, or cycle the whole route in reverse.

This tour is a little too long for two riding days and a little too short for three. Strong cyclists may be able to get to Deqing the first day, or they may choose to ride to Fengkai on the second day and spend the night there. A short third day's ride into Wuzhou would leave plenty of time to explore the town before dark.

If you want to combine this tour with Tour No. 4, you can do it as a side trip to the previous tour, cycling from Zhaoqing to Wuzhou and back, and then continue on Tour No. 4's final cycling segment from Zhaoqing to Guangzhou.

CONNECTIONS. The easiest way to travel from Hong Kong to Guangzhou with a bike is by ferry. Get advance tickets for the overnight ferry at the China Ferry terminal on Canton Road in Kowloon. Boats depart Hong Kong daily at 9:00 P.M. and arrive in Guangzhou the following morning at 7:00 A.M.

To continue on to the starting point for Tour No. 6, take a boat from Guangzhou to Shanghai. For information, see the Connections section of Tour No. 4.

INFORMATION. This tour is best in fall through spring. Summer months in southern PRC are too hot for enjoyable touring. Remember to cycle on the right in the PRC.

In Guangzhou, do not leave luggage or any valuables unattended in ferry terminals or other public places. If you are taking a riverboat to begin or end this tour, be especially attentive to security on the boat.

Guangzhou to Gaoliang: 89.2 km

From Guangzhou, cycle or take a riverboat to Zhaoqing. (If you cycle, follow the Zhaoqing to Guangzhou segment of Tour No. 4, in reverse.) Spend a few days in Zhaoqing exploring Qixingyan Park, then head west along the Xijiang River. Along the way, broad rice paddies, sugarcane fields, and gardens stretch from the roadside to the foothills. Brick-walled villages are reflected in roadside fishponds, and bamboo outhouses are perched on stilts over the ponds. The road is level at first, but becomes hilly after about 30 kilometers. Road surfaces vary from good pavement to dirt roads. Watch for sand-filled potholes that are nearly invisible until your front wheel drops into them. After a series of grades, drop into the village of Gaoliang for the night.

WHERE TO STAY. In Gaoliang, the Shunda Zhaodaisuo is 0.1 kilometer down the lane to your left at the end-of-day point. Get an upstairs room and look down into the home life of the villagers. Village pigs are kept out of the hotel by low boards across the entryway.

WHERE TO EAT. The Shunda Zhaodaisuo has a dining room that serves country-style food.

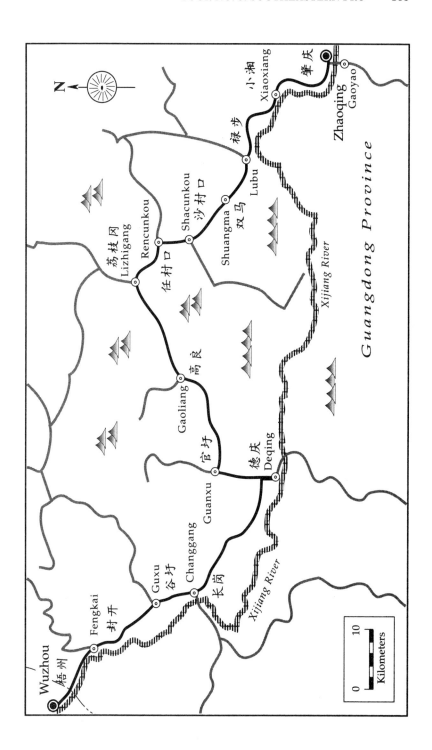

WHAT TO DO. Gaoliang is not a tourist spot. Relax, clean your bike in the courtyard, and watch Cantonese opera with locals who come over to view the hostel's television.

Log:

0.0 At the Qixingyan Park entry gates in Zhaoqing, reset and head right (W) on the main road.

2.4 X circle; go straight.

7.5 R:T; stay straight, heading toward the mountains.

13.8 Enter Xiaoxiang village. This stretch is very rural, with nice riding along the river. The hills are reforested with pine trees.

31.1 Y, at Lubu; bear left, leaving the river and heading up into mountains.

33.6 Y; stay left on the main road.

34.0 Start up a grade.

38.0 Descend into the village of Shuangma, in a small valley with rice paddies, red dirt, and yellow-brick houses.

44.9 Top of the grade. You are now entering Deqing County.

53.2 L:T, at Shacunkou; stay straight.

54.2 Village of Bozhi, which has several restaurants.

58.4 Rev R:Y, at the village of Rencunkou; stay straight.

64.4 Pass through Yongfeng.

68.1 Cross a bridge into Lizhigang.

68.3 Y, as you leave Lizhigang; go left (SW), heading into the mountains.

72.0 Begin climbing switchbacks.

75.4 Top of a grade.

85.0 Pass through a village with small restaurants.

89.2 EOD; L:T, in Gaoliang; go left to the Shunda Zhaodaisuo.

Gaoliang to Deqing: 34.4 km

Deqing is a typical southeastern PRC river town that makes its living shipping local forestry products down the Xijiang River to Guangzhou. It is the destination of this segment's ride because it is large enough to have lodging options open to foreigners.

WHERE TO STAY. The Huaqiao at the end-of-day point or the Feng Shun are your options. Those who continue to Fengkai for the night should try the Apricot Blossom Hotel, at mileage point 59.0 in the next segment's route log.

WHERE TO EAT. Town streets in the area of the Huaqiao have food stalls and restaurants, and the Huaqiao has its own dining room.

WHAT TO DO. There are no official tourist attractions, but local street life can be interesting.

Log:

0.0 At the L:T in Gaoliang (previous segment's EOD), reset and continue straight (SW).

5.2 Pass through a village.

14.6 L:T, at Maxu village; continue straight.
20.0 Pass through Guanxu; stay to the left through town.
31.6 R:T; go straight, entering Deqing on Jiefang Lu.
33.3 Feng Shun Hotel is on the right. Pass it and head through town toward the river. Turn right at the levee.
34.4 EOD; the Huaqiao Hotel is on the right.

Deqing to Wuzhou: 80.8 km

As you leave Deqing, the road is fairly level through the foothills, with eucalyptus-lined roads and logging-truck traffic. After the town of Fengkai, the road follows the banks of the Xijiang River into Guangxi Province and Wuzhou. Wuzhou is famous for its huge snake market, and other markets selling dogs and cats for culinary purposes. From Wuzhou, catch a riverboat ferry back to Guangzhou. The ferry wharf and ticket hall are on Xijiang Lu two blocks east of Zhongshan Lu.

WHERE TO STAY. The Yanjiang Hotel at the end-of-day point is basic and inexpensive. For more upscale lodging, continue past the

Riverboats along the Xijiang River at Wuzhou

A Wuzhou back alley scene

end-of-day point on Xijiang Lu, cross the big Guijiang bridge, and the Hebin Hotel is on the right, across from Hebin Park.

WHERE TO EAT. Wuzhou is a large town with many restaurants. Locals here include many things in their diet that Chinese from the northern provinces would not dream of eating. But do not worry about them slipping you cat when you ordered pork: the cat is much more expensive! If you do want to try the cat, ask for *Longfenghu*, or "Dragon, Phoenix, and Tiger." It is a dish of snake, chicken, and cat. Interesting street food can be had in night markets on side streets off of Zhongshan Lu.

WHAT TO DO. While in Wuzhou, visit Zhongshan Park and the zoo (where other visitors may find you more interesting than the caged primates). The teahouse in Zhongshan Park is a good place to relax. Another possibility is a side trip north to Guilin, the famous scenic area with limestone karst hills along the Li River. Store the bike at your hotel and take a bus to Guilin. As of this writing, the route to Guilin via Yangshuo was in a closed area. Check with the local Gong An before trying to cycle there or you may run into trouble.

Log:

0.0 At the Huaqiao Hotel in Deqing, reset and go left along the levee.

0.3 Turn left and head away from the river on Jiefang Lu.

2.7 L:T; turn left toward Wuzhou. Bear left (NW) near the brick smokestack.

12.5 L:T; stay straight.

13.8 Pass through a village.

31.4 T, at the village of Changgang; turn right (N).

32.5 Y; bear left.

40.6 Large T, at Guxu; turn left (NW).

45.3 Ascend a short grade.

55.4 Enter Jiangkou.

58.2 Cross a bridge and enter Fengkai.

58.7 X circle; continue straight.

59.0 Rev L:Y, with the Jiangbin Hotel on the left; continue straight. For an interesting break, disconnect and go left along the riverfront. Explore the street markets and eat clay-pot rice dishes. (For those who opt to spend the second night in Fengkai rather than Deqing, the Apricot Blossom Hotel is also on this street on the left.) Return to the Y and reconnect to continue.

79.0 Enter Wuzhou city limits along Xijiang Lu.

80.5 X, with Zhongshan Lu. A right turn here leads to the city center.

80.8 EOD; Yanjiang Hotel is on the right, Xijiang River and the boat docks are off to the left.

TOUR NO. 6: EAST-CENTRAL PRC

THE LAND OF FISH AND RICE
Shanghai to Ningbo

Distance: 614 kilometers; 26-km and 6-km side
trips
Estimated time: 10 riding days; 1–2 days for side trips
Best time to go: March–June, September–November
Terrain: Mostly level, a few grades
Maps: Nelles Map No. 3 of Central China,
provincial maps of Jiangsu and
Zhejiang, city map of Shanghai
Connecting tours: Tour Nos. 4, 5, and 7

This tour begins in Shanghai and heads west across Jiangsu Province to Suzhou. Passing Wuxi on the north shore of Lake Tai (Taihu), the route proceeds south through Yixing and Huzhou to Hangzhou, capital of Zhejiang Province. From Hangzhou, bear east along the south shore of Hangzhou Bay to Shaoxing and Cixi. End the tour in Ningbo, and ferry back to Shanghai.

Jiangsu and Zhejiang are two of China's richest provinces, and have been a center of Chinese culture for at least a thousand years. They were formerly the ancient kingdoms of Wu and Yueh. Marco Polo visited the major cities on this tour, and even then was astounded at the dense population and high level of culture.

Jiangsu Province straddles the Yangzi River and is laced with waterways and lakes, including Taihu, the second-largest lake in the PRC. The scenery is predominantly flat and watery with lively scenes of canal life: *sampans*, cormorant fishermen, and Grand Canal barges. West of Taihu, and south to Hangzhou, the terrain gets hilly with stretches of bamboo groves, cedar forests, and tea gardens. After Hangzhou, the northeastern part of Zhejiang Province returns to flat watery scenery.

Since this is the most densely populated and fastest-growing part of the PRC, you will see more truck traffic than flute-playing boys on the backs of water buffalo. The highlights of this tour are cultural: the ancient cities of Suzhou, Hangzhou, Shaoxing, and Ningbo.

Suzhou is known as the "Venice of China" because of its numerous canals and bridges. The industrial ugliness of Wuxi is balanced by the misty lakeside scenery of Taihu. Yixing, China's "pottery capital," produces teapots and other ceramics of the highest grade, and tours of the workshops are available. Also near Yixing are Linggu and Zhanggong caves.

Hangzhou is a former dynastic capital, and is home to one of China's

One of Suzhou's many narrow alleys

premier tourist attractions: West Lake (Xihu). Countless vistas, parks, islands, and pavilions around Xihu delight visitors and have been the subject of poetry for a thousand years.

Shaoxing is not on the main tourist trail and still retains a lot of "old China" atmosphere. A stroll through any canalside neighborhood presents scenes of *sampans* moving produce, craftsmen in open-fronted workshops, oldsters knitting and chatting on the sidewalk, or a mother cooking lunch in her alleyway kitchen. In Ningbo, there is Moon Lake, and more water-life scenery on the western outskirts.

Scenery is not the only attraction on this tour through "the land of fish and rice." Culinary culture is well developed here. Even the smallest towns have restaurants and truck-stop eateries with good food at ridiculously low prices. In the larger towns, restaurants provide true gourmet dining, from famous sweets in Suzhou to braised pork ribs and Taihu fish in Wuxi, from excellent teas and pastries in Hangzhou to China's best wines in Shaoxing and great seafood in Ningbo. You may even gain weight on this tour!

CONNECTIONS. If you reach Shanghai by boat, ships from Guangzhou dock at the Gongpinglu Wharf. Refer to the Shanghai city map in your conventional guidebook for directions from that wharf to lodgings. (If you have chosen the Pujiang Hotel—which is no longer inexpensive—it is about 1.9 kilometers from the wharf area.)

Shanghai street scene

If you reach Shanghai by air, you will arrive at Hongqiao Airport. In 1993 there were no city maps available at this airport. Buy a map of Shanghai before arriving or pick one up at one of the large hotels on the way into town. If you arrive after dark, taxi into town in one of the micro-van taxis, or store your bike in the terminal until the next day, and then ride into town. There is a baggage deposit office on the north end of the Departures hall.

As soon as you arrive at the end point for this tour—Ningbo—make arrangements at your hotel for boat tickets back to Shanghai, and be sure to get the best tickets available: even the best cabins are not too good. Buying tickets at the crowded passenger terminal ticket hall is difficult, and good tickets are usually presold to scalpers. If you want to really save money, buy *san xi* tickets and sleep in the ship's passageways with the poorer voyagers. You get the same free hot water and smelly rest rooms, but no bed. This overnight boat leaves Ningbo at about 4:00 P.M. Ask at your hotel for information on other departure times. The boat from Ningbo docks in Shanghai at about 3:30 A.M. at Shiliupu Wharf in the Haitan district. You must get off the boat even though it is early, so be prepared with lights, food, et cetera. Ride north from the terminal along the riverside promenade to the intersection at Nanjing Lu near the Peace Hotel. Navigate to other lodgings from this central location.

If you are leaving the PRC from Shanghai's Hongqiao Airport, start at the west end of Nanjing Lu and continue west to Hongqiao Lu and the airport. There are airport signs all along the route.

Those heading north from Shanghai to begin Tour No. 7 should take the overnight ship to Qingdao. Ships leave Shanghai on even-numbered days at 1:00 P.M. from the Gongpinglu Wharf. Buy tickets ahead of time at the second-floor ticket hall on Jinling Lu by the Orient Hotel. The ticket window is on the left of the hall, with a sign that says "FOREIGN GUEST TICKETS." To change money near the ticket office, go west one block on Jinling Lu, then north on Sichuan Lu one block to Nanjing Lu. On the northeast corner is a CITIC bank that cashes TCs. It may also be possible to obtain tickets through your hotel.

INFORMATION. If Shanghai is your point of entry to the PRC, spend several days getting used to the roads and riding style of locals before setting out on the tour. Some of Shanghai's main streets are closed to bikes during business hours, but there are always side roads a few blocks away where bikes are permitted. A bicycle is the best way to explore this great city.

The route log for the segment that takes you into town from the airport leads you to the Bund, the broad road along the waterfront in the Haitan district. This route passes many well-known hotels and ends up a few blocks from the Peace Hotel, a landmark on every map of Shanghai.

Although there are only nine to ten riding days on this tour, budget at least three weeks to allow for time in Shanghai and for layovers in the cultural cities along the route. Remember to ride on the right in the PRC.

Shanghai Hongqiao Airport to Haitan District: 16.2 km

Exit customs and the Arrivals hall onto street level, facing east. The domestic airline terminal is to your left. Departures are upstairs, and foreign airline offices are upstairs from the Departures hall. The ride into central Shanghai is along busy, wide avenues for 7 kilometers, then the streets are narrow and congested with thousands of bicycles. This route across Shanghai passes old-style apartment buildings with inner courts, alleyways with vegetable markets, open-front noodle stalls, and high-rise modern hotels. You will want to return to sections along this route and explore the back alleyways. Plan to spend a few days exploring Shanghai by bike, especially the back streets in the older "Chinese" sections of town.

In the 1920s and 1930s, Shanghai was the financial heart of Asia. Commerce, banking, food, and nightlife made it China's most vibrant city. Mao Zedong's socialist experiment destroyed the old Shanghai, but could not suppress the vigor, elegance, wile, and sophistication of the Shanghainese. Now that prosperity is once again legal, Shanghai is making a comeback. The city is alive with international trade and in-

Along the Bund, Shanghai

dustry. The Pudong area across the Huangpu River from the central city is developing into the PRC's industrial joint-venture showcase.

Ten years ago it was hard to find a decent restaurant in Shanghai; now it is hard to find one that is not good. Even Hong Kong movie stars are investing in Shanghai restaurants. In Shanghai, all provincial cuisines are represented, even Chinese Muslim foods from the northwest. It is not uncommon to see northern-style noodle stalls where chefs twist and pull dough into noodles as fine as "dragon whiskers."

WHERE TO STAY. Lodgings in Shanghai are listed in all conventional guidebooks, and there are quite a few high-end hotels near the airport. For the last few years Shanghai has been on a building spree, but no matter how many hotels are built, it is still difficult to find a reasonably priced room. If you didn't pre-book lodging, there are hotel reservation kiosks to the left of the customs exit on the Arrivals floor of Hongqiao Airport.

WHERE TO EAT. There are still state-owned restaurants and dining halls, but now you can choose from thousands of "mom-and-pop" places that are all trying hard to please. The local cuisine is basically Jiangsu style with influences from other provinces and Europe: sweetish soy-braised meats, seafood of every variety, fava bean and beancurd dishes, cold dishes of duck, "drunken" chicken steeped in wine, and many varieties of sweet pastries. Street stalls have inexpensive bowls of noodles with pork chops, meat sauce, beancurd sauce, or pork and salted mustard greens.

WHAT TO DO. My favorite thing to see in Shanghai is the everyday street life in the old "Chinese" section of town south of Huaihai Lu and Renmin Lu, around Yuyuan Gardens: old people sit along the sidewalks and knit or chat, colorful laundry hangs everywhere, and hawkers sell rice cakes from carts that explode rice in a cannonlike device. You may even see a merchant on the corner who sells rice-grain–size baby crickets: some for singing, others for fighting! Other good places to people-watch are the riverside promenade along the Bund and Renmin Park. A stroll along Nanjing Lu will give you an idea of what is currently in style in the PRC: Shanghai is still the fashion center of China.

Log:

0.0 At Hongqiao Airport, as you face east at the Arrivals exit doors, reset and go right (S). Remember to ride on the right in the PRC.

0.2 Merge with traffic from the airport Departures area, keeping to the right.

0.4 X; go straight (SE). Shanghai International Airport Hotel is on the left as you leave the airport area.

0.7 You are now heading (SE) along a tree-lined road.

1.5 Y; bear left (E) on Hongqiao Lu. Notice a huge stainless-steel statue of women waving ribbons.

1.8 Cypress Hotel is on the right.

2.6 Zoo entrance is on the left.

4.7 New Garden Hotel is on the right.

5.2 X; go straight (E).

5.8 X; continue straight ahead (E). Stay in bike lanes.

6.3 L:T; go straight (E). The Westin Shanghai and Yangzi New World hotels are on the left here.

6.7 X; go straight. You are now on Yanan Xilu. A skybridge sign says "WELCOME TO SHANGHAI." Hongqiao Hotel is on the right.

6.9 X; stay straight (E). Bank of China is on the right by the Rainbow Hotel. Change money here if you didn't at the airport.

7.1 Skybridge sign: "JING AN SI."

7.5 Road narrows.

7.6 Rev L:Y; stay straight (E).

7.8 X; go straight.

9.0 X circle; bend left and exit (ENE).

9.4 Road, still Yanan Xilu, curves back to (E).

10.5 Y, at intersection of Nanjing Xilu (on left) and Yanan Xilu (on right); turn right here. Nanjing Road is closed to bicycle traffic during business hours (8:30 A.M.–5:30 P.M.). At this point, find your position on a local map.

10.9 Shanghai International Equatorial Hotel is on the right.

11.0 X; turn right (S) onto Huashan Lu and pass the Jingan Hilton Hotel on the right 0.1 km later.

11.3 Road name changes to Changxu Lu.

11.4 L:T; turn left (E) onto Julu Lu, a smaller road. This is the bike route heading east to the waterfront Haitan district.

11.8 Cross Fumin Lu.

12.4 Cross Shanxi Nanlu.

12.8 Cross Maoming Lu.

13.1 Cross Ruijin Lu; there is a market area through here.

13.5 Cross a road and in 0.2 km merge into Jinling Lu, heading east.

14.8 Cross Xicang Nanlu.

16.2 EOD; road ends at the Bund, with the Dongfang (Orient) Hotel on the right. (The ticket office for ships to Qingdao, beginning point for Tour No. 7, is on the second floor.)

Shanghai to Kunshan: 65 km

The main cycling on this tour actually begins after you have explored Shanghai. Use your Shanghai city map to get to the starting point at the North Railway Station, the main train station in Shanghai. From the train station, leave the city and ride west on flat roads bordered with truck gardens and light industry. Stop in Nanxiang at Guyi Yuan Garden. Built in the Ming Dynasty, it is considered one of the best gardens south of the Yangzi River.

Continue through wide fields of rapeseed, which turn the countryside a brilliant yellow when they flower in the spring. Roadside canals are busy with riverboats towing logs and barges. The road remains level through Taicang, then Kunshan Mountain rises out of the plain. Kunshan, also called Lu Du, "Deer Capital," is modernizing but still has Jiangsu Province canal-town character in the older parts of town.

WHERE TO STAY. The Kunshan Binguan is a good stopping place; telephone (05224) 552104. If you turn right (west) at mileage point 64.8 in the route log below, the Ludu Hotel is about 100 meters down Qianjin Xilu on the right, and the Garden Hotel is 150 meters farther on the right, near the next large intersection.

WHERE TO EAT. These hotels each have restaurants, and there are more in the commercial district along Renmin Lu.

WHAT TO DO. Kunshan is not a tourist destination; it is included as a stop on this tour because the mileage from Shanghai to Suzhou may be too far for some cyclists to ride in one day. Nevertheless, the downtown streets and canal boat scenes are interesting.

Log:

0.0 At the east entrance to the train station X circle, in front of the Zhongya Hotel, reset at the NW corner of the X and head W on Tianmu Zhonglu.

0.3 X; bear right (NNW) and head toward the bridge. The train station is off to the right. A bridge sign says no bikes allowed, but many cyclists are using it.

1.3 Once across the bridge, make a hairpin right turn and head (S) along the small road on the east side of the bridge.

1.6 X; turn right (W) onto Jiaotong Lu, go under the bridge, and join traffic heading out of Shanghai.

7.7 Road curves to the (N), approaching a T.

7.8 T; turn left (W) toward Jiading.

9.2 X; stay straight (W).

11.1 Taopu area; you are now heading through villages and farms.

11.6 T; turn left (W). The freeway is on the right now.

14.6 Cross a narrow bridge over a canal with boat traffic.

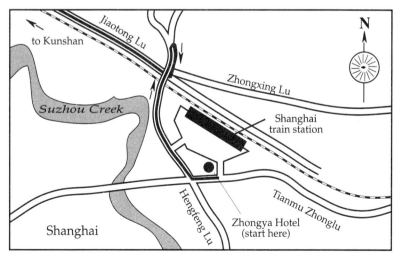

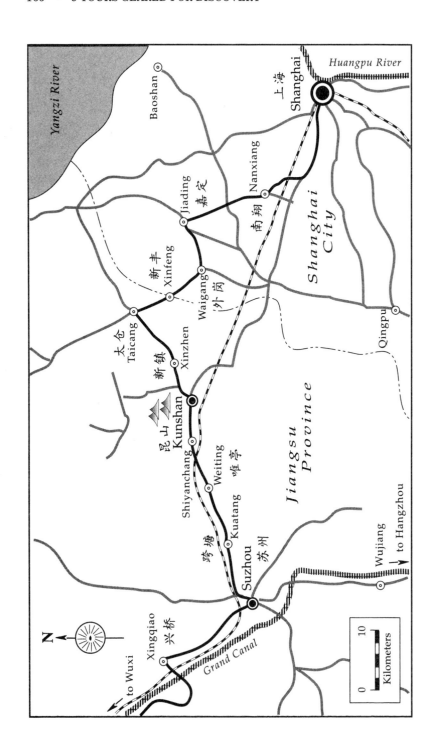

15.1 Sinope gas station is on the right as you head (W).

15.9 Y; bear left (WSW) toward Nanxiang. Guyi Yuan wall is on your right after the turn.

16.5 Entry gate to the Guyi Yuan on the right. Disconnect here and explore this elegant Ming garden. The entry fee is RMB 2.00 per person. Take a break at the tea pavilion along the lake or have lunch in the dining hall.

17.2 Pass through the town of Nanxiang.

17.5 Y; bear right (NW) and leave Nanxiang.

19.2 X; stay straight (N).

22.3 X; stay straight. A right turn leads to the freeway.

26.6 Tian Yi restaurant is on the right (with a yellow tile face); it is a friendly place with good food.

28.6 Y; turn left (W). The fork heading straight goes 1 km into Jiading.

30.2 X, with a signal; go straight (W).

30.7 Y; go left (SW).

32.0 Pass an industrial plant on the left.

34.6 Y; go right (NW). This is the village of Waigang.

40.9 Pass an inspection station and leave Shanghai City Administrative Area. The next village is Xinfeng.

47.1 Cross a bridge over a wide canal (NW).

48.6 Cross a smaller canal and enter Taicang.

48.8 X; turn left (SW) off the main road onto a smaller road.

56.1 L:T, with a bridge on the left; go straight (W), entering Xinzhen.

60.0 View Kunshan Mountain rising up out of the flats ahead.

63.3 Y; turn left, then cross a canal bridge, heading south.

63.5 Y; go right (W) into Kunshan on Huancheng Beilu. (This intersection is the starting point for the next segment.)

64.2 T; turn left (S) onto Tinglin Lu.

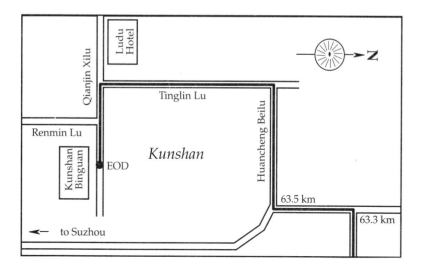

64.8 T; turn left (E) onto Qianjin Xilu.

65.0 EOD; Kunshan Binguan on the right. Just before the hotel is a R:T at Renmin Lu. Head south on Renmin Lu to get to restaurants, department stores, and bookstores.

Kunshan to Suzhou: 41 km

Continue through canal-laced countryside and enter Wu County, in ancient times known as the Kingdom of Wu. As you approach Suzhou, notice the distinctive village architecture: moon bridges, horn-shaped roof peaks, and whitewashed walls.

Suzhou is a water city, filled with canals and bridges, and has been called the "Venice of China." Since it is a major destination for both native and foreign tourists, Suzhou may end up being preserved as a "Disneyland of Chinese Culture." Fortunately, so far the only fast-food joints are traditional wonton and steamed-bun stands. Local street life is still the real thing. Plan to spend at least two days in Suzhou.

Suzhou offers visitors from more developed countries a glimpse of a traditional recycling practice. A modern sewer system would be difficult to install and a waste of good fertilizer, so human waste is carefully transported by canal barge to nearby farms. In the morning, women empty wooden chamberpots at canalside pickup stations. The pots are then cleaned with long bamboo whisks and left to air on the sidewalk. Nothing is wasted, and the dense urban area is surprisingly clean and odor-free.

In the old saying that dictates "Eat in Guangzhou," the next phrase is "Women in Suzhou": Suzhou has long been famous for its beautiful women and the sex business. Not much has changed; men are likely to be accosted and propositioned by pedicab drivers and pimps who hover around tourist hotel gates.

WHERE TO STAY. The Dongwu Hotel, at the end-of-day point, or the Suzhou Hotel are good options. Refer to your conventional guidebook for more lodging choices.

WHERE TO EAT. There are simple dumpling stalls and noodle shops along most streets. For more complex Suzhou cuisine, try the Deyue Lou, across the street from the famous Songhe Lou (Pine and Crane). The Songhe Lou is the oldest continually operating restaurant in China, but locals advised that the Deyue was better. The Songhe Lou is located in the Suzhou Bazaar area, and is listed on most conventional guidebook maps. Try dishes of braised pork and beancurd, and steamed freshwater eels. Suzhou is also famous for sweets, which include *songzi zongzi*, a type of pine-nut brittle, and *zhimapiantang*, crisp slices of sesame candy. Both are available in the alleyway teahouse near Hanshan Temple.

WHAT TO DO. Suzhou is famous for classic Chinese gardens. In addition to the Master of the Nets and Humble Administrator's gardens, Hanshan Temple on the west side of town is a must-see. Near this temple you will find wonderful old moon bridges and an alley with a traditional teahouse tucked in between Hanshan T-shirt shops.

Moon bridge and canal scene in Suzhou

There are a number of art studios along Shiquan Jie near the Dongwu Hotel.

Log:

0.0 At the Kunshan Guesthouse, reset and ride back toward the Y at the previous route log's 63.5 mileage point, where you entered Kunshan.

1.5 Y; reset and continue from this point.

0.0 Y; reset on the SW side of the intersection and head (E). The road immediately curves right, bearing (S) along the east side of town.

0.8 X; stay straight (S).

1.4 Cross a canal bridge (SSW) with log-barge traffic jams.

1.9 T; turn right (NW) onto Chaoyang Donglu.

2.3 City bus terminal is on the left.

2.6 Large X; go straight. Kunshan train station is to the left.

3.2 R:Y; bear right (NW). There is a white wall on the right after the turn.

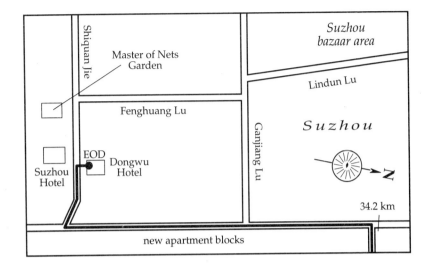

3.4 Cross a canal.

3.5 L:Y; bear left (NW), then curve left (W) on route 312.

5.0 You are out in the countryside now. Canals are on the left with long canal boats. There is plenty of traffic along here, but there are also good shoulders and pavement.

9.2 Y; follow main traffic flow to left. There is a new bridge to the right.

9.8 Pass under a railroad trestle.

13.7 Cross a canal and enter Wu County.

18.0 Sign: "ENTERING WEITING."

19.6 Great scenery on the left: canals, moon bridges, and old houses.

27.1 Sign: "ENTERING KUATANG." This is the Suzhou outskirts.

34.2 Large X circle; reset before continuing on.

0.0 Reset and head around the X circle. Exit left (S) on a new road lined with six-story gray cement apartment buildings.

1.1 Cross a canal.

2.6 Signal X; stay straight. Sign: "URBAN DISTRICT TO RIGHT."

3.9 Second signal X; turn right (SW), then curve to (W).

4.7 Cross a canal (W).

4.9 Enter the narrow, tree-canopied Shiquan Jie.

5.3 EOD; the Dongwu Hotel is across the canal bridge on the right. If you aren't staying at the Dongwu, continue on 0.3 km to the Suzhou Hotel on the left; in another 0.1 km the entry alley for Wang Shi Yuan (Master of Nets Garden) is on the left.

Suzhou to Wuxi: 55.6 km

This short segment continues through canal country, with many glimpses of waterborne life and long boat trains along the Grand Canal. Near Wuxi, the route follows a busy truck route lined with cheap restaurants and inns, all hastily constructed to benefit from the economic liberalization. The girls who come out and wave are not just being friendly: they are hired to attract truck drivers at lunchtime.

Wuxi is pronounced *woo-shee*, and means "without tin." A couple of thousand years ago, Wuxi was a tin-producing area, but the tin mines petered out; hence the town is "without tin." The city and surrounding districts are somewhat ugly and industrial, but the parklands near Taihu Lake are scenic.

WHERE TO STAY. The Yunhe Hotel at the end-of-day point is adequate. For upscale resort atmosphere, try the Hubin on the road out to Turtle Head Island. There are more hotels in the downtown area straight ahead from the intersection at mileage point 50.0 in the route log below.

WHERE TO EAT. There are several popular restaurants across the street from the Yunhe Hotel. In Wuxi, do not miss the rich saucy pork ribs called *Wuxi paigu*. Other good local dishes are cold sliced beef with Zhejiang vinegar, and cold fava beans with sesame oil.

WHAT TO DO. Explore Turtle Head Island and see the plum blossoms at Mei Yuan in the spring.

Log:

0.0 At the Dongwu Hotel gates in Suzhou, at EOD point in the previous route log, reset and ride back toward mileage point 34.2 in the first part of the previous route log.

0.4 Cross a canal bridge and head (E).

0.5 X, just past the bridge; go straight. The road bends left, then (E).

1.3 Large T; go left, heading (N).

2.6 L:T, with a signal; stay straight (N).

4.1 Cross a canal.

5.0 Top of a bridge over a larger canal.

5.3 Large X circle, at mileage point 34.2 of the first segment of the previous route log; reset on the NE corner.

0.0 X circle; reset and continue north.

0.1 Pass under a railroad trestle.

0.3 T; turn left (W).

1.1 Cross a canal, then curve right (N).

2.1 R:T circle; go straight through, heading (W) over a canal after exiting the circle.

2.7 L:Y, heading to a railroad station; go straight (WSW).

4.5 Huqiu pagoda is ahead to the left. You are leaving the city area now.

5.8 L:T, with a turnoff to Huqiu (Tiger Hill); continue straight (W).

10.5 Suzhou New District is to the left. Descend into an underpass, go under a railroad in 0.2 km, then exit the underpass, heading (NW).

10.9 R:Y; go straight (WNW).

11.7 Start over the Grand Canal bridge, heading (SW).

16.1 Large X circle; go straight through, exiting (NW).

16.9 Good restaurant is on the left.

19.0 Sign: "WU COUNTY."

A Grand Canal vista along the road to Wuxi

22.7 L:Y; stay straight (NW), toward Wuxi.

25.0 Outskirts of Wuxi, with industrial ugliness and lumberyards.

30.0 Head (NNW), with a busy canal on the right.

30.8 Y; bear right (NW) along the canal. (The main road bears left.)

31.5 R:T; stay straight (NW).

32.8 Go under an underpass.

34.0 X; stay straight (W), on the main road.

39.4 Leaving the town of Huazhuang, you are now back on tree-lined roads.

43.0 Enter Wuxi County, heading (N).

44.1 L:T; go straight (N), toward Wuxi.

44.6 L:Y; stay straight.

45.5 R:Y; stay straight.

46.6 A small restaurant is on the right. The *Wuxi paigu* here are excellent.

47.0 X circle; turn left (W).

47.4 Cross a canal.

47.7 R:T, at Zhongqiao intersection; turn right (N) onto Hubin Lu. (This intersection is mileage point 2.6 on the side trip to Turtle Head Island.)

48.1 Large X; go straight (N).

48.3 Fei Hong Hotel is on the left.

48.8 Customs building is on the left.

49.0 Start onto the bridge over the canal harbor. Exit the bridge in 0.2 km.

50.0 L:Y; turn left (NW) onto a larger street. The fork leading straight goes to the Grand Canal and the central city area.

50.3 EOD; Yunhe Hotel is on the right.

Side Trip to Turtle Head Island: 25.8 km

To get to Turtle Head Island, backtrack from the Yunhe Hotel to the Zhongqiao intersection and head west. At Turtle Head Island, see theme-park "dinosaurs" and "dragons," take boat rides, and enjoy the lakeside scenery. Just before entering the park, go left into Dafu to see the aquarium.

0.0 At the Yunhe Hotel in Wuxi, reset and head left on the road in front of the hotel.

0.3 T; turn right (S).

2.6 T; turn right (W), at the Zhongqiao intersection, still on Hubin Lu.

4.7 Y; stay left (SW). The road is lined with large plane trees.

5.9 L:T, entrance road to Hubin Hotel; disconnect here and go left to explore the lakeside parks and grounds around the Hubin. (**Note:** *do not* reset your cycle computer at this point.) When you have finished your explorations, return to the entrance and reconnect.

6.1 Tourist parking area is on the right, near some shrimp ponds.

7.3 X; turn left and cross the bridge over to Turtle Head Island.

7.9 Exit the bridge and turn right to get to the park entrance. The aquarium is to the left in the village of Dafu. Continue along the

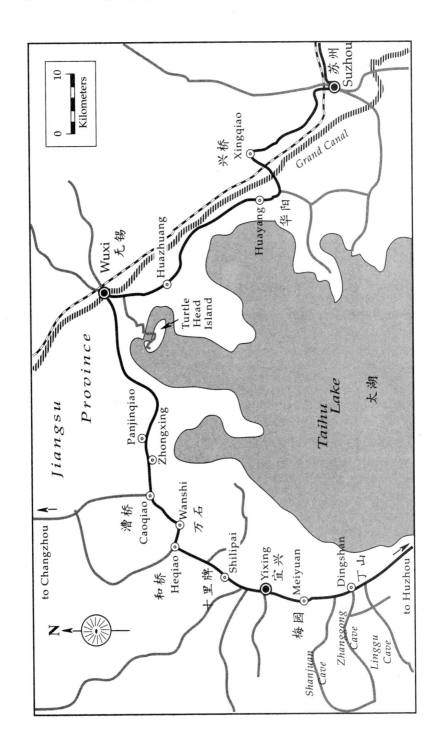

road to the park entry gate, a few hundred meters from the bridgehead. Pay RMB 10.00 per person to enter and ride all the way around to the tourist area.

12.9 Tourist park area on the other side of the island. When you have finished seeing Turtle Head Island, retrace the route back to the Yunhe Hotel in Wuxi.

Wuxi to Dingshan: 76.1 km

From Wuxi, head southwest along a rolling foothill road on the west shore of Taihu. Once you are out of the foothills, the road continues along canals through level terrain. You may see fishermen in punts cormorant fishing, beating the water with sticks to rustle up fish for their birds to catch. After 20 kilometers, the road joins a busy north–south truck route.

As you approach Yixing, pass roadside stalls selling pottery, marble products, and grotesque rocks from Taihu. Yixing styles itself the "Pottery Capital" of China, and it is easy to see why: canals swarm with boats loaded with huge pots, and even streetlight posts are made of pottery.

WHERE TO STAY. Find accommodations in Yixing at the Yixing Binguan, telephone 702811, 702822, or 702179. The Dingshan Shanghai Hotel, telephone 741811 or 741885, is 14 kilometers farther down the road. There is also the Tao Reng Yuan Hotel at mileage point 0.3 on the next segment's route log.

WHERE TO EAT. The Yixing Guesthouse and Shanghai Hotel have restaurants, and there are small private restaurants nearby.

WHAT TO DO. The town of Yixing is nothing special, but the teapot factories in Dingshan are worth a visit, as are the caves southwest of Dingshan.

Log:

0.0 At the Yunhe Hotel in Wuxi, reset and head right (NW) toward the big X circle.

0.2 X circle; exit left (SW) in 0.2 km. The Wuxi Grand Hotel is on the left.

1.0 Head (W) along a wide road with bike lanes.

1.5 X; go straight.

2.2 T; turn right (N).

2.6 T; turn left (W) toward Yixing.

5.8 R:T; stay straight. (A right turn leads to Nanjing.)

6.7 Mei Yuan garden entrance on right.

6.9 L:T; stay straight. (A left turn here leads to Turtle Head Island.)

8.1 Great Wall Hotel is on the right.

9.6 Leave Wuxi city limits.

10.4 R:T; stay straight. You are into a hilly area now.

11.3 You can see Taihu off to the left.

13.4 R:T, at the road to Hukang; stay straight (SW).

18.5 Y; bear right (WNW) and cross a small bridge.

20.0 Enter Wujin County.

Taihu lakeside scenery

21.5 T; turn left (SW) onto a busy highway.

22.2 L:T; stay on the large road as it curves right (W).

27.2 R:T; stay straight, through the town of Zhongxing.

34.0 X circle, at the Caoqiao intersection; go through (WSW).

34.3 Enter Yixing city limits.

40.4 Enter Wanshi.

45.0 Dong Jiao Ting restaurant, with good food, is on the right.

45.5 R:T; in Heqiao; stay straight (SW) toward Yixing.

51.0 L:T; stay straight (SW).

54.6 Enter Shilipai.

58.4 China Yixing Pottery Commercial Town is on the left.

58.6 X circle, with stainless-steel statue; go straight (SW).

59.1 X; go straight (SW) along Yibei Lu.

59.3 Cross a canal.

59.8 L:T; turn left, leave the highway, and head (SE) into Yixing downtown streets.

60.3 X; turn right, then cross a bridge. Now you are on Renmin Beilu in downtown Yixing.

60.7 X; go straight.

61.3 X; go straight.

61.5 Cross a bridge over a canal.

62.1 Cross a bridge and enter Yixing Guesthouse grounds, an optional EOD. If you don't stay at the Yixing Guesthouse, continue on to the Shanghai Hotel, 14 km farther down the road, in Dingshan. Reset at Yixing Guesthouse to continue.

0.0 At Yixing Guesthouse gate, reset and ride (N) on Renmin Lu.

0.3 L:T; turn left and head out to the highway.

0.6 T, at the highway; turn left (S).

9.6 R:T, at Chuanbu; continue straight (S) toward Dingshan. (The right turn leads 15 km to Shanjuan Cave, another possible side trip.)

10.0 Cross a canal bridge.

13.5 L:T, at a signal; turn left (E) off the highway.

14.0 EOD; Shanghai Hotel in Dingshan is on the left, just before the intersection.

Side Trip to the Purple Sand First Teapot Factory: 6 km

The unglazed teaware produced in Yixing is made from a special sandy clay with a purple-brown color. Tea connoisseurs consider this type of teaware the best for making a high-quality brew. When the first casks of tea from China arrived in Europe, the Chinese worried that the purchasers might not have the right equipment to brew the tea, so teapots from Yixing were included. This teaware has become a favorite with collectors throughout China and the rest of the world,

Cormorant fisherman work a canal near Yixing.

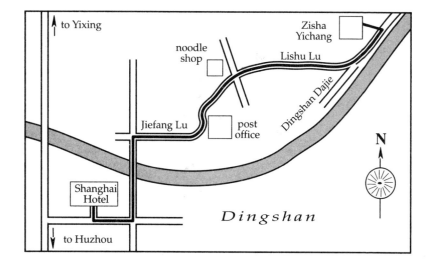

with phenomenal prices being paid for pots crafted by famous artisans of the past. The whole area makes pottery, but much of it is coarse utility ware like pickle jars and water urns. The mostly female artists at Purple Sand First Teapot Factory produce the highest grade of purple-sand teaware, and it is a real treat to see their amazing craftsmanship in progress.

Log:

- 0.0 At the Shanghai Hotel gates in Dingshan, reset and ride (E). At the first intersecton, turn left (N).
- 0.1 Cross a bridge over a canal crowded with boats full of pottery.
- **0.4** X, at Jiefang Lu; turn right (E).
- **1.0** Large X circle; go past the post office and exit left (NE).
- 1.6 Road curves back to E.
- 1.7 X; go straight (E).
- 2.2 Cross a canal bridge. You are now on Lishu Lu.
- **2.5** T, at Dingshan Dajie; turn left and ride along the canal.
- 2.9 Cross a canal bridge with boat docks on the right.
- 3.0 On the left is the Zisha Yichang (translates literally as Purple Sand First Factory), where the highest level of teapot craftswomen work. Disconnect and register at the gate to tour the teapot museum and workshops. To continue on the main tour route, retrace your route to the Shanghai Hotel in Dingshan.

Dingshan to Huzhou: 60.7 km

This segment's hilly ride begins at Dingshan Shanghai Hotel. As you leave Jiangsu and enter Zhejiang Province, the road quality improves, but traffic is still heavy. Along the road, hillsides are planted with tea gardens and bamboo groves. Finish the day in the town of Huzhou on the south shore of Taihu. Huzhou is a typical midsize Zhejiang town, but not a tourist destination.

WHERE TO STAY. The Bailu Hotel is Chinese style and somewhat dirty, but cheap. The Huzhou Hotel comes closer to foreign tourist standards, with prices to match.

WHERE TO EAT. The Meilongzhen Winehouse across from the Bailu Hotel has excellent Zhejiang cuisine. For a local snack, try the Ding Ou Xiang dumpling shop across from the Huzhou Hotel.

WHAT TO DO. Cruise the old downtown side streets for local color. There is nothing here that could be called a tourist attraction.

Log:

    0.0 At the Shanghai Hotel gates in Dingshan, reset, turn right (W), and head back to the highway.

    0.4 T, at the highway; reset.

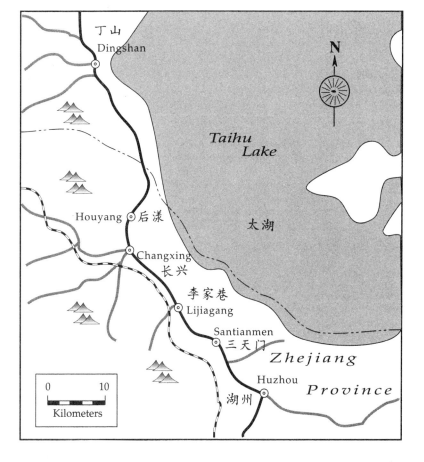

Ducklings are herded home for the night in Zhejiang.

0.0 T; reset and turn left (S) onto the highway.
0.3 Tao Reng Yuan Hotel is on the left.
1.1 X circle, with stainless-steel ring sculpture; go around and exit straight. (A right turn leads to Zhanggong and Linggu caves, another possible side trip.)
12.4 Top of the hill; Taihu is visible on the left.
13.1 Pass under blue signs and enter Changxing County, Zhejiang.
20.7 R:T; go straight.
26.0 Cross a bridge over a canal.
27.8 Pass the village of Houyang.
33.0 Enter Changxing township.
34.1 Cross a canal bridge, then come to a Y; stay to the left.
35.7 Cross a canal bridge with a coal-fired power plant on the right.
47.4 Top of a 2-km grade, with mountains, pines, bamboos, and hillside tea gardens.
49.1 Enter Santianmen.
52.6 L:T, to Baique; stay straight on the main road.
53.3 Cross a large canal bridge; the road curves left.
56.6 Enter Lungxi.

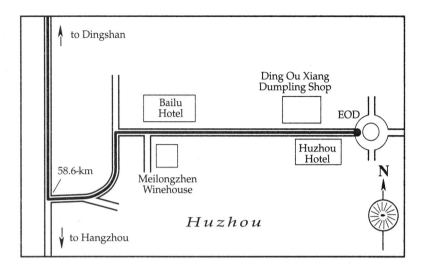

58.6 Signal L:T; turn left (NE), leaving the highway. **Enter Huzhou** downtown streets.

59.0 Y; bear left on the larger street.

59.3 R:T, with a customs house on the left; turn right. **The Bailu Hotel** is on the left just after this turn. Meilongzhen Winehouse is in the alley across from the hotel.

59.4 X; go straight.

60.1 Huzhou Hotel is on the right 800 m past the Bailu.

60.3 EOD; X circle, with a post office.

Huzhou to Hangzhou: 92 km

Continue over more hills through bamboo farms, terraced tea gardens, and cedar forests. As you approach Hangzhou, the terraces level onto flatter terrain with rice paddies. Hangzhou is a premier tourist spot in China. The main attraction is Xihu (West Lake) and the parks and temples in the surrounding hills.

WHERE TO STAY. Hangzhou is a major tourist city, so budget lodgings for foreigners are scarce. The hotels mentioned in the route log below are good, but expensive. Budget cycle tourists should plan to stay on the outskirts of Hangzhou and cycle in for sightseeing. There are cheap inns before entering the city limits, and in the first few kilometers after crossing the Qiantangjiang bridge in the next segment's route log.

WHERE TO EAT. Places to eat are not hard to find in Hangzhou. The newer hotels all have fine dining rooms, and excellent smaller restaurants are located at the end-of-day point along the side streets east of Xihu. For cheap eats, alleys off the side streets usually have noodle

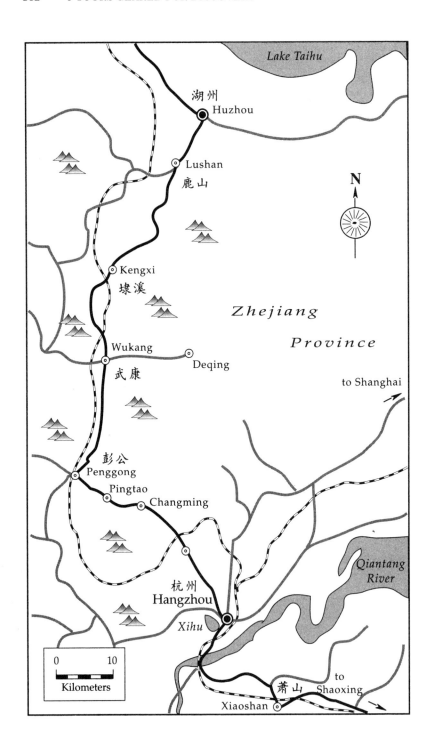

stalls and pan-fried dumpling stands. Lungjing shrimp, Tungpo pork, West Lake vinegar carp, steamed buns, and endless snack foods—you will not starve in Hangzhou! Lungjing is the local tea specialty, with a clear yellow color, bright fresh taste, and lots of caffeine. Put a big pinch of this tea in your water bottle each day, and not only will the boiled water taste better, you will pedal faster. Beware of fake or low-quality Lungjing tea sold by hawkers in tourist areas around the lake.

WHAT TO DO. Plan to spend at least one layover day here exploring the lakeside parks and boating to the islands. Tea culture aficionados should visit the China National Tea Museum southwest of Xihu.

Log:

0.0 At the Bailu Hotel in Huzhou, reset, turn right at the gate, and backtrack to the main highway at mileage point 58.6 on the previous route log.

0.7 Signal L:T, at the main highway; reset and continue.

0.0 Signal L:T, at the highway; reset and head (SE) toward Hangzhou.

1.3 L:T, to Shanghai; stay straight, curving to the right, and cross a bridge (S) just after the intersection.

1.9 Cross a large bridge.

2.3 You are in the countryside again.

8.0 Enter Lushan; continue straight.

21.2 L:T, to Donglin; stay straight (SW).

28.0 Cross a canal bridge and enter Kengxi.

28.4 X; stay straight.

Young women attracting lunch customers at a roadside restaurant

33.9 Cross railroad tracks on a bridge. There are many small inns through here.

35.1 Enter Deqing County. There are tea gardens and forested hills to the right.

40.0 Pass a village and enter Sanqiao Zhen.

43.4 Enter Wukang.

43.5 X; go straight (SSW).

49.5 L:T; go straight.

55.6 Crest the grade and coast down through bamboo crafts stands selling seat covers, chairs, et cetera. There is a railroad in the valley to the right.

59.0 Y, in Penggong; stay left on the main road.

64.5 Enter the village of Pingtao.

65.7 Cross a canal bridge (SSE).

70.0 Pass through Changming.

82.3 L:T; continue straight (S). (A left leads to Qiantangjiang Number Two Bridge.)

84.7 X; continue straight and enter the urban area of Hangzhou. The road has bike lanes now.

86.0 Signal X; stay straight (SSE) on Moganshan Road.

86.5 Xincheng Hotel is on the right.

87.4 Dunhuang Hotel is on the left.

87.5 X; continue straight.

88.0 Zhijiang Hotel is on the left.

88.2 R:T; stay straight.

89.2 Silver Star Hotel is on the left.

89.6 X; continue straight. (The right turn is onto Tianmushan Lu and the left is onto Huanchengbeilu.)

89.8 X; cross and continue straight.

90.3 R:Y, heading toward Xihu; stay straight.

90.9 R:T; stay straight.

91.1 Entrance to Wanghu Hotel is on the left.

91.3 EOD; signal Rev R:Y. Xihu is on your right.

Hangzhou to Shaoxing: 64.7 km

As you leave Hangzhou, skirt Xihu and ride over the southern hills. Cross the Qiantang River and roll through flat farmland and canal towns. Head east through Xiaoshan, passing busy textile markets just before entering Shaoxing. Shaoxing is an old cultural center that is still relatively undiscovered by tourists. It is also the hometown of Lu Xun, China's greatest modern writer.

WHERE TO STAY. Budget lodging can be found at the Donghu Hotel, and luxury accommodations at the Shaoxing Hotel. Even if you do not stay at the Shaoxing, stop in to get a local map. The Huaqiao Hotel is on Shangda Lu just as you enter town, and there are cheap inns on the outskirts of town.

WHERE TO EAT. Shaoxing has no lack of restaurants; you will find small eateries and wine shops down the side alleys along Jiefang Lu. Sidewalk restaurants that open at dusk along Jeifang Lu display fresh vegetables and meats for you to select and have cooked in their out-door kitchens. For a taste of historical food culture, try *Huixiangdou* (spiced beans) and *Chou doufu* (fragrant fried beancurd) at Xian Hen Wineshop. At any restaurant you can drink fresh Shaoxing wine and eat *Gancai shao rou*, a local dish of braised pork with savory dry-cured cabbage.

WHAT TO DO. Visit the memorial and home of Lu Xun. Drink *jiafan* rice wine and hang out with locals at the historic Xian Hen Wineshop, the scene of one of Lu Xun's stories. Soak up traditional street life along the numerous canals and back alleys.

Log:

- 0.0 At the Y near the Hangzhou Wanghu Hotel (mileage point 91.3 in the previous route log), reset and head south along the lake on Hubin Lu.
- 1.0 Road bends right (SW) around the lake edge.
- 1.3 Road name changes to Nanshan Lu.
- 3.1 L:T; continue straight (SW).
- 3.5 Road bends right (W).
- 4.1 Zheng Si temple complex is on the left.

Canalside houses in Shaoxing

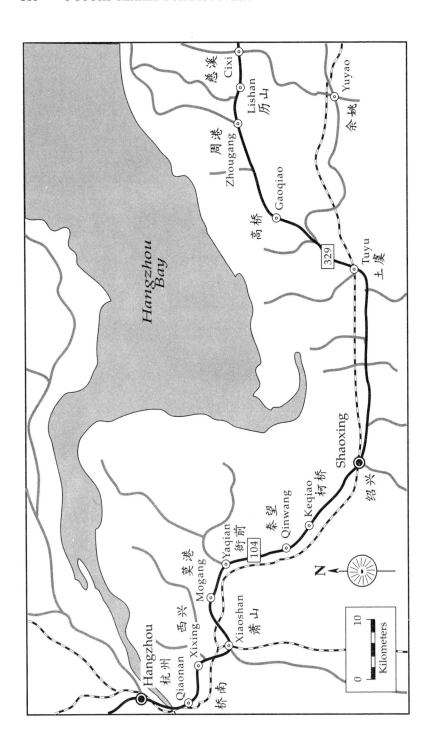

5.1 Signal R:T; reset here. The road is now Hubao Lu. (A right turn here leads to the National Tea Museum.)

0.0 Signal R:T; reset and continue straight (SW) on Hubao Road, heading up a hill.

1.0 Crest of the hill, with green parklands and tourist stalls.

2.0 Hubao Park is on the right.

2.8 R:T; turn right and curve left uphill onto the bridgehead of the Qiantangjiang bridge.

3.3 Bridge guard kiosk. Guards tell you to walk your bike on the sidewalk and stay off the narrow automobile carriageway.

4.6 Guard kiosk on the other side of the bridge. The road bends left as you exit the bridge onto flat terrain.

5.3 Pass under a tollgate (no toll for bikes).

5.4 Second tollgate.

6.5 Curve (E) on a wide road with trees, fields, a small canal on the right, and light traffic.

8.0 Inn on the left.

8.6 Pass through a village, heading (E).

9.6 X; go straight (E).

10.0 Village of Miaopu.

12.9 L:Y; go straight. Sign says "LEFT TO SHAOXING."

15.4 Y; stay left and cross a canal just past the intersection, heading (ESE).

18.0 Y circle; go around and exit left, heading (E).

18.4 X, at a signal; continue straight (E).

18.6 Pass through downtown Xiaoshan.

19.6 Xiaoshan bus station is on the left.

20.1 X circle; go around and exit (E), straight ahead.

21.2 Pass under a railroad trestle. There are wide bike lanes along this stretch.

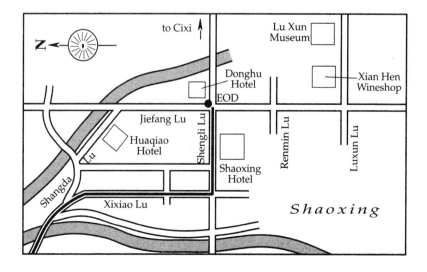

24.9 L:T; stay straight (ESE) on route 104 toward Shaoxing. (The left goes to Qiantangjiang Second Bridge, back to Hangzhou.)

30.5 Pass through Tianlifu village.

32.5 L:T, in Yaqian; stay straight, then the road curves right (SE).

36.4 L:T; stay straight (SSW).

41.2 L:T, with bridge; stay straight.

46.4 Enter Keqiao, heading (SE).

47.7 Shaoxing textile markets are on the left, with many food stalls.

49.8 L:T; stay straight. Railroad tracks are on the right. This busy stretch has heavy truck traffic.

57.6 Cross a canal bridge and enter Shaoxing. Pagodas are off to the right.

57.8 Y; bear right (S) onto Xixiao Lu. The left fork is Shangda Lu, and the Huaqiao Hotel is down it on the right.

58.5 X; turn left (E) onto Shengli Lu.

58.9 Stone bridge is on the right: this is the back entrance to the fancy Shaoxing Hotel; continue (E).

59.6 EOD; the intersection of Shengli Lu and Jiefang Lu. The Donghu Hotel is on the NE corner of this intersection. Lu Xun Park is 1.1 km down (S) Jiefang Lu on the left.

Shaoxing to Cixi: 75.1 km

Leave Shaoxing and continue east on well-paved tree-lined roads, passing lakes, fishponds, and more canal scenery. Leave route 104 and enter Yuyao County, traveling through flat and often windy farmlands on the south shore of Hangzhou Bay.

Cixi is not a tourist destination yet, but is making an attempt to draw visitors with Sishan Park. The local economy is growing rapidly, with new industries sprouting in surrounding villages and farmlands.

WHERE TO STAY. The Hangzhouwan Hotel is brand-new and expensive, but cheap inns line the road just west of town.

WHERE TO EAT. Nicer restaurants in the area have excellent seafood from Hangzhou Bay. The road through Cixi is lined with cheap food stalls serving steamed buns and wonton.

WHAT TO DO. Downtown Cixi is packed with pedicabs: why not take a pedicab tour of the town and let someone else pedal for a change? There are some charming old villages north of the main route if you want to explore the area. Go 8.3 kilometers east of Cixi on the main road and turn left (north) to get to the villages of Xiaolin and Xinpu.

Log:

0.0 At the SE corner of Jeifang Lu and Shengli Lu in Shaoxing, across the street from the Donghu Hotel, reset and head (ESE) out of town on Shengli Lu.

1.2 R:Y; turn right (S).

1.7 Y; stay left on the main road, heading (E) after curving left.

3.4 Cross a canal bridge.

Happy wonton maker at a Cixi food stall

8.0 Pass a series of open ponds with boats and willow trees.
9.0 L:T; stay straight (E).
26.1 Milepost 1534 km on route 104.
28.4 R:Y; keep to the left (ESE). Enter Tuyu.
28.7 Y; cross a bridge, then go left.
28.9 Head (N) under a railroad trestle. You are now on route 329.
30.6 Milepost 92 km on route 329.
31.0 Middle of a long bridge, which you exit in 0.6 km (E).
32.0 Tollgates (no toll for bikes); continue straight (E).
32.2 X, with a signal; continue straight (E).
33.2 Y; bear left, heading (NE).
43.4 Y; stay left, heading (NNE). Sign: "WELCOME TO YUYAO COUNTY."
44.3 A good cheap inn is on the left, others are on the right.
47.2 L:Y, leading to Lanhui; stay straight (NE).
48.6 Milepost 110 km on route 329.
55.9 L:T; stay straight.
56.8 X; stay straight (E).
59.7 Big post office building is on the left.
62.9 Pass under a blue arched sign: "WELCOME TO CIXI TOWNSHIP," then enter the village of Zhougang.
64.6 L:T; stay straight (E).
65.5 R:Y; stay on the left leg of the Y, heading (E). A gas station is on the left just after the turn.

67.5 L:T; stay straight (E).
69.5 Enter the urban part of Cixi township; the road is cement now.
71.1 L:Y, to Xinzha; continue straight (E).
73.9 Sign: "WELCOME TO CIXI."
74.5 R:T; stay straight (E).
75.1 EOD; signal X, at Sishan Lu. To the right 1 km is Sishan Park and the Hangzhouwan Hotel.

Cixi to Ningbo: 67.8 km

As you leave Cixi, pass through stretches where old villages are being torn down to make way for "progress." Ascend a gentle grade out of Cixi, then coast toward Zhenhai through terraced fields with roadside duck farms and brick kilns. Enter Ningbo from the northeast.

Because of its proximity to the sea, Ningbo canal scenery has a different character than Suzhou. To enjoy this scenery, continue north from the Huaqiao Hotel on Changchun Lu to Xijiao Lu. Then head west out of town on Xijiao Lu for canalside scenes of life on *sampans* and junks. Cross canal bridges and head out onto country lanes for something more idyllic than downtown Ningbo.

WHERE TO STAY. The Ningbo Huaqiao is an older western-style lodging with standard tourist prices, but the rooms are nice and the location is good. Cheap Chinese-style inns in Ningbo city were not open to foreigners in 1993. Get out of the main part of town to get lodging at Chinese prices.

WHERE TO EAT. The Huaqiao Hotel has a good clean dining room, but nearby restaurants provide better atmosphere and prices. For inexpensive meals, walk east from the Huaqiao to Moon Lake and turn left. There are numerous small eateries across from the lakeside park. Side streets east of Changchun Lu just before the end-of-day point have brightly lit restaurants that serve fresh seafood and Ningbo specialties. For a Ningbo style breakfast, go to the Ningbo Hotel dining room and try the buffet of rice porridge with pickled vegetables and pastries.

Ningbo cuisine is based on the local seafood catch, which includes yellow croaker, shrimp, crab, and just about every other creature that lives in the water. Also try the local noodle specialty: *Ningbo Niangao*. If you are adventurous, there is a raw fermented crab dish that locals love, but it is considered strange by many other Chinese.

WHAT TO DO. In Ningbo, Moon Lake and the park along Wangjing Lu are both good spots to hang out and people-watch. In the morning there are dances at Moon Lake Park, where you can learn the local steps!

Log:

0.0 At the signal X at Sishan Lu in Cixi, reset at the SE corner and head (ESE) on route 329, the main road through town.
0.4 Signal X; continue straight (E).
1.7 L:T; stay straight (E) on the main road.

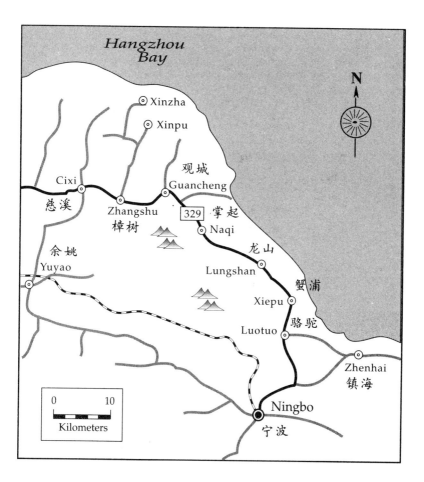

3.5 X; continue straight.

8.3 L:T, to Xinpu; stay straight (E) and pass through Zhangshu.

11.9 L:T, to Sanguan; stay straight (E).

16.5 Pass through Guancheng.

19.4 Pass through Shiqiao.

28.0 Pass through Lungshan. There are mountains off to the right.

29.5 L:T, to Yenhai; stay straight.

37.3 R:T; stay straight (E) as the road curves to the left.

41.4 Top of the hill. Pass under a banner: "ENTERING ZHENHAI" and coast (S) on route 329.

48.0 Enter township of Luotuo.

48.6 L:T; stay straight (S) on the main road.

48.8 Cross a busy canal.

52.8 R:Y; stay straight as the road curves left (SE).

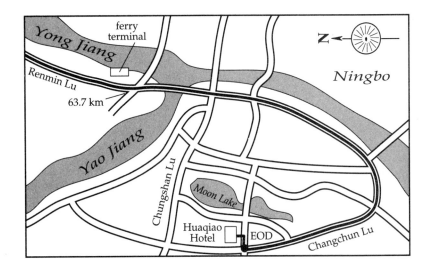

57.8 Y; stay right on the main road, heading (SW), and merge with a road coming in from the left in 0.2 km.

59.0 L:Y; head due (W) into the intersection, then bear left (SW). The road continues to curve left into the Kungpu district.

60.2 Cross railroad tracks heading (SW), then curve right, back to the (W). The railroad is on the right of the road.

60.8 L:T; stay straight (W), then cross another railroad in 0.1 km.

61.9 T; turn left (S) onto Renmin Lu, and cross more railroad tracks.

62.0 Y; bear left on Renmin Lu, across a large X.

63.1 Y; bear left (S) and wind down Renmin Lu through old wooden Ningbo-style houses.

63.7 Ningbo ferry passenger terminal is on the left. Reset at the signal near the south end of the terminal.

0.0 Ferry terminal; reset and continue south on Renmin Lu.

0.1 Manao Hotel is on the right.

0.5 Cross Xinjiang bridge over the Yao Jiang.

0.8 X; go straight.

0.9 Waterfront park is on the left.

1.3 X, with a bridge to the left; go straight (SW).

2.5 Large X circle, with fountain; exit heading (W) onto tree-lined Lingqiao Lu, which turns into Changchun Lu.

2.8 X, with Nanyuan Hotel on the left; continue straight (WNW).

3.7 X, with Jinlong Hotel across to the left; continue straight.

4.1 EOD; X, Liuting Jie. The Ningbo Hotel is ahead to the left. Turn right here and the Huaqiao Hotel is a block down on the left. Past the Huaqiao is Moon Lake and lakeside parks, shops, and restaurants.

THE MOUNTAINS OF SHANDONG
Qingdao to Taian

Distance: 378 kilometers
Estimated time: 5 riding days
Best time to go: April–June, September–November
Terrain: Some level, some steeply mountainous
Maps: Nelles Map No. 2 of Northern China, map of Shandong, city map of Qingdao
Connecting tours: Tour Nos. 6 and 8

The first of the three northeastern PRC tours begins with an overnight ferry trip from Shanghai to Qingdao. Spend a few days in Qingdao enjoying its architecture, beaches, seafood, and beer; then ride west into the garlic and wheat country of Shandong Province. During the late spring, the roadside is piled with sacks of garlic bulbs and bundles of garlic shoots. The Shandongese are famous throughout China for their heavy consumption of the "stinking rose."

On the third day of cycling, you will leave the more developed coastal region and climb into the mountains. Follow tree-lined sand roads through backward villages where primitive inns are the only lodging option. In this poor area, farmers struggle to get more growing space; stone retaining walls have completely transformed some of the mountains into terraced fields. After a roller coaster of mountain villages, drop into a broad valley at Laiwu and head across flat farmlands to Taian. Taian is the home of Taishan, the most famous of China's mountains.

CONNECTIONS. The starting point for this tour, Qingdao, can be reached from Shanghai, the end point of Tour No. 6. It is possible to fly to Qingdao from Shanghai, but trying to transport your bike on domestic Chinese flights is not recommended; besides, Qingdao Liuting Airport is inconveniently located 26 kilometers north of the city.

The overnight ferry from Shanghai is inexpensive and docks at this tour's starting point. The ship to Qingdao leaves Shanghai from Gongpinglu Wharf on even-numbered days at 1:00 P.M., and docks in Qingdao at 3:30 P.M. the following day. Buy tickets ahead of time at the second-floor ticket hall by the Dongfang (Orient) Hotel (see the Connections section for Tour No. 6). The ticket window is on the left of the hall, with a sign that says "FOREIGN GUEST TICKETS." To change money near the ticket office, go west one block on Jinling Lu, then north on

Stone-terrace wheat fields in rural Shandong

Sichuan Road one block to Nanjing Road. On the northeast corner is a CITIC bank that cashes TCs. It may also be possible to obtain tickets through your hotel.

To get to Gongpinglu Wharf, start at the boat ticketing hall on East Jinling Lu. Go one block west, then head north on Sichuan Road. After crossing the bridge over Suzhou Creek, turn right on the next large road and work your way east. At Gongping Lu, turn right (south) toward the wharves. Push your bike through the boarding lines and pay RMB 20 per bike shipping fee before boarding.

The ship's restaurant has not earned any culinary stars, so be sure to bring fruits, snacks, et cetera. If you are drinking beer, bring your own cup: the beer is cheap, but the plastic mug is not. City maps of Qingdao are on sale at the ship's store. When you disembark in Qingdao, go to the left (E) from the wharf and exit the dock area via the automobile exit gate rather than through the passenger terminal. Show your tickets to the gate guards as you leave.

Another option to reach Qingdao is the train from Beijing. Enter the PRC at Beijing Shoudu International Airport, spend a few days in

Beijing, then take the train to Qingdao. Combine this tour with Tour No. 8 to end up back in Beijing.

INFORMATION. Allow at least eight days for this tour, exclusive of time spent in Shanghai before ferrying to Qingdao. There is a longer-than-average day that may be broken into two smaller days; alternate lodging options are listed in the route logs.

Arrival in Qingdao: 1.5 km

This segment describes how to get from the Port of Qingdao to nearby lodgings and central Qingdao. As you leave the wharf area, you will notice many of the buildings don't look very Chinese. Qingdao was once a German concession and many downtown streets still retain a broken-down European flavor. The Germans left more than architecture in Qingdao: The local beer is considered the best in China.

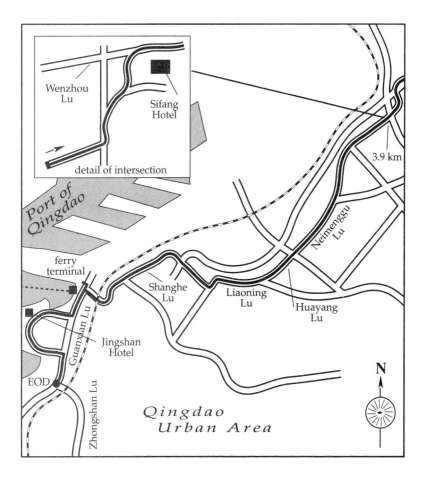

If you arrive in Qingdao by train from Beijing, refer to local tourist maps to find your way north from the train station to the Port of Qingdao and the starting point of the next segment.

WHERE TO STAY. Consider the Jingshan Hotel, the Hoping (Peace) Hotel, or recommendations in your conventional guidebook. Upscale hotels are near the beaches on the south side of the peninsula. If you arrive by train from Beijing, consider the Qingdao Railway Hotel, telephone: 269963, or the Huaqiao Hotel, telephone 268888, both in the vicinity of the train station and near the No. 6 Beach on Qingdao Bay.

WHERE TO EAT. In Qingdao, eat seafood. Try the razor clams, fresh scallops, and lobster-type crustaceans. Look for plastic basins with live shrimp and shellfish in front of restaurants in downtown market alleys and along the beach.

WHAT TO DO. Plan to spend a couple of days in Qingdao sightseeing. Ride along the rocky coast and visit the beaches. Check out Lu Xun Park and Xiaoqingdao Island just east of the first tourist beaches, and visit the Qingdao Beer Factory.

Log:

- 0.0 At the Port of Qingdao wharf, disembark and go left to exit through the automobile exit gates. In front of the auto exit gates, reset and turn right (WSW) onto Xinjiang Lu. The International Seaman's Club is on the right.
- 0.1 L:T, with a signal; go straight (WSW). Another 80 m on the right is the Peace Hotel, which accepts foreigners.
- 0.2 Ship passenger terminal ticket hall is on the right.
- **0.5** R:T; turn right (W) down a side street. The tall white building in the distance is the Jingshan Hotel.
- 0.8 The entrance to the Jingshan Hotel is on the right. To continue to downtown, take a left here and head uphill to Guanxian Lu.
- 1.0 Turn right (SW) onto Guanxian Lu.
- 1.5 L:T, with a railroad trestle on the left. Turn left to get to Zhongshan Lu and the old downtown area. To get to beach tourist areas, continue straight for 5 km around the peninsula.

Qingdao to Jiaozhou: 66.7 km

The route out of Qingdao is complex, but after 7 kilometers, you are riding on flat roads through truck-garden villages and light industrial facilities. Pass Laoshan Mountain recreation area to the east, then bear west through the garlic fields of Chengyang. Cross the Dagu River and end the day in Jiaozhou. Jiaozhou is a small provincial city with no pretensions as a tourist destination, but the food is good and the people are friendly.

WHERE TO STAY. The Haiwei Inn is cheap and very Chinese. Big breezy rooms on the upper floors have no private baths, but the price is right. The Lianyi Binguan (United Friendship Guesthouse) is closer to western standards.

WHERE TO EAT. From the end-of-day point, go 550 meters south

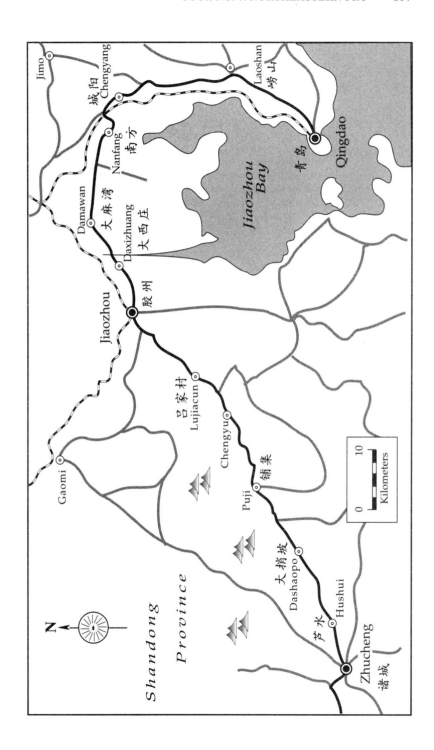

on Guangzhou Lu and you will find a night-market "food street" on the left with numerous small eateries offering seafood and meat dishes. At night, fruit and snack stalls lit with candles line Guangzhou Lu.

WHAT TO DO. There's not much to do in Jiaozhou; but if you like billiards, open-air snooker games continue late into the night near the night market, or drop in for a Chinese movie. Some residents show videos in their courtyards for a small fee.

Log:

0.0 At the auto exit gate of the Port of Qingdao (the gate with the "PORT OF QINGDAO" sign), reset and turn right (WSW) onto Xinjiang Lu.

0.1 L:T, with a signal; turn left and go under the railroad trestle. Just past the trestle is a Y; turn sharply left, almost a hairpin turn, and head (E) uphill on Shanghe Lu.

1.0 Crest a hill and head 50 m down to an X; turn right (S).

1.1 Jog in the road; turn left, heading (SE).

1.4 T; turn left (E). In 0.1 km, the road curves to the right along Liaoning Lu.

1.8 L:Y; turn left (E) onto Huayang Lu.

2.2 X; continue straight (ENE) on Huayang Lu, following the electric streetcar lines.

2.4 Begin heading up a gentle hill.

2.7 Crest the hill.

2.9 X, with a Y ahead; go straight at the X, then go left at the Y.

3.8 Pass under the "world's most complex intersection" sign. Study it and continue straight on Neimenggu Lu.

3.9 Complex X circle; enter and bear left (NNE).

4.0 Y, with a larger road heading left; turn right. Immediately come to another Y; bear left at the second Y and descend to Wenzhou Lu. (See map on page 195 for detail.)

4.2 T, at Wenzhou Lu; turn right (E). The Sifang Hotel is on the right after this turn and the long-distance bus station is on the left.

4.7 Ramp; stay to the right. No bikes are allowed on the ramp.

5.0 X circle; go around and exit (E). This is a newer commercial area.

5.9 Underpass; stay right and do not descend into the underpass.

6.1 X circle; go around and exit (E). Jiadingshan Park is on the left.

6.4 Begin heading (NE) up a gentle grade with wide bike lanes, apartment blocks, light industry, and monochrome scenery.

7.7 Crest the hill and coast down (NE).

10.0 Pass under high-tension lines. An electric substation is on the left.

12.1 R:T; go straight (N), then curve left uphill.

14.2 Large X circle; go around and exit (N).

17.0 Crest of a gentle rise. Laoshan Mountains are to the right.

20.2 Enter Nanliang.

25.1 Liuting bridge; exit it in 0.2 km.

A Shandong farmer tends pigs on a roadside.

26.0 L:T, to Qingdao Liuting Airport; stay straight (NNW).

26.3 Liuting Interchange bridge, with "NO BIKES" sign; stay on the dirt path along the right side of the ramp.

26.4 Small tunnel on the left 160 m past the ramp; turn left (NW) and go under the ramp. Continue (NW) past an open square until you see the highway ahead.

26.9 Highway; cross to the north side and head (WNW) on route 308. Here you will find numerous restaurants and inns.

28.9 Mileage point 24 km on route 308.

29.3 Chengyang Industrial Development Area is on the left.

30.9 R:T; continue straight (WNW) through Chengyang.

31.7 Cross a bridge (W).

34.2 L:Y; bear left (W) onto route 204, a slightly smaller road flanked with garlic fields and roadside cigarette hawkers.

34.9 Pass under a railroad trestle.

36.6 Nanfang. There are several truck-stop eateries here.

39.2 Enter Tiejiazhuang (W) along tree-lined roads.

41.5 Enter Lihongtan village.

41.7 R:Y; continue straight.

42.5 Cross railroad tracks, then go under a dragon-style welcome sign.

43.4 L:T; stay straight (W).
46.0 Enter Zhangjiazhuang (W). There is an earth-dam reservoir on the right.
47.3 Enter Jiaozhou city limits.
47.6 Cross a bridge over the Dagu River.
48.5 Village of Lijiazhuang, with restaurants.
52.5 R:T; stay straight (WSW), then cross a bridge.
53.0 Pass through Damawan.
57.7 R:T, to Diankou; continue straight.
63.1 L:Y; stay straight (WSW). (The left fork heads to Jiaonan.)
64.1 L:Y; stay straight (W) along Jiaozhou Donglu.
65.5 X circle; go straight (W). There is a lotus sculpture in the center of the circle.
65.8 Jiaozhou Park is on the left.
66.3 L:T, with street markets; continue straight (W).
66.7 EOD; signal X. This cross street is Guangzhou Lu and the Haiwei Inn is on the SE corner. Go south 150 m and the Lianyi Binguan is on the left.

Jiaozhou to Zhucheng: 67.8 km

Leave Jiaozhou on a country road through wheat and garlic fields. Near the village of Puji, the terrain gets hilly. The road is flanked with stone-terraced apple orchards, and herds of goats graze the grassy shoulders. Now you are well into the land of garlic and *jiaozi*: for lunch, dine on a plate of these pork-filled dumplings with fresh garlic shoots. End the day at Zhucheng, a small city similar to Jiaozhou.

WHERE TO STAY. The Lantian Grand Hotel is acceptable but not grand. They will not let you take bikes up to your room. Park in the hallway behind the hotel lobby.

WHERE TO EAT. The restaurant downstairs in the Lantian Grand is passable and there are small stalls around the bus station across the street. Do not wait too late for dinner, because the hotel restaurant closes early.

WHAT TO DO. There are no tourist attractions in Zhucheng; it is just a place to spend the night. Check out the usual downtown market scenes, play snooker on far-from-level tables.

Log:

0.0 At the NE corner of Jiaozhou Lu and Guangzhou Lu in Jiaozhou, the previous route log's EOD, reset and head (W).
0.8 X; continue straight (W).
2.0 You are out of the downtown area.
3.7 X, at Liuzhou Lu; turn left (S).
4.5 Road doglegs right, curving (SW) to (W).
5.2 R:Y, to Gaomi; continue straight (SW) on the main road.
7.3 X; go straight. Farmhouses here look prosperous.
16.0 Cross a bridge over a shallow riverbed, then enter Lujiacun. There are gentle grades through here.
16.6 Pass through Lujiacun (S).

Passing through a mud-brick Shandong village

23.0 Pass through Chengyu village.
24.6 L:Y; stay straight (SW).
34.0 Cross a bridge, leaving it in 0.3 km.
34.4 Enter the village of Puji.
34.9 L:T; stay straight, then the road curves right (SW).
41.1 R:Y; stay straight on the main road.
46.0 Pass through Dashaopo village.
52.0 Cross a small bridge (W).
52.8 Curve right and merge with another road. In 0.2 km, you are heading (W) through a village.
66.1 X circle; go straight (W) on a wider road with bike lanes.
67.3 X; go straight.
67.8 EOD; Lantian Grand Hotel is on the right. The Zhucheng bus station is across the street on the left.

Zhucheng to Mazhan: 63.9 km

As you leave the modernizing part of Shandong Province behind, you will see why Shandong is considered a poor province. The route rolls through small market towns and then gets steeper after Mengtuan, where the pavement ends and sand roads begin.

In Dongdeshui village you will see yellow-mud houses, brush fences, and villagers grinding corn by hand on stone mills. It feels like a kung-fu movie set, but it is real. Continue climbing through stone-terraced wheat fields, then coast into the village of Mazhan and spend the night at a country inn.

Stock up on road snacks before you leave Zhucheng, or before the paved road ends. The selection in small villages is meager. After the paved road ends, there is no lodging until Mazhan.

WHERE TO STAY. There are few choices in Mazhan. Spend the night at the rustic Yinbin inn, a brick-floored bare-bulb joint with pit toilets and a friendly pig out back. The rooms do not have running water or heating. The Yinbin is a typical country inn with its own restaurant and a courtyard that is locked at night. Up the road there are a few more inns of the same quality.

WHERE TO EAT. Stop for an early dinner or late lunch at Mr. Zhang's place, 2.2 kilometers before Mazhan, and have supper at the Yinbin. In the morning, there are breakfast stalls near the village center that sell porridge and fried doughsticks.

WHAT TO DO. At the Yinbin we asked, "What's there to do in Mazhan?" The maid looked at us oddly and said, "Why, there's *nothing* to do in Mazhan!"

Log:

0.0 At the Lantian Grand Hotel in Zhucheng, reset and head (W).

0.2 X circle; go straight (W).

0.7 Start across a bridge (W) with white marble railings.

1.5 R:T; turn right (N). A park with a lake is on the right.

2.1 Start across a bridge, and leave it in 0.4 km.

2.7 L:T circle, at Wanjia Zhuang; turn left (W) onto a smaller road to Mazhan. There are open street markets at this intersection.

3.9 R:Y; continue straight (WNW).

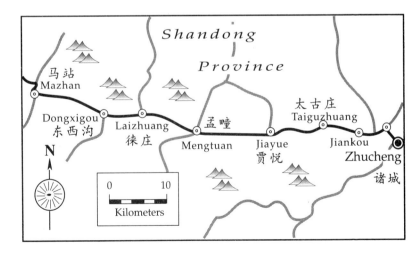

10.0 R:T, at Jiankou village; continue straight (W).

14.9 Cross a bridge (W).

18.4 X, with a flashing red light; go straight (NW). There is a school on the right after the X.

20.2 Cross a bridge and enter a village.

21.3 L:T; stay straight through the town of Jiayue.

24.0 Leave Jiayue (SW).

28.2 Enter another village, which you leave in 0.7 km.

33.5 R:T; stay straight toward Mazhan.

34.0 Pass through the village of Mengtuan.

36.0 Ascend a steep hill, which crests in 0.8 km. There are big mountains ahead.

37.0 Pavement turns into a sand road; head straight (N), into the hills. Notice the rock retaining walls and terraced fields.

38.0 Pass through a poor-looking village.

41.4 Dongdeshui village—authentic Chinese country style!

45.0 R:T, in Laizhuang; continue straight (W). You are now in Yishui County, with rocky fields and sand roads.

46.3 R:T, heading to Quanziya; continue straight (W).

48.1 Village of Gaojiashiling.

50.0 Leave the village of Minquantou, then head downhill.

52.3 L:T, in old village of Dongxigou; stay straight.

55.7 Eshankou village.

56.9 Peak can be seen in the distance and an open plain is ahead as you head (SW).

58.0 Start uphill again (N).

59.5 Cross a small bridge, then climb again.

59.7 Village of Guojiayu is to the right.

61.7 A brightly painted restaurant is on the left. Mr. Zhang Minglai, the owner, cooks Shandong country-style meals and shows videos in the dining room.

63.7 Start across the Mazhan east bridge.

63.9 EOD; T, village center of Mazhan. Go right (N) 380 m and the Yinbin inn is on the right.

Mazhan to Yiyuan: 73.1 km

After leaving Mazhan, continue west through terraced fields of garlic, wheat, and peanuts, then begin a tough ride on sandy mountain roads through remote thatch-roofed villages.

The mud-walled village of Shangliu could be the set for a "chow mein Western": dustdevils blow across the deserted street; the old country store with stone counters sells fertilizer, seeds, and kerosene. In another sleepy village, inbred-looking children peer out of brick shacks, and young men play snooker on dusty tables along the roadside.

In the valleys, cottonwood-lined roads meander through lush truck gardens, then climb back onto dry rocky ridges. The craggy peaks of Yishan and Fenghuangshan overlook the route from the north. After 60 kilometers, the sand road finally merges with pavement as you drop into Yiyuan. Yiyuan is a larger town with plain but comfortable hotels and lively street markets.

WHERE TO STAY. The Jingshan Hotel is reasonably priced, has private bathrooms, and is close to downtown market areas. It rates about one star—at least four stars higher than the inn in Mazhan! Park bikes under the stairwell by the elevator. Alternately, stay at the Xiyuan Hotel on the left just past this segment's end-of-day point.

WHERE TO EAT. There are small private restaurants on both sides of the road in the market area, and the Jingshan Hotel has a dining room if you do not want to go out. Cruise the market areas and try *huoshao,* grilled muffinlike breads filled with meat or garlic greens. Also look for bamboo skewers of bright red candied *shanzha* (haw) fruits.

WHAT TO DO. Yiyuan is the liveliest town since Qingdao. A stroll down the shaded street markets north of the Jingshan Hotel is filled with interesting sights.

Log:

0.0 At the T in the village center of Mazhan, reset and head (N).
0.1 Covered market area is on the right.
0.3 Yinbin Fandian is on the right.

Taking a break along the high road near Yishan

0.8 Cross the Mazhan north bridge, heading (NNW) on a paved road.
2.4 Village of Shenlidian.
3.4 L:T; turn left (W) and leave the paved road.
3.6 Cross a river-bottom causeway (W).
4.7 Village of Donghuangzhuang.
7.2 Village of Xiwangzhuang.
8.0 Village of Yaxia. Now you are heading (W), in steep terrain.
10.6 Crest of a hill. You are riding along the ridge.
14.9 Village of Dongyugou. Cross a bridge and head uphill.
19.0 Crest of a steep hill, with terraced fields on the right.
22.0 Village of Shangliu. Kerosene is available in the store on the right.
23.9 Crest of a grade, with a good restaurant for a lunch stop.
28.0 View Yishan and Fenghuangshan mountains on the right.
30.2 Enter the town of Yishan.
30.9 Y, after crossing a bridge; bear left (W) toward Yiyuan, then curve right to (NW).
36.6 Top of a steep grind; coast down (W).
37.2 Village of Jiushan (Nine Mountains).
37.5 L:Y; stay straight (NW) on the main road, which curves right (N) and passes a few stores.
39.4 Crest a grade through a rocky cut.
39.8 Cross Entou bridge.
42.0 Enter the village of Baisha (White Sand).
42.8 R:Y; stay straight (W) on the main road to Yiyuan.
42.9 Pavement is broken. Watch out for bees along this stretch.
50.3 Village of Shangzhi, with a steep climb out.
53.0 Top of the climb. Head downhill (WNW) on a smooth sand road.
54.0 Village of Baxianguanzhuang.

Villagers on the road through Yishui Zhen

56.0 Crest a hill, then ride down a steep stretch.

61.0 Village of Jiaojiayu.

61.5 Now you are rolling along a wider sand road lined with huge trees. You are out of the mountains and onto the Yiyuan plain.

63.8 Rev L:Y, at Yuezhuang where the sand road ends; merge onto the asphalt road heading (W).

70.5 Enter the outskirts of Yiyuan, heading (W) over rolling hills.

72.5 X, with Jingshan Hotel on the right corner of a willow-lined cross street; continue straight (W).

73.1 EOD; X circle. To get to the Xiyuan Hotel, continue around the X circle, exiting on the far left side across a bridge (the next segment's starting point is on the east end of this bridge). The Xiyuan Hotel is on the left 0.2 km from this bridge.

Yiyuan to Taian: 105 km

Ride west out of Yiyuan through the valley below Lushan Mountain, then ascend to dry rocky high areas with orchards and sulfur mines. Ongoing road repairs along this stretch may make for slow going. Leave the mountains and drop into the city of Laiwu, then traverse a broad valley into Taian. If you prefer to go slower through the mountain areas, spend the night in Laiwu and head to Taian the next day.

The main attraction in Taian is Taishan: the most famous of China's five holy mountains. Taishan's fame attracts pilgrims and tourists from all over China, so be prepared for crowds. Old crones with bound feet hobble down the stone steps and porters haul incredible loads of water and supplies up the slopes. Many of the Chinese tourists are from places few foreigners visit, and may find you at least as interesting as the mountain! If you want to avoid the crowds and see more of the mountain itself, ride your bike up rather than taking the tourist bus. The pines and granite are a nice change from red dust and sand roads. Do not bring luggage if you intend to lock your bike and continue the climb by foot: there is no safe place to leave it unattended.

WHERE TO STAY. The Huaqiao Hotel has an international class exterior and lobby, and it is priced accordingly. The Xidu is Chinese style and reasonable, with the usual seedy amenities. At the Xidu, they charge for bike storage in the alleyway west of the main building. Other lodging options are listed in your conventional guidebook.

WHERE TO EAT. You can dine inside your hotel or at small private restaurants along the road near the Xidu. Head south down Qingnian Lu to get to more department stores and restaurants. A local sweet snack worth trying is haw jelly (*shanzha gao*), a thick red confection that tastes like quince jelly.

WHAT TO DO. You can catch a bus or ride your bike to the Taishan tourist area where the stone stairs begin. Tour buses pick up passengers in the large traffic circle by the train station. Hawkers board these buses to sell maps and guidebooks to tourists. They are persistent: you will probably have to buy a map to get rid of them. Taishan is not a budget tourist spot: the cable car up to the peak has "special" prices for foreigners, and the snack shops by the bus stop are a ripoff.

Log:

0.0 At the bridgehead on the west side of the large X circle in Yiyuan, reset and head across the bridge (W).

0.2 Xiyuan Hotel is on the left.

0.4 L:T, to Tangshan; go straight (WSW) on Dongfeng Lu.

3.3 L:Y; continue straight (W). Do not go left here.

4.2 Cross an earth dam and reservoir off to the left.

5.0 A hillside village is just to the right at this point, as you head (SW) up a slope. There is a switchback ahead. (**Note:** This area was under construction when the route was logged. Watch for mileage discrepancies and adjust metering if necessary.)

5.5 Switchback uphill to the (NE).

6.3 Crest through a dry rocky cut (W).

11.2 Cross a bridge and enter the village of Lucun on a wide new road.

13.0 Leave Lucun. Lushan Mountain looks over the valley from the north.

13.4 Cross a bridge (W).

16.0 Climb a dry barren mountain with rock terraces, stony orchards, and sulfur mining.

20.0 Crest the grade, then coast down.

21.4 River bottom with cottonwoods.

22.1 Top of a steep climb (W). Crest through a stone cut.

26.8 Cross a bridge (W) over a wide, sandy river bottom into the village of Shiwanzizhuang.

28.1 Enter Tieche Xiang.

28.4 Village of Dongtieche. There is a good little restaurant on the left just before the grove of trees and open market area.

30.4 Village of Chengling; head up a grade out of the village.

31.7 Top of the grade; head down (W).

33.0 Less steep now.

35.8 Village of Shangchen.

36.6 X; continue straight toward Laiwu.

41.4 Rev R:Y; merge (SW) onto a paved road in the village of Beizuihong.

47.0 Start across a single-lane bridge (W).

48.8 Enter Laiwu, on a wider road with bike lanes.

49.6 X, with a signal; go straight (W) on Chengguan Donglu.

51.2 X, with a signal; go straight (W).

51.6 Bank of China is on the left.

51.7 X, at Changzheng Zhonglu; go straight (SW).

52.5 Bus station and Chezhan Hotel are on the right. The Laiwu Hotel is on the NW corner of the next X. (If you wish to break this

Grinding corn on a human-powered mill near Dongtieche

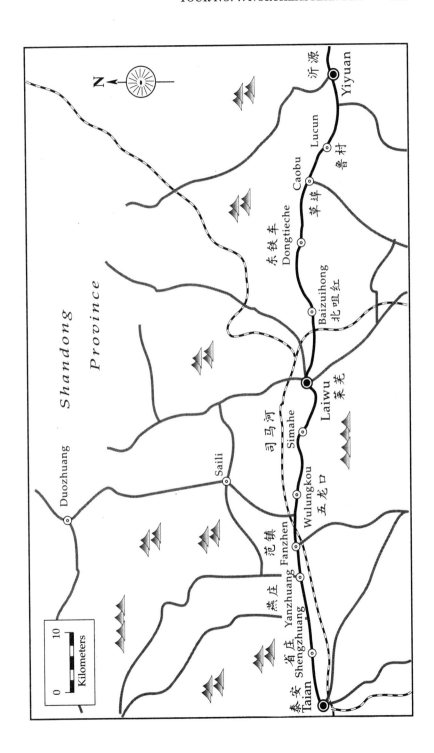

segment into two riding days, this is the recommended overnight spot.)
52.9 Jiaotong Binguan is on the right.
53.0 Leaving downtown Laiwu (W) on Chengguan Lu.
55.0 T; turn left (S).
55.7 T; turn right (W) onto a smaller tree-lined road.
60.5 Open market area is on the left.
60.6 L:T; go straight (W).
61.6 Cross Fangxia bridge.
62.1 R:T; stay straight (W).

A quiet country road near Yiyuan, Shandong

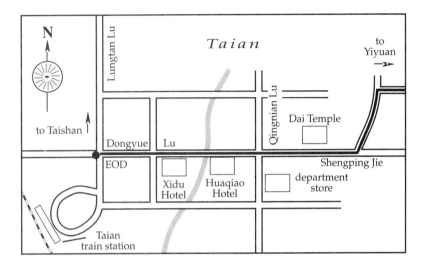

63.1 R:Y; stay straight (W). After this intersection, the road curves left and goes under a new elevated highway; stay on the older highway. Red-brick aqueducts can be seen in the wheat fields.

69.8 Pass through a village.

74.1 X, with a right turn going to Saili; continue straight (W). (**Note:** The first segment of Tour No. 8 backtracks from Taian to this X and heads N.)

76.3 Go through a short tunnel under the new highway.

78.3 L:T; stay straight (W). There is a railroad trestle ahead.

79.0 Go under the railroad trestle. The road here is lined with garlic fields.

90.2 R:T, at a village; continue straight (W).

96.0 Area called Shengzhuang. Taishan is visible in the distance to the right.

99.0 L:T; stay straight (W).

100.5 R:T; stay straight (W).

101.8 T; turn left (S).

102.0 X; turn right (W) onto Shengping Jie.

102.8 X, at Hushan Lu; continue straight (W).

103.3 Entrance to Dai Temple is on the right.

103.5 X circle, at Qingnian Lu; go straight.

103.8 Huaqiao Hotel is on the left.

104.2 Xidu Hotel is on the left.

104.4 X circle; go straight (W). The road is now called Dongyue Lu.

105.0 EOD; large X circle. The road to the left leads two blocks to bus and train stations; the road to the right, Lungtan Lu, heads up to Taishan.

ACROSS THE YELLOW RIVER PLAIN

Taian to Beijing

Distance: 565 kilometers
Estimated time: 7 riding days
Best time to go: April–June, September–October
Terrain: Some steep mountains, then level plains
Maps: Nelles Map No. 2 of Northern China; maps of Shandong, Hebei, and Beijing
Connecting tours: Tour Nos. 7 and 9

Ride east from Taian through garlic and wheat fields, then head north across the mountains on unpaved roads. The scenery is rocky and dry, with thatched-roof villages and stone-terraced *shanzha* orchards. Cross a pontoon bridge over the Yellow River and the scenery changes again. Farmhouses made of yellow-mud bricks are sheltered from the dusty wind by windrows of cottonwood trees.

As you leave Shandong Province and enter Hebei Province, the culture takes on a northern flavor. Horsecarts jangle along the country roads and many restaurants specialize in Chinese Muslim food. Roadside hawkers sell dried red dates (*zaozi*) and crisp Tianjin pears. In many places it is hard to obtain a bowl of rice: everyone eats dumplings, noodles, and bread.

To avoid closed areas in Hebei Province, the route stays close to Tianjin before the final stretch into Beijing. Willows and cottonwoods line the flat, well-paved roads. Pedal into Beijing in the late afternoon and end this tour at Tiananmen Square, under the portrait of Chairman Mao.

CONNECTIONS. To reach the start of the tour at Taian, you can cycle in by combining this tour with Tour No. 7. Or you can take the train to Taian from Beijing. If Beijing is your entry point to the PRC, see the Connections section of Tour No. 9. From the Taian train station, cycle one long block north on Lungtan Lu to the intersection with Dongyue Lu. This intersection is the starting point of the tour.

After exploring Beijing, do Tour No. 9 and visit the Great Wall. When you are ready to leave Beijing, begin by deciding how you will pack your bike, if at all. There are no boxes supplied at Beijing Shoudu International Airport, and loose cardboard is not easy to find. You will have to pack your own cardboard and strapping tape from Beijing to

Passing a hay wagon near the Yellow River

the airport; otherwise, the bike will be loaded onto the plane "as is." Set aside the equivalent of US$20 per person for airport departure taxes.

INFORMATION. Before you leave for Taian (either from Qingdao via Shanghai, or from Beijing), buy a detailed map of Beijing and work out Beijing lodging options and their position relative to this tour's end point at Tiananmen Square. If you are entering the PRC at Beijing, have your travel agent pre-book hotel space, preferably in the central city area where you can easily bike to tourist attractions. Near the end of this tour, use information in your conventional guidebook to call Beijing and make hotel reservations.

Autumn is the prime tourism season in Beijing, and at that time inexpensive rooms can be hard to find. A warning: the days are over for super-cheap lodgings in seedy but charming Beijing hotels. *Zhaodaisuo* (hostels) and *luguan* (small inns) can be found down many side streets, but the Gong An has forbidden them to accept foreigners. While Beijing prices may be high, if you average in the bargain lodgings along this route the overall cost is reasonable.

曹龙旅馆

Characters for the Caolong Inn in Zaoyuan

Taian to Zaoyuan: 101.4 km

From Taian, ride east about 40 kilometers and head north through Yangzhuang to Saili. Yangzhuang is a town dedicated to garlic culture: bulbs, greens, and shoots are piled along the roadside. Have lunch and fill your water bottles in Saili, then ascend into the dry mountains, climbing through terraced *shanzha* (haw) orchards with ginger plants beneath the trees.

Crest after a series of switchbacks, then coast down sand roads through villages with roofs of thatch and slate tile. Watch for bees swarming from roadside hives.

The mosque minaret in Bucun signals the beginning of Chinese Muslim cultural influence. You are out of the hills now, and will not ride in the mountains again unless you continue on to Tour No. 9 and ride north of Beijing. End the day in Zaoyuan, a small crossroads town on the edge of the Yellow River plain.

WHERE TO STAY. On the left a few hundred meters past the end-of-day point is the Cao Long Inn, a seedy truck stop like the one in Mazhan, but with more traffic and restaurants nearby. The owner, Mr. Li, is courteous and welcoming. He may even do some calligraphy for you. There is another inn a few hundred meters into the next segment's route log, on the left.

WHERE TO EAT. The Cao Long Inn has a restaurant in the attached brick building in front of the inn compound, and there are many others on both sides of the busy street. Try the garlic shoots and pork (*suantai rousi*) and cold mixed chicken shreds (*liangban jisi*).

WHAT TO DO. There is nothing to do in Zaoyuan. The interesting spots on this segment are the mountain villages and the foothill towns. Time your riding to linger there and roll into Zaoyuan at dusk.

Log:

0.0 At the SE corner of the intersection of Lungtan Lu and Dongyue Lu in Taian (the EOD of the last segment of Tour No. 7), reset and head (E) on Dongyue Lu.

0.5 X circle; go straight (E).

0.7 Xidu Hotel is on the right.

1.1 Cross a bridge (E), then a signal X. The Huaqiao Hotel is on the right.

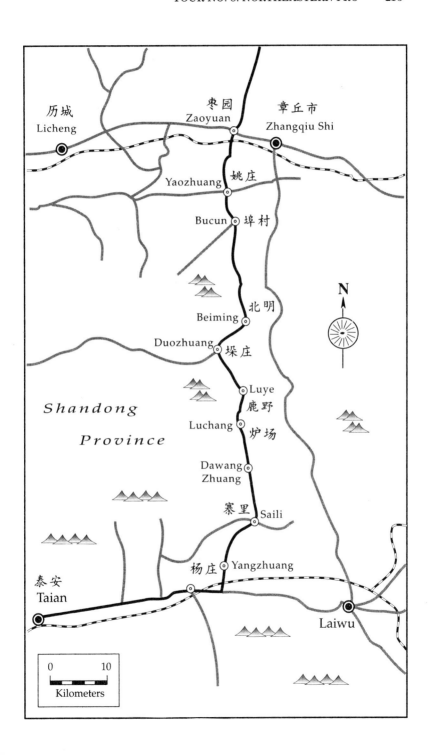

1.4 X; go straight (E). Shops and department stores are to the right down Qingnian Lu. Pick up a variety of local dried fruits, snacks, instant coffee, et cetera, here.

1.6 X circle, with Dai Temple on the left and a large tree in the middle of the X; continue straight (E).

2.2 X; go straight (E).

2.9 X; turn left (NE).

3.1 R:T; turn right (E) and leave Taian.

6.0 R:T, to Weijiazhuang; go straight (E) on a tree-lined road.

8.6 X; continue straight.

14.8 L:T, to Shankou; continue straight (E).

19.6 Cross a low cement bridge over a polluted creek.

20.8 L:T, to Qingyang; continue straight.

26.0 Pass under a railroad trestle and enter a market area.

26.7 R:T, to Jiaogu; continue straight (E) past garlic fields.

28.7 Tunnel; go under the new highway overpass.

30.9 X; turn left (NE) toward Saili. Do not miss this turn. There are run-down stores on the NW corner.

31.2 Cross a bridge over the highway.

32.4 Cross a railroad crossing.

33.1 Enter Yangzhuang, a town dedicated to garlic culture.

37.0 R:Y, in the village; continue on the main road to the left as it curves right (NE).

41.6 Enter Saili (NE).

42.2 X, in downtown Saili; continue straight (N). This is a good place to stop for lunch and fill water bottles.

48.1 Enter Dawang Zhuang.

48.2 Y; bear left (WNW).

48.7 X; go straight (WNW).

51.0 Now you are climbing (N) through foothill orchards of *shanzha*.

53.4 Doufushi (Tofu Stone) village is along the river below. Grades get steeper and the area feels wild.

54.3 Pass the village of Luchang; there are steep switchbacks after this.

58.0 Crest of the grade. Pass carved stone gateposts in the pass and coast down steeply. Watch for falling rocks.

61.7 Enter Luye; cross a bridge (E) and come to an X; stay straight.

62.3 Road turns into hardpacked dirt, heading uphill again.

63.7 Maojialin village is on the right.

64.8 Crest of the grade as you enter Jinan city limits.

69.2 Roll into Duozhuang and cross a bridge.

69.5 Y; bear right (E). About 30 or 40 m after the turn is a dirt-floored two-table restaurant where you can soak up some local color over a beer. Expect lots of downhill after this.

73.2 Cross a bridge. Wheat and garlic plots are all along the river.

73.7 Enter Nanming village.

77.9 Pass carved stone pillars. The river is on the left now.

84.7 R:T, to Wenzu; continue straight (N).

88.4 Enter Bucun village and head (N) through town.

89.0 Mosque minaret is off to the right.

A dirt-floored, two-table restaurant in Duozhuang

89.2 X circle; go straight (N).

90.1 Railroad crossing; cross (NE) onto a narrower tree-lined road.

93.2 X; go (N) across a busy E–W highway. The road to the left leads to Jinan, the Shandong provincial capital.

99.0 Jog in the road; go right (E), then in 0.1 km go left (N).

99.5 Enter Zaoyuan; continue (NE).

100.1 Cross double railroad tracks (N).

100.4 T; turn left (W) and roll onto the main street of Zaoyuan.

101.4 EOD; signal X.

Zaoyuan to Huimin: 113.7 km

Continue north along flat country roads through Daozhen, Weiqiao, and the poor, dirty village of Taizi. Now that you are on the Yellow River plain, most roads are lined with cottonwoods and willows. After a stop in Qingcheng, cross the levee and drop onto the Yellow River floodplain. Share a wobbly pontoon bridge with horsecarts and trucks, and ride across the muddy waters known as "China's Sorrow."

As you roll off the dusty levee into the village of Qinghe, the scenery changes again. Everything is the color of Yellow River mud and the wind easily lifts the dusty soil. Ride through more open country, possibly into a head wind, then cut west to end the day in Huimin. This segment is longer than most on this tour, so you will be glad of the comfortable accommodations available in Huimin.

WHERE TO STAY. The Huimin Binguan has large comfortable rooms and is not too expensive.

WHERE TO EAT. Do not waste time looking for an outside restaurant; the hotel restaurant is excellent. Try the lamb with Muslim spices (*huixiang yangrou*) and the sugar-mixed tomatoes (*tangban xihongshi*).

WHAT TO DO. This segment's ride is a long one. You will probably be content to eat and relax in your hotel. The area near the clock tower at the end-of-day point has a theater and other restaurants.

Log:

- 0.0 At the signal intersection in Zaoyuan, yesterday's EOD, reset and head (N).
- 9.7 X, in Xiuhui village; go straight through downtown (NE).
- 10.2 X; go straight (N).
- 15.1 X; go straight (NNE) on the main road.
- 15.4 R:T; go straight and in 0.1 km ascend a bridgehead.
- 15.8 Cross the bridge over the freeway (which was under construction when this route was logged).
- 16.6 X, as you enter Zhangqiu; go straight (N) onto a wider road.
- 19.0 Enter Daozhen.
- **20.2** Road doglegs right; don't go right. Instead, cross a culvert on the left and go straight (N) on a dirt lane. There is a high brick wall on the left. (Road contruction when this route was logged made a detour necessary. This log entry and the following three will get you onto the correct road. As you leave Daozhen, if you *don't* come to this dogleg to the right, you are on the new road and should re-synchronize your computer with log entries after entry 21.1, if necessary.)

Characters displayed on restaurants serving Muslim food

20.4 Corner of the brick wall; turn left (W) on the dirt path and follow the wall.

20.7 Wall ends; keep going (W) across the fields until you come to the paved road.

21.1 T, at paved road; turn right (N). (This is the end of the detour around road construction.)

25.3 Enter a village.

26.5 X; go straight (N).

29.9 L:T, to Dapo village; go straight (N) toward Weiqiao.

34.0 Rev R:Y; continue straight.

34.8 L:T; turn left (NNW) and cross an older small bridge into Weiqiao. A new bridge is under construction just past the old bridge.

35.1 T; turn right (E) and head up to the next intersection.

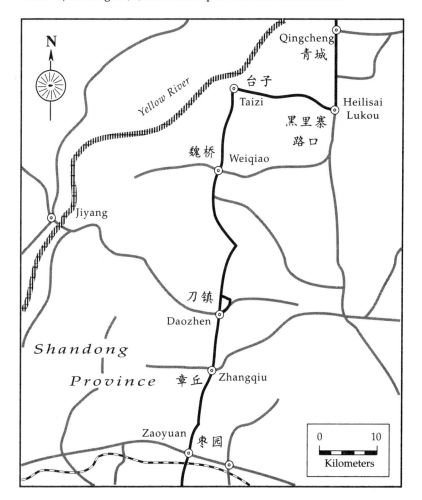

Crossing the Yellow River pontoon bridge alongside mulecarts

35.2 T; turn left (N). (If you took the new bridge, this is a L:T; be sure your computer is correct at this intersection.)

36.0 Leave Weiqiao.

36.7 L:T; stay straight (NE). There are ponds off to the right.

39.2 Cross a bridge over a canal (NNE).

43.0 Enter the backward village of Taizi.

44.1 R:T, in the village center; turn right (E). Do not go straight on the dirt streets.

46.5 Small restaurant, a possible lunch stop, is on the right.

51.5 X; stay straight (E) toward Heilisai Lukou.

52.9 Road doglegs (ESE).

54.5 Road doglegs left (E).

57.2 X; stay straight (E).

60.4 T, at Heisaili Lukou; turn left (N) onto a paved road. A gas station is on the right just after the turn.

64.0 R:T; stay straight (N).

68.9 Qingcheng railroad station is on the right. Continue through Qingcheng toward the Yellow River.

69.7 R:T; continue straight. There is a pagoda off to the right.

76.6 Pass through Muli Xiang.

77.1 X, on top of levee; go straight (N) downhill over a cobbled road.

78.3 Start across a pontoon bridge over the Yellow River.

78.9 Leave the bridge, heading up to a levee on the north side. Pay a RMB 1.00 toll.

79.0 T, at the top of the levee; go left (W) on a bumpy, dusty road.

79.6 R:Y; go right and roll off the levee onto a paved road, curving right (N) into the village of Qinghe. There are low-rent mud-walled inns on both sides of the road in Qinghe.

83.7 X; go straight (N) toward Huimin. The road curves right (NE) after this.

91.0 T; turn left (NNW), toward Huimin.

91.2 Cross a bridge.

99.5 R:T, in Madian; go straight (NW).

104.4 Start across a bridge (NW).

110.3 Cross an irrigation canal.

111.3 X circle, with a horse statue; go around the circle to the third exit road, in 0.1 km exiting the X circle (W). Roll along a wide avenue with new buildings under construction. It looks like they knocked down the old town and started over.

113.6 R:T; stay straight. Turn right here to get to the Huimin Binguan. It is one block down on the left.

113.7 EOD; X, with the imperial-looking clock tower on your right.

Huimin to Yanshan: 76.1 km

Continue northward across open, dry country, passing orchards and roadside stalls selling Chinese red dates (*zaozi*). There is a possible overnight stop in Qingyun, but the quality of lodging in Qingyun is not great and the local Gong An are snoopy. After Qingyun, cross a bridge and enter Hebei Province. As you roll into Yanshan, the main street is lined with hawkers whose wares are spread out on tarps, including rows of freshly killed rats. What are freshly killed rats sold for? We didn't ask!

WHERE TO STAY. For lodging in Qingyun, go left (west) 30 meters from mileage point 39.1, and the yellow-tiled Huaqing Binguan is on the right. It is run by the government and is visited by the Gong An. In Yanshan, the Yanshan Binguan is a newer hotel, a good choice if you want something better than the Huaqing Binguan. The Youyi Binguan Hotel is 1.2 kilometers farther, on the next segment's route log.

WHERE TO EAT. In Qingyun, small restaurants are across the street from the Huaqing Binguan. The Yanshan Binguan is a new hotel with good dining facilities. Streets around the town clock intersection also have cheap restaurants.

WHAT TO DO. Yanshan is just an overnight stop, with no tourist attractions. Foreigners are pretty scarce in this region, so your explorations in the downtown area will likely draw a crowd of locals.

Breakfasting on wonton soup at a roadside stall

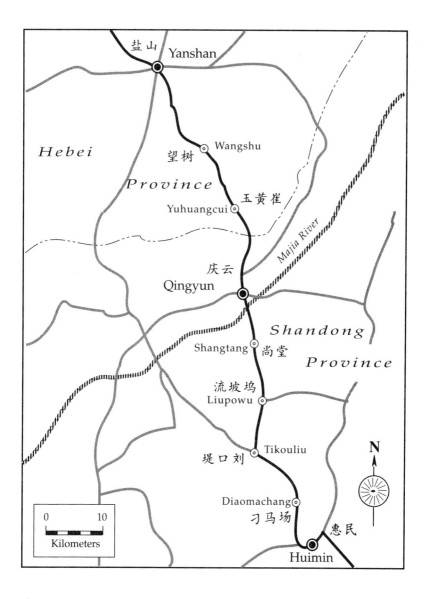

Log:

0.0 At X by the big clock, the previous route log's EOD, reset and head (W) on the main road.

1.1 T; turn right (N) on Xiguan Jie.

5.3 Merge onto a larger tree-lined road (N).

7.6 Pass through the village of Diaomachang.

9.8 Cross a canal bridge.

15.0 Dogleg right, then cross a bridge.

15.2 Y, in Tikouliu; head right (NE), then curve back to (NW).

18.1 R:T, with a brick bridge on the right; stay straight (N).

21.2 X, at Liupowu; stay straight (N) toward Qingyun.

26.5 Enter Qingyun Xian. There are fewer trees and a newer road.

30.0 R:T, at Shangtang; continue straight.

36.7 Cross a bridge over the Majia River (W).

39.1 X, in Qingyun, possible overnight stop; reset here.

0.0 X; reset and continue (N) out of town.

5.2 Y; stay left (N) on the main road. Chinese red dates (*zaozi*) are for sale at roadside stands.

8.0 Cross a bridge into Hebei Province. When off the bridge, roll down into a village, curving left (NW).

13.1 Village of Yuhuangcui.

19.2 Cross a small bridge.

21.1 Enter the village of Wangshu (NNW).

34.5 Strip of truck-stop restaurants and inns.

34.8 X; go straight and enter Yanshan.

35.5 R:Y; turn right, entering Yanshan city streets.

36.5 X, with a town clock on the left, the main downtown X; go straight (N).

37.0 EOD; entrance to Yanshan Binguan is on the right.

Yanshan to Cangzhou: 47 km

The route to Cangzhou continues through dusty farmlands and villages, where you will share the road with slow-moving hay wagons and jangling mule carts. Cangzhou is a very old city that was known to early western cartographers: it appears on antique maps that are too old to list Shanghai. This area and the town of Jiuzhou are mentioned in *Tales of the Water Margin*, one of China's most famous literary classics. One restaurant in Jiuzhou, the Lincong Huangdi, takes its name from that story.

WHERE TO STAY. Stay at the Jiujiang Hotel, the Wushu Hotel, or one of the cheap inns on the way into town. For those suffering from acute culture shock, the Jiujiang has satellite TV with CNN and BBC.

WHERE TO EAT. There are many good restaurants along the old downtown streets. The Muslim restaurant across from the city park near the Wushu Hotel is excellent. Try the yellow braised beef (*huangmen niurou*) and sweet spring rolls filled with date paste (*chunjuan*). For starch, northerners here eat *chaobing*, a flat bread cut into shreds and fried like noodles. A block south of the Jiujiang Hotel, there are several places on the same side of the road that are not bad, but the food at the Jiujiang itself is overpriced and not memorable.

WHAT TO DO. Cangzhou is the largest town on this route since Taian, and has new and old sections of town to explore. There is even an amusement park on the north side of Xinhua Lu just before the turn onto Renmin Lu, at mileage point 46.0 on the route log below.

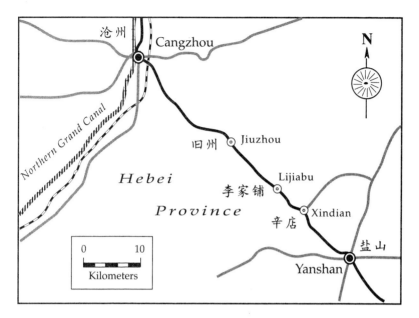

Log:

0.0 At the Yanshan Binguan gates, reset and head (NNE).

0.4 X; turn left (W). A post office with a radio tower is on the right after the turn.

1.2 The Youyi Binguan, a smaller hotel than the Yanshan Binguan, is on the right.

2.0 T, at the highway; turn right (NW).

5.7 Pass under a skybridge and begin travel on a divided road. The left carriageway is for autos only, and the right carriageway is for "mixed" traffic, including horsecarts and bikes.

9.9 Pass through the village of Xindian.

24.0 Cross a 100-m bridge over a river.

25.4 Village of Jiuzhou. Lincong Huangdi restaurant is on the right.

27.2 L:T; stay straight (N) on the main road.

34.9 L:T; stay straight (NW).

35.4 Cross an aqueduct bridge.

36.6 Enter Cangzhou city limits, passing roadside brick kilns.

38.0 Enter Cangzhou's industrial development area.

38.5 X, with a road merging in from the right; stay straight.

40.5 X; go straight (NW). The road to the left goes to Dezhou, the road to the right goes to Tianjin.

42.0 X signal; go straight (W).

42.4 Stay right, in the bike lane, and descend into a railroad underpass.

42.8 Exit the underpass, heading (W).

43.2 R:T; turn right (N) onto Jiaotong Lu.

Frying doughsticks at a roadside stall

43.8 X, with radio tower on the right; turn left (W) onto Xinhua Lu, the main street into downtown Cangzhou. (This X is the starting point for the next segment.)

44.3 Cangzhou Wushu Hotel is on the right, a yellow building behind gates. This is the older downtown area.

44.8 Bohai Mansions and a clock tower are on the left.

45.0 X; go straight, then cross a bridge in 0.2 km.

46.0 Large signal X; go right (N) on Renmin Lu.

47.0 EOD; Jiujiang (Holy River) Hotel is on the left.

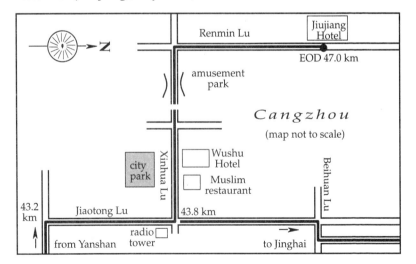

Cangzhou to Jinghai: 77.4 km

As you leave Cangzhou, breakfast on hot sesame *shaobing* biscuits at one of the stalls along Jiaotong Lu. Roll out of town amid jangling horsecarts hauling steel re-bar for new buildings. The highway parallels the railroad and the Northern Grand Canal into Tianjin City administrative area. Truck traffic is heavy, but the road is wide, well paved, and relatively flat. In May, hawkers line stretches of the highway selling delicious Tianjin apple-pears (*xueli*). If you have never tried this crisp, sweet fruit, do not miss the opportunity.

WHERE TO STAY. The Jinghai Binguan is comfortable and reasonably priced.

WHERE TO EAT. Turn right at the intersection by the Jinghai Binguan Hotel and go up about a block. There are several small restaurants on the right that serve good northern dishes. Tianjin cookery influences are evident: some dishes are seasoned with *dong cai*, a type of garlic-cured dried cabbage. Try the *jinjiangrousi*, shredded pork sauteed with rich sweet bean sauce and served with raw scallions to wrap up in beancurd skins and eat like a burrito.

WHAT TO DO. There are no tourist attractions in Jinghai.

Log:

0.0 At the intersection of Xinhua Lu and Jiaotong Lu in Cangzhou, at mileage point 43.8 in the previous route log, reset and head (NNE).

1.2 Large signal X; turn right (ESE) onto Beihuan Lu.

1.7 Signal L:T; turn left (N) to head out of town.

2.2 Stay to the left in the smaller mixed-traffic lane. Do not use the automobile overhead bridge.

2.5 Cross railroad tracks (NE).

3.1 Double railroad crossing.

3.5 Rejoin traffic from the automobile overhead, heading (N). This is a wide new road, with railroad tracks now on the right.

9.0 Enter Xingji, which has food and lodging.

10.2 Leave Xingji, heading (N).

17.5 Enter Zhouguantun.

18.4 Leave Zhouguantun.

20.5 Start across a bridge into Qing Xian County.

23.0 X; go straight.

24.1 Tollgate (no toll collected on bikes).

30.5 Enter Qingxian, a larger town.

32.6 L:T, with an inn on the left; stay straight (N) through Qingxian.

33.8 Road curves to (NE).

43.5 X; go straight. In May, Shandong apple-pears are for sale along the roadside.

47.0 Y; go right and, after the Y, head up to a bridge with canal-lock gates on the left. Cross the bridge (E).

52.0 Stay to the right in bike lanes and go down into a railroad underpass. In 0.2 km, go under the railroad tracks themselves.

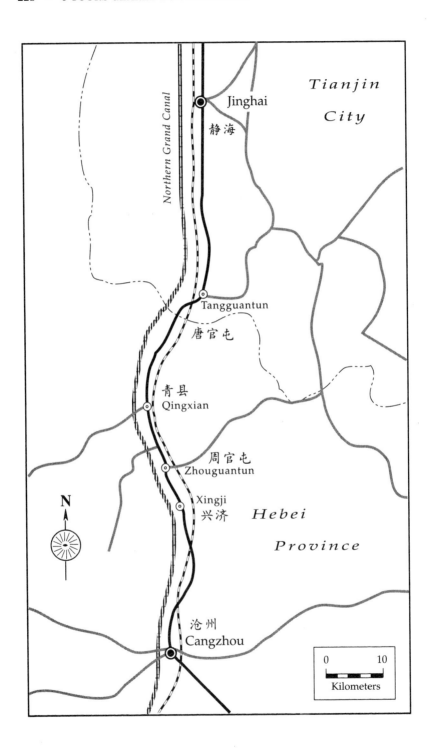

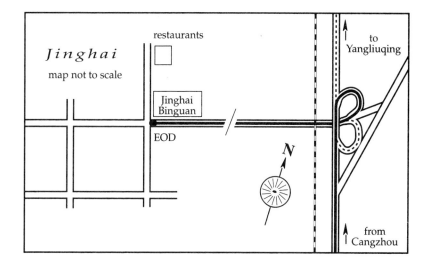

You are now in the Tianjin City area, Qinghai Zhen. Approach a Rev R:Y; stay straight.

52.5 Pass under a new freeway in Tangguantun.

56.0 Pear orchards are on the right, railroad tracks are on the left.

63.4 L:T, heading under a railroad at Chenguantun; stay straight (NE). There are plenty of restaurants through this stretch.

68.8 X, in Dongshuangtang; stay straight.

75.0 R:T, to Xiaowang Zhuang; continue straight (NE).

75.4 Jinghai bus station is on the right.

76.0 R:Y; go straight (NE), not right toward Tianjin.

76.3 Cross a bridge over the road into Jinghai. You want to get onto that road heading (SW), so you must turn right just after crossing the bridge and loop around to the right. (Note that this bridge is the 1.0-km point on the next segment's route log.)

76.5 Now pass under the overpass, heading (SW).

77.0 Exit the cloverleaf X, heading (SW) into Jinghai.

77.4 EOD; Jinghai Binguan is on the right, just before the X with the clock tower on the left.

Jinghai to Langfang: 88.6 km

As you leave Jinghai, breakfast on northern-style crepes at a *jianbing* cart, then continue north on a quieter side road. Cross the Duliu Jianhe River at Duliu, then enter the shaded streets of Yangliuqing. Cut west across the Daqing River, then back north through open countryside and mud-brick villages. Villages here produce bean noodles, which hang out drying on roadside racks. Stop at a lively streetside food market for an afternoon snack as you enter the medium-size city of Langfang.

WHERE TO STAY. The Langfang Binguan is in a courtyard behind a faux imperial gate. The older section on the east side of the courtyard is seedy but has character: high lattice windows are held open with sticks, and the showers actually work! Check in at the far end of the courtyard. Another option is the Mingzhu Hotel at mileage point 0.7 on the next segment's route log.

WHERE TO EAT. At the food stalls on the way into town (at mileage point 86.1 in the route log below), try the grilled lamb skewers with cumin. These merchants are good "recyclers": they sharpen old bicycle spokes and use them as skewers for their product. As you leave the Langfang Binguan hotel compound gates, there is a small Muslim restaurant just to the left (east) . The owner is from Xian, in the northwest, and his sons work the *shaobing* ovens in front of the restaurant. Have *yangrou paomo*, a crumbled hard biscuit soaked in lamb soup; *shoulamian*, hand-pulled noodles; and of course the sesame *shaobing*. It is a good place for breakfast in the morning, and you can take a bag of *shaobing* for the road.

WHAT TO DO. Across the road from the Langfang Binguan is a small street market and down the alley is a city park with a nearby movie house and video-game parlors that are all the rage with Chinese youth.

Log:

0.0 At the NW corner of the X in front of the Jinghai Binguan in Jinghai, reset and head (ESE).

0.5 Descend into an underpass (E) under the railroad tracks.

0.9 Come out of the underpass, with a big X circle ahead. Do not enter the X circle; instead bear right (S) onto a ramp. Continue right (SW) around this curved ramp until you are heading (N).

1.0 Just after 1.0 km, cross over the bridge that was mileage point 76.3 in the previous route log, with railroad tracks off to the left.

Jianbing *(crepe) cart near Jinghai*

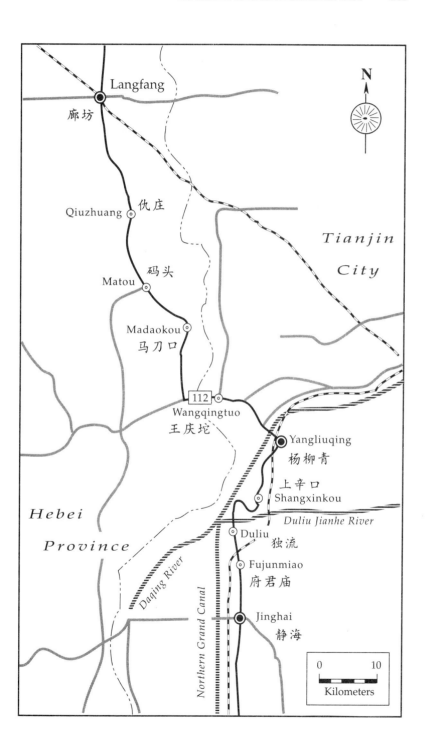

1.5 Cross double railroad tracks angling out to your right. You are on a tree-lined road now, with less traffic and noise.

7.0 Village of Fujunmiao.

8.7 Pass under railroad tracks and continue (N). Mud-wall and plastic greenhouses can be seen along here.

10.5 X; go straight (N).

13.9 Cross a small bridge. Enter the village of Duliu.

14.4 Cross a wider cement bridge (NE) with canal-lock gates on the right side.

15.0 Cross another bridge with locks. You have crossed the Duliu Jianhe River.

19.3 T, in Xiqingchu; turn right (E), toward Yangliuqing.

20.3 Newer commercial district in Shangxinkou, for about 0.7 km.

21.1 R:T; continue straight (E). After that, in around 0.1 km, the road curves left, back to the (N).

21.6 R:T, to Laojuntang; continue straight (NE). You are on willow-lined streets, now leaving Shangxinkou.

23.6 Jog in the road; dogleg right, go under railroad tracks, then dogleg left. In 0.1 km, you are heading (N).

23.8 R:T; continue straight (N).

26.6 Enter Yangliuqing, heading (NE) through town.

26.8 X; go straight (NE) on Xinhua Lu.

27.4 L:T; turn left (NW) here, onto Jianshe Lu. To explore downtown Yangliuqing, disconnect here and go straight for several blocks along tree-lined streets for food or lodging. (**Note:** *do not* reset your cycle computer; when you're done exploring, reconnect and continue from this intersection.)

27.8 Yangliuqing train station is ahead. Follow the road as it doglegs right (E) in front of the train station entrance.

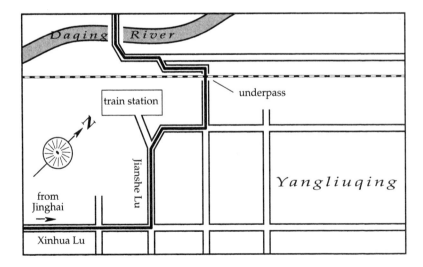

28.1 X; turn left (NW) onto a tree-canopied street with outdoor snooker halls, and head toward the railroad tracks.

28.2 Come to a bike-path underpass and go under the railroad tracks. On the other side, turn left (W) and ascend a ramp.

28.4 Merge with the road (SW). The train station and tracks are now on your left.

28.6 Head uphill and curve right (NW) toward a bridge.

28.8 Cross the bridge (N) over the Daqing River.

30.8 Rev R:Y; merge onto route 112 heading (W).

35.3 Rev R:Y; merge again onto a larger road (WSW).

38.5 R:T, in Wangqingtuo; go straight (W) through town.

38.8 R:T; stay straight (W).

44.6 R:T; turn right (N) onto a smaller country road.

46.8 Pass through the village of Madaokou, which you leave in 1.2 km.

52.3 R:Y; stay left on the main road as it curves left, back to (NW) in 0.1 km. Bean-thread noodles are drying on racks by the roadside.

53.1 X; go straight on the main road as it curves right, back to (N).

55.1 L:T; stay straight (N).

60.2 L:Y; stay straight (WNW).

61.0 Enter the village of Matou.

61.2 Cross a small bridge heading (NW).

Chinese gypsy cart

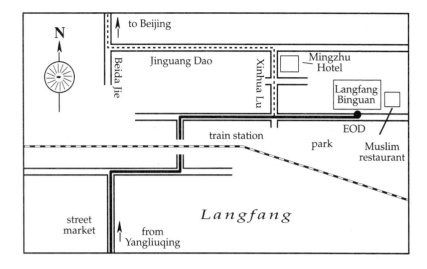

61.6 X, in the market area of Matou; stay straight (NW).
62.5 Rev L:Y; merge into a larger road, heading (N).
64.6 X; stay straight (N).
70.0 Enter Qiuzhuang. The road is wide here.
83.5 L:T; stay straight (NNW).
83.9 Cross a bridge.
84.7 R:T, to freeway; stay straight (N). Bike lanes start as you enter the Langfang urban area.
86.1 Signal X; go straight (N). Street-food markets are on the left.
87.1 Signal T; turn right (E). Before the turn, a mosque minaret is visible straight ahead.
87.3 L:Y circle; go left (N) and descend to an underpass.
87.5 Go under the underpass.
87.7 T; turn right (E). The Langfang train station is on the right in 0.1 km.
87.9 Bus station, a big white building, is on the right.
88.1 X, with a clock tower on the left; go straight (E).
88.6 EOD; the Langfang Binguan is on the left, with a gaudy-colored imperial-style gate.

Langfang to Beijing: 60.9 km

The final segment of this tour takes you into Beijing along farm roads and brick-walled northern villages. Huge cottonwood trees line most of the route, and their "cotton" drifts in the air and blows across the road in the spring. As you close in on Beijing, the traffic gets worse, but wide roads and bike lanes make this a "bike-friendly" city. By now, you are probably riding just like the locals. Close to the end point, use the city map of Beijing in your conventional guidebook to navigate to your lodgings.

When Beijing was the Qing Dynasty imperial capital, there were great city walls surrounding the metropolis and each wall had several gates. The streets inside the walls were laid out on a grid with the Forbidden City at the center. Now the walls have been torn down and major thoroughfares have been laid out in their place. Major street and intersection names are derived from the names of the old city-wall gates. For the cyclist, Beijing's wide avenues are a welcome change from the clogged downtown streets of Shanghai and Guangzhou.

Although Shanghai has been designated as the country's industrial-growth showcase, business is booming in Beijing. International firms are falling over themselves to open offices and participate in joint ventures to tap the world's largest market: 1.2 billion people who are ready to enjoy a taste of prosperity. When the government decided to allow small private enterprise, it should have termed the policy "Let 100 restaurants bloom!" But the number is in the thousands now. Competition from new eateries has even forced stodgy state-owned operations to shape up and put a smile on their face. The nation's political capital, Beijing is also its cultural capital: museums, architecture, antiques markets, opera, sports, and, now, even rock and roll.

The best way to see Beijing is by bicycle! It is flat, major street signs have English subtitles, and, if you have a map and a compass, it is impossible to get really lost. In fact, getting lost in the back alleys called *hutong* is the best way to see the real Beijing. Peer through gateways into walled courtyards to see the way Beijingers lived before the advent of high-rise apartment blocks. Stop at a neighborhood noodle stall for lunch, and watch them pull the noodles by hand.

WHERE TO STAY. To get to some easy-to-find options, ride 3 or 4 kilometers east from Tiananmen and you will find the International Hotel and others farther down in the vicinity of Jianguomen. There are other options west of Tiananmen along Fuxingmennei Dajie.

WHERE TO EAT. One good area for night life and restaurants is Xidan, north of Changan Jie on Xidan Beidajie. The Wangfujing district just east of Tiananmen also has a lot of restaurants, as well as the world's largest McDonald's. Try the night market (*yeshi*) north of Wangfujing in Dongsi district, where block after block of stalls serve the "small eats" (*fengweixiaochi*) of various provinces. Small noodle shops are in nearly every alley: in summer try the spicy cold noodles (*malaliangmian*) along with pickled and cold mixed snack dishes displayed as you enter. When the weather is warm, beer gardens and cafes spill out onto the sidewalks of larger streets. For breakfast, itinerant merchants set up shop on street corners, selling wonton in soup, steamed buns, and *jianbing* crepes.

WHAT TO DO. The first thing to see is the Forbidden City, the former imperial residence. Only after experiencing the grandeur of its huge walls and courtyards can one appreciate the power and wealth that was imperial China. Another must-see is the Summer Palace (Yiheyuan), about 18 kilometers northwest of the city (see the first 18 kilometers of the route log for the first segment of Tour No. 9). The Qing dowager empress Ci Xi misspent the budget of the imperial navy embellishing this complex of pavilions and courtyards along Kunming

Lake. Those interested in antiquities and scholarly art items should visit the stores along Liulichang Jie, just off Nanxinhua Jie west of Qianmen. North of the railway station near Jianguomen is the Beijing Ancient Observatory, with an outdoor display of curious devices for measuring celestial events. For listings of concerts, operas, and plays, refer to the tourist magazines provided in major hotels.

Log:

0.0 At the Langfang Binguan gates, turn right and head (W).

0.1 Gong An building is on the right.

0.4 X; turn right (N) onto Xinhua Lu.

0.5 Post office is on the left.

0.7 X; go straight (N). The Mingzhu Hotel, an alternative lodging for the previous segment, is just before the clock tower on the right.

1.0 X circle, at Jinguang Dao; go around and exit left (W).

1.2 Langfang city government buildings are on the right.

1.8 T, with Bank of China straight ahead; turn right (N) onto Beida Jie. This is a busy street with department stores and shops.

2.6 Signal X; continue straight (N).

3.9 X; go straight (N).

8.5 X; go straight (N). Pass wheat fields and brick kilns.

12.0 Enter the market town of Fengheying; go straight through.

12.9 T; turn left (W), onto a narrower tree-lined road.

16.5 L:T, to Dapiying; stay straight (NW).

17.7 Village of Shawo, with cornstalk fences.

19.5 Y; stay left (W).

19.6 L:T; go straight (W).

20.7 T, at Caiyu; turn left (W).

23.3 X; go straight (W).

27.6 Lihuachang village.

30.1 Cross a bridge and enter the village of Qingyundian.

30.4 Road curves (N), then in 0.1 km it curves back (W).

30.6 Cross a bridge over an aqueduct.

30.9 Leave Qingyundian (W). Follow signs to Nanyuan.

31.2 L:Y, to Weishan Zhuang; stay straight (W).

31.5 Road curves right, heading (NNW).

33.0 R:T; stay straight (NNW).

37.4 Enter the village of Nandahongmen.

37.7 X, at a wide highway; go straight (N). Across the X on the left is a small teashop on the corner, run by two old men who hang a birdcage in front. You are now entering Beijing city limits.

37.8 Cross a canal.

38.4 Village of Nangong.

42.2 Enter Yunhai Zhuang.

42.8 Y; stay left, (W).

45.8 Rev L:Y; continue straight as the road curves right, back to (N) in 0.1 km.

46.8 Enter Donggaodi.

47.2 X; go straight and approach a Y.

47.5 Y; bear left (WNW) around the SW end of apartment buildings.

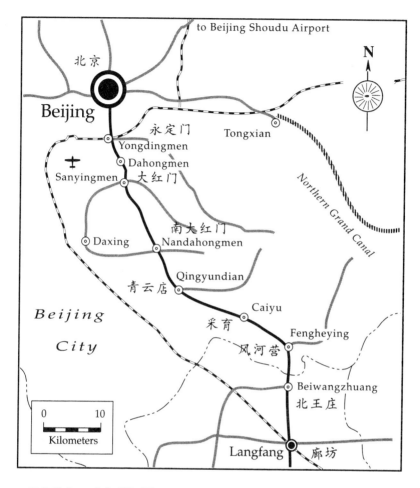

47.9 T; bear left (W). There are bike lanes after this turn.

49.2 T; turn right (N) toward Dahongmen. You may see airplanes taking off and landing on the left at the Beijing southwest airport.

50.6 Cross railroad tracks. The Western Hills are to the left in the distance.

51.8 Climb a rise onto a railroad overpass. Pines are growing along the roadside.

52.5 Cross railroad tracks.

52.7 Signal X, at Dahongmen Lukou; go straight on Nanyuan Lu.

53.7 Cross a bridge (N) near truck gardens and apartment blocks.

54.7 X, with no bikes allowed straight ahead; turn right (E) to bypass that section.

54.8 X; turn left (N) and stay in bike lanes.

55.0 Road tends (W) and then back (N).

Ending the tour at Tiananmen, Beijing

55.1 X circle, in Shazikou district; go straight (N).

56.6 Pass under a railroad trestle.

56.9 Cross over an eight-lane freeway and a river (N). Now you are on Yongdingmen Neidajie heading toward Qianmen.

57.9 Entry to Tiantan (Platform of Heaven) is on the right.

58.2 Beijing Natural History Museum is on the right.

58.5 X, at Tiantan Lu; go straight (N).

59.0 X; go straight.

59.9 Qianmen (Front Gate); turn right (E), going around the gate.

60.1 X, with Tiananmen Square visible straight ahead; go straight (N).

60.9 EOD; north edge of Tiananmen Square, with Tiananmen and Mao's picture to the left. This main avenue is Dong Changan Jie. Head east to get to the Wangfujing district (New China bookstore, McDonald's, department stores), Dongdan Park, and Jianguomen (Friendship Store, hotels). Consult your Beijing road map and conventional guidebook for your stay in Beijing.

TOUR NO. 9: NORTHEASTERN PRC

NORTH TO THE GREAT WALL
Beijing to Badaling Great Wall and back

Distance: 209 kilometers; 29 kilometers to the airport

Estimated time: 2–3 riding days; 2 hours to the airport

Best time to go: April–June, September–October

Terrain: Some flat, some steep and mountainous

Maps: Maps of Beijing, map of Beijing administrative area

Connecting tour: Tour No. 8

This tour begins and ends in Beijing, and can be done on its own, or combined with Tour No. 8, Taian to Beijing. After you have explored Beijing, head north and see the Summer Palace on the way to the Great Wall. The final stretch into Badaling is a steep climb through ragged mountains laced with crumbling sections of the Great Wall. Spend the night at an inn in Badaling and watch the sun rise from the Great Wall before the buses arrive with thousands of tourists.

From the Great Wall, you can retrace your route back to Beijing or continue on a loop that takes you to a rural hot-spring town for the night. Head east from the Great Wall through Yanqing, then cut south on a wicked descent through narrow tunnels and gorges. The road finally levels out near the site of the Ming Tombs. Leave the busy highway and ride along canals to the hot-spring village of Xiaotangshan. After your hot-spring stop, return to Beijing.

CONNECTIONS. The commonest way in and out of Beijing is by air at Beijing Shoudu International Airport. If you are arriving in and departing from Beijing by air, get your hotel to store the bike shipping carton for your return flight.

Those arriving at night should consider hiring a minivan taxi for transporting their bikes to their hotel. Daytime arrivals can ride into downtown Beijing by following the Beijing to Beijing International Airport route log in reverse.

When you are ready to leave Beijing, begin by deciding how you will pack your bike, if at all. There are no boxes supplied at Beijing Shoudu International Airport, and loose cardboard is not easy to find. You will have to pack your own cardboard and strapping tape from Beijing to the airport; otherwise, the bike will be loaded onto the plane "as is." Don't exchange all your money before arriving at the Beijing airport;

set aside the equivalent of US$20 per person for airport departure taxes.

INFORMATION. Allow three days for this loop to the Great Wall, unless you want to linger at the Ming Tombs area or spend more than a night at Xiaotangshan. It is not a hard ride, but sections of downhill are fast and dangerous. Be sure your tires and brakes are in good shape for those sections. Because lodging is limited around the Badaling area, it is not a bad idea to have bivvy gear in case no rooms are available.

Beijing to Badaling Great Wall: 76 km

Get an early start from Tiananmen Square and cycle north to the Summer Palace (Yiheyuan). It is possible to make a quick stop at the Summer Palace on the way up to the Wall, but the Summer Palace really requires a day to do it justice. If you decide to stop and see it on this tour, rather than as a day trip from Beijing, plan to spend the

The Badaling Great Wall snakes over distant mountains.

night in the surrounding area, or ride as far as Wenquan and find lodging there.

The road is well paved and lined with huge trees until Wenquan. Pedal up a very gentle grade until the military town of Nankou, then pump up a boulder-strewn valley past jagged ridges and occasional stone farmhouses. As you near Badaling, you will see crumbling sections of the Great Wall along the ridges. Foreign and Chinese tourists all go to the Badaling Great Wall, and it sometimes seems as though they are all there at once. Even Chinese who are accustomed to crowds complain that you cannot take a picture on the Wall because of all the people in the way. The village of Badaling is the strip northwest of the Wall and is pretty much devoted to Great Wall tourism business.

WHERE TO STAY. There are several inns on the left 0.5 to 0.9 kilometer below the eastern Great Wall tunnel portal. Arrange lodging as soon as you arrive; there are not many choices. It is possible to camp in the area, but check the area closely before laying out your bedroll: many level spots beside the road have been used as a public lavatory.

WHERE TO EAT. There are plenty of noodle stalls and small restaurants on the east side of the Wall. For those who want something "finger-lickin' good," there is even a Kentucky Fried Chicken franchise!

WHAT TO DO. See the Wall at its best near sunset or at sunrise before the tour buses arrive from Beijing. In the tourist area by the ticket booths, there are sometimes performances of traditional dance and acrobatics.

Log:

0.0 At Chairman Mao's picture at Tiananmen Square, reset and head (W) on Dong Changan Jie.

1.9 You are now in the Xidan district, on Xi Changan Jie.

2.4 Minority Culture Palace (Minzu Wenhua Gong) is on the right.

2.6 Minzu Hotel is on the right.

4.6 Xidan McDonald's is on the right. You are now on Fuxing Dongwaijie.

5.3 X; turn right (N) on Sanlihe Lu.

5.6 Stay to the left on the main road.

6.0 X, at Yuetan Nanjie; go straight (N).

7.0 X, at Fuchangmenwai Jie; go straight (N).

8.1 X, at Donggongzhuang Nanjie; go straight (N). Beijing Mandarin Hotel is on the right.

8.7 T, with a park ahead; go left (W) on Shahemenwai Jie.

9.3 Capital Sports Arena is on the right.

9.4 X, at Baishiqiao Road; turn right (N).

11.4 Cross Xueyuan Nanlu. The area is less urban now.

12.6 X; go straight, onto Haidan Lu.

13.6 X; go straight (N).

13.9 X circle; stay straight (N) through Haidan Zhuang.

14.8 Signal L:T, at Haidan Dajie; turn left (W). Do not miss this turn.

15.3 Entrance to Beijing University is on the right.

15.7 X; turn right (N) onto Yiheyuan Lu.

16.6 Another entrance to Beijing University is on the right.

17.0 T; turn left (W) toward Yiheyuan.

17.8 L:T; continue straight, bearing right (WNW) as you leave the intersection. The hills of the Summer Palace (Yiheyuan) are ahead.

18.3 Y, with the left fork going to the entrance to the Summer Palace (Yiheyuan); go right (N) on Yuanmingyuan Xilu. To visit the Summer Palace, disconnect here and go straight. (If you choose to stay overnight in this vicinity for a longer visit at the Summer Palace, there are several inns along here.) After your visit to the Summer Palace, reconnect. (**Note:** *do not* reset your cycle computer after this side trip.)

18.6 L:T circle; turn left, exiting (W). Yiheyuan rooftops can be seen on the hill after the turn. You are now on a smaller road.

19.3 On the left is the wall around the Summer Palace.

19.9 Y, with a large tour-bus parking area; bear right (NW).

20.2 Y; bear left and head up to a canal bridge.

20.4 Cross a canal bridge and come to an X; turn right (N), toward Wenquan, on a willow-lined road with a canal on your right.

21.0 L:Y; stay straight on the main road as it curves right (NW).

25.0 R:T, in a village; stay straight (W).

31.1 Enter Wenquan Xiang. Mountains are to the south.

32.7 L:T; stay straight (W).

33.2 Good restaurant is on the right in a newer building.

33.4 Enter the village of Wenquan. (This is a possible overnight stop for those riders who choose an extended side trip to the Summer Palace.)

33.6 Y; go right (N) toward Nankou.

33.8 Cross a canal over the Wenquan bridge (N).

42.7 T; bear left (W) toward Nankou.

43.7 Road bends right, crosses Nanfang bridge, and heads (N).

43.9 Pass under a railroad trestle. The road widens and is no longer lined with trees. There is a Muslim restaurant on the right.

44.6 Muslim restaurants are on the left, and an inn is out back.

50.0 Armored-tank practice roads parallel the road.

55.1 T; turn right (E), entering Nankou, a military-base town.

55.4 Cross Nankou west bridge (E), then cross railroad tracks.

56.5 Entrance to a military installation is on the right. Dongda Jie curves left through town and back to (NE).

56.6 R:T; continue straight on Dongda Jie as it curves left. Nankou is the last town before Badaling.

57.6 Large X circle; go around and exit the far side (NW), then bear left onto a two-lane road climbing into the jagged mountains ahead.

59.3 Cross Nankou north bridge over railroad tracks. The road levels a bit, and you can see orchards, stone farmhouses, rock fences, and boulder fields.

65.5 Sections of the Great Wall are evident along the ridges here.

71.5 Go through a tunnel and enter Yanqing County.

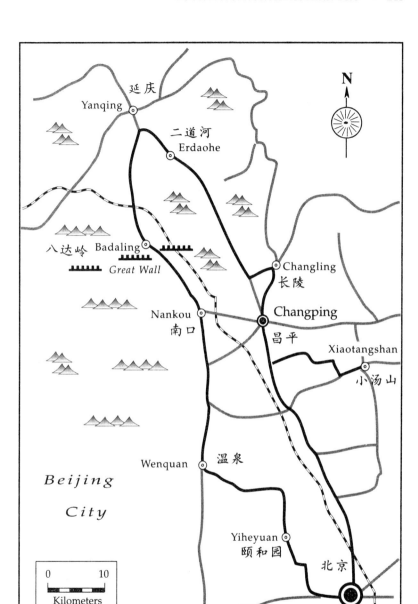

71.9 Tourist area is on the right.
74.3 Inn is on the left; you must go ahead, then backtrack, to get to it.
74.5 Rev L:Y; go straight. The inn is down the other leg.
74.7 Go under railroad tracks.

75.0 Tourist area and restaurants are on the left.

75.2 Leave the tourist area and ascend switchbacks.

75.8 Signal at a tunnel through the Great Wall.

76.0 EOD; the other side of the tunnels, looking down on the tourist area on the northwest side of the Great Wall. This is Badaling.

Badaling to Xiaotangshan: 78.1 km

The reward on this segment is the incredibly fast (and dangerous) downhill ride from Badaling through tunnels and high mountain gorges. The scenery is worth it. The road levels out in the vicinity of the Ming Tombs, then you join busy southbound traffic toward Changping.

A little past Changping, leave the highway and follow a cottonwood-lined canal road east to Xiaotangshan. Xiaotangshan is a backward little village but it has a drawing point: a hot spring. The hot spring is in a sanitarium-type setting, with many geriatric clients. Do not expect this to be a "resort" type of atmosphere; it is rustic. Next to the bathing house is a primitive inn, and the town has only a few places to eat.

If you are not in a mood for such rustic lodging, plan on riding back to Beijing directly from the Great Wall, by retracing the previous segment's route log, or bypassing the turnoff to Xiaotangshan.

WHERE TO STAY. The nameless inn at the hot spring is the place to stay in Xiaotangshan. This was the cheapest lodging of all the tours in this book (US$1 for two), and if you stay here, you will understand why. If you arrive after 5:00 P.M., you must wait until 8:00 A.M. to "take the waters."

WHERE TO EAT. There are small places around the market square to the right at the end-of-day point. The inn is too small to have its own eating facility, but some guests light a fire in front of their room and cook there!

WHAT TO DO. Take a soak in the hot spring. The hot spring is included in the price of your lodging. Be warned: it is *hot*! Lock your room with a padlock and do not leave valuables unattended in the dressing room. Even the locals use long poles to hang their coats and bags high on the wall to keep them out of the wrong hands.

Log:

0.0 At the stone portal of the Great Wall in Badaling, reset and head down (W).

0.9 Zhaodaisuo (an inn) is on the left.

1.1 Badaling train station is on the right.

4.0 Village of Xibozi.

5.4 Y; go right (NW). Now you are up on a high plateau with orchards and dry, stony fields.

5.9 Railroad crossing; cross (N), then coast downhill.

8.0 Village of Dafutuo, with bald, terraced, dry hills.

10.3 Village of Xinbao Zhuang.

At the gate of the Badaling Great Wall

14.2 Cross railroad tracks and enter a huge X circle.

14.5 Take the first exit out of the X circle, heading (ENE). The second exit, heading (N), goes to downtown Yanqing (3 km to its central district).

16.2 R:Y, with the straight fork leading to Zhangjiakou and the right fork leading to Beijing; turn right (SE) onto a narrower tree-lined road.

17.1 Pass under a railroad trestle.

17.3 Rev L:Y; merge into a larger road.

30.5 You are now down from the first steep section; head (SE) through the village of Duibaishi in foothills along a creek.

32.9 Truck-stop cafes are on the right, in Beidi, just before a tunnel.

33.1 Enter the tunnel, exit in 0.1 km, then cross a bridge over a gorge. This tunnel is narrow and not lit, and there are no separate bike lanes.

34.3 Enter a tunnel; exit in 0.2 km. Watch for trucks; use your safety flasher.

38.5 The road levels out a bit in Guniangtai, then it gets steep again.

39.2 An inn is on the left in Guozhuang. Fruit orchards and incredible jagged mountains are on the right.

41.2 L:T; pass it and head (SE).

43.0 Reservoir is on the right; head (SE) here.

45.0 Road levels again.

46.2 Sign: "LEFT TO DINGLING."

46.4 L:T; turn left (E) off the main road and head toward Dingling. The suffix *ling* means "imperial tomb"; this valley is filled with *ling*.

47.2 Zhaoling, one of the Ming Tombs, is on the left.

49.0 T; go right (SE). (A left turn goes (NW) to Dingling tomb.)

49.3 Cross a bridge (E).

49.5 Cross a bridge.

49.9 T; turn right (SSW), then cross a bridge. (A left turn heads (ENE) to Changling and Mutianyu Great Wall.) Just across the bridge on the left is a restaurant.

50.7 L:T; stay straight (SSW).

51.4 Start across Qikung bridge. Shanling Shuiku reservoir is on the left.

52.4 X; go straight (SW), toward Changping. (A left turn goes around the lake.)

52.8 Y, the road splits into a double carriageway around Mingling Shen Dao Park; stay right (SW).

55.1 Road merges back into a two-way road.

55.8 X; go straight (SW), then curve left (S) and exit the ornate Mingling Gate.

56.2 Shipai Fang stone gate monument is on the left.

56.4 Signal T; go left (SSW) and merge onto the main highway.

57.9 Large X circle; bikes must stay to the right, then go *under* the automobile traffic, through a pedestrian/bike maze. The idea is to get through the maze and out the other side heading (S) in 0.5 km. A left turn leads into Changping.

59.4 Large X circle; go around and exit the circle in 0.2 km, heading (S).

60.6 Pass through Shuidun.

62.1 R:Y; bear right off the highway and drop down to a road along a canal. (If you are going directly back into Beijing, do not turn right, but reset and continue straight.)

62.2 Turn left (E) at the canal, and pass under the highway in 0.1 km. The canal is to the south of the road.

66.8 X; turn right (S) and cross a narrow canal bridge, then enter a village.

67.5 Leave the village, and you are back on a tree-lined road.

67.8 Paved road doglegs left (E).

69.6 R:T; head right (SSW) onto a smaller farm road. There is a small store on the corner.

71.0 X; turn left (E).

72.3 X, at Baishan Lukou; stay straight (E).

72.6 Rev R:Y, merging with the road you are on; stay straight (E).

75.0 X, with a left turn leading to the Aviation Museum; stay straight (E).

77.2 Y, with the main road heading right; go left (E) on the narrower road leading into Xiaotangshan.

77.5 X; go straight (E).

78.1 EOD; T, at the market square of Xiaotangshan. Go left (NNW) here and 50 m farther on your left is the hot-spring building. There is no sign. Look for the old building with a steel gate on the left leading back into the inn compound. Baths close at 5:00 P.M.

Xiaotangshan to Beijing: 54.9 km

After a boiling-hot bath in the Xiaotangshan hot spring, have breakfast in the market area and then retrace the route back to the main highway heading into Beijing. Once you are on the highway, expect constant truck and auto traffic all the way to the city center at Tiananmen. It is noisy, but the road surface is good and bike lanes are wide.

WHERE TO STAY. See this information in Tour No. 8.

WHERE TO EAT. See this information in Tour No. 8.

WHAT TO DO. See this information in Tour No. 8.

Log:

0.0 At the T at the market square in Xiaotangshan, reset and head (W) out of town.

0.5 X; go straight.

1.0 Merge back onto a larger road (W).

3.1 X; go straight.

5.4 L:Y, heading to Shahe; stay straight.

5.8 X, with a restaurant ahead; turn right (N).

7.3 X, with main road doglegging left; go left (W).

9.0 L:T, with a small store on the corner; continue straight (W).

10.7 Road doglegs right (N) toward a canal.

11.7 Cross a bridge to the north side of the canal, then turn left (W) onto the canal road.

16.1 Approach the highway.

16.2 Go under the highway. In 0.1 km, turn right and loop back up to the highway.

16.4 Rejoin the highway and reset.

0.0 At the highway, reset and continue across the bridge (S).

2.3 X; continue straight.

6.8 L:T, leading to Xiaotangshan; stay straight (S).

6.9 Start across a bridge with stone pillars on each side.

8.3 X; go straight (S).

9.2 Cross Shahe Nanqiao bridge.

17.3 X circle; go around and exit straight (S) in 0.2 km.

19.5 X circle, with a horse statue in the center; exit (S) in 0.2 km.

20.6 R:T; go straight (S). This is the Qinghe area.

21.1 Cross a river and stay straight on the main road (S).

24.0 X; go straight (S) down Xueyuan Lu.

Morning tourist invasion at the Great Wall

24.9 X; go straight. This is Chengfu Lukou.
26.8 X; bear slightly right, then back (S) in 0.1 km.
27.8 Stay straight (S) and pass under Ji Men Qiao bridge.
28.7 Y; bear left (SSE) on a larger road.
28.9 X; bend back (S).
29.5 Cross double railroad tracks.
30.4 Xizhimen bridge is ahead. Stay in the right bike lane.
32.8 Pass under Fuchengmen bridge.
34.6 Pass under Fuxingmen Qiao.
34.8 Turn right and curve around a ramp up onto Changan Lu.
35.0 On Changan Lu, you are heading (E) toward the Xidan district.
38.5 EOD; Tiananmen Square in Beijing.

Beijing to Beijing Shoudu International Airport: 29 km

When you are ready to leave Beijing, transport your bike in a mini-van taxi or ride out to the Beijing Shoudu Airport. Get from Tiananmen Square to the Friendship Store, and begin the route log at nearby Jianguomen intersection. The route described here was logged while the Airport Expressway was under construction, and some areas may have changed. Nevertheless, the route should be easy to find because of airport signs all along the route.

Log:

0.0 At Tiananmen Square, reset, head east on Changan Donglu about 4 km to the Beijing Friendship Store, then go back (W) along Jianguomen Waijie.

0.6 X, at Jianguomen intersection; reset on the NE corner.

0.0 Reset and turn right, heading (N) from X at Jianguomen.

0.4 Pass the International Post Office Building on the right. (If you want to mail a package home from Beijing, do it here.)

1.7 Pass under Qiaoyangmen bridge.

2.7 Pass under Dongsishitiao bridge.

3.3 R:Y; bear right just before Dongzhimen, heading (NE) on the off-ramp.

3.5 X, at the end of the ramp; turn right (E).

3.6 L:T, at the first left after the last turn; go left (N).

3.8 Road divides, with Dongzhimen north bus station stop on the left; continue past the bus stop (NE).

5.1 X; go straight on Jichang Lu.

5.7 X; go straight (NE) on a tree-lined road with iron fences.

6.2 Sanyuan bridge; go under it and then go straight through the X.

9.4 Holiday Inn is on the right.

12.2 Airport Expressway ramp is on the right; stay straight (NE).

14.7 Another ramp; stay with the main traffic flow, do not go onto the ramp.

18.0 Pass through Sunhe.

21.1 Y; bear right (S). Follow signs to Capital Airport (Shoudu Jichang).

21.5 X; turn left (E).

24.0 Pass through a village, your last chance for cheap Chinese food.

24.4 Road doglegs right and heads up over a bridge. The Huayi Hotel is on the right.

24.6 Top of a bridge over the new freeway.

25.0 Exit the bridge at a T; go left (NE). Just after the turn is a Y; go left, heading (N).

25.4 Merge onto a tree-lined road with bike paths, heading (NNW).

26.8 L:T; go left, leaving the tree-lined road. If you arrive at the old airport terminal building at mileage point 27.0, you missed this turn.

26.9 Road bends right (N). The Capital Airport Hotel is on the right.

27.3 You are now heading (N), with airport control towers ahead. Go around the north side of the old airport.

27.6 You are now heading (E), and the old airport is on the right.

27.7 Road bends left (N). X circle and taxis are ahead.

28.1 T, at a road that fronts the terminal; go left (W).

28.4 Arrivals door; go upstairs for departures.

A rock climber at the Great Wall can't pass up the challenge.

PHRASEGUIDE

This phraseguide covers many common situations a cycle tourist will encounter. The phrases are worded so the answer can be a nod of the head, a written number or money amount, or a physical action such as pointing. As you use this phraseguide, have a pencil and paper ready to record answers to your inquiries.

Restaurants

A Chinese meal usually consists of some cold dishes, one hot dish per person, and a soup, along with a starch such as rice, noodles, or bread.

Show the waiter or proprietor the first phrase after this paragraph to explain why you are showing him this book. Then, use phrase No. 10 to say how many dishes you want, phrase No. 11 to order starchy food, and phrase No. 6 to order beverages. If you want certain combinations of ingredients, point to them in the table of main and side ingredients found later in this phraseguide; or use the phrase No. 18 to ask them to point out the items they have. For each dish, point at one main ingredient and one side ingredient.

Use phrase No. 12 to get a total price before giving them the go-ahead on your meal with phrase No. 13.

1. We are using this book to communicate with you. Please read the phrases we point to and write or indicate your answer.
   Women yao yung zheben yu nin goutong. Qing du xiamian women suo zhichu de juzi, bing xiexia huo zhichu ninde daan.
   我们要用这本与您沟通。请读下面我们所指出的句子，并写下或指出你的答案。

2. Where can we wash our hands?
   Xishou de difang zai nali?
   洗手的地方在那里？

3. Please get us a bowl and boiling water to scald the utensils.
   Qing gei women yige dawan he kaishui, rang women tang yixia zhexie canju.
   请给我们一个大碗和开水，让我们烫一下这些餐具。

4. Please help us select a meal of local specialties.
Qing bangzhu women jiao yige you zhege difang fengwei de cai.
请帮助我们叫一个有这个地方风味的菜。

5. Please show us your appetizer plates.
Qing gei women kan nimen de xiao cai, lung cai.
请给我们看你们的小菜、冷菜。

6. We want to drink beer/soda/tea/boiled water.
Women xiang he pijiu / qishui / cha / kaishui.
我们想喝啤酒/汽水/茶/开水。

7. Please show us what brands of beer you sell.
Qing rang women kan nimen mai shenme paizi de pijiu.
请让我们看你们卖什么牌子的啤酒。

8. Please let us see the kitchen and what you have to eat.
Qing rang women kan chufang, kan you shenma cai keyi chi.
请让我们看厨房，看有什么菜可以吃。

9. We would like the same dishes they're having.
Women yao chi gen naxie ren chi yiyang de cai.
我们要吃跟那些人吃一样的菜。

10. We would like ( ) cold dishes, ( ) hot dishes, and one soup.
Women yao ( ) lung cai, ( ) re cai, yige tang.
我们要( )冷菜，( )热菜，一个汤。

11. We'd like rice/bread/noodles/dumplings
Women xiang chi fan / mantou / mian / jiaozi.
我们想吃饭/馒头/面/饺子。

12. Please write down the number of dishes and the total price.
Qing xie xia lai women dianle jidao cai, duoshao qian.
请写下来我们点了几道菜，多少钱。

13. That price is OK. Go ahead and prepare our meal.
Zhege jiaqian keyi. Qing ni kaishi zhunbei womende cai.
这个价钱可以，请你开始准备我们的菜。

14. This is too expensive! We want cheaper dishes.
Zhege cai tai gui! Women yao jiao bijiao pianyide
这个菜太贵，我们要叫比较便宜的。

15. Please fill our water bottles with cool boiled water, OK?
Qing nin zhuang lung kaishui, haoma?
请您装冷开水，好吗？

16. We would like to pay our bill now.
Xianzai women yao fu zhangdan.
现在我们要付帐单。

17. Thanks for a great meal!
Xiexie nin zuo zhemma haochide cai gei women chi!
谢谢您做这么好的菜给我们吃。

18. On the following table, please point out what you can cook for us.
Qing kan xiamian de biaoge, zhichulai naizhong cailiao shi keyi zhu gei women chide.
请看下面的表格，指出来那一种材料是可以煮给我们吃的。

19. Can you make a dish of the ingredients I'm pointing at?
Wo zhichulai de cailiao ni nengbuneng zuocheng cai?
我指出来的材料你能不能做成菜？

20. We'd like Muslim-style dishes.
Women xiang chi qingzhen cai.
我们想吃清真菜。

21. We're vegetarians. Please prepare the food without meat.
Women chisu. Qing bu yao yung rou chao women jiao de cai.
我们吃素。请不要用肉炒我们叫的菜。

Main ingredients	*Zhuliao*	主料
beef	*niu rou*	牛肉
chicken	*ji rou*	鸡肉
lamb	*yang rou*	羊肉
pork	*zhu rou*	猪肉
spareribs	*paigu*	排骨
clams	*heli*	蚵蜊
crabs	*pangxie*	螃蟹
eels	*shan yu*	鳝鱼
fish, slices	*yu pian*	鱼片
fish, whole	*quan yu*	全鱼
scallops	*xian bei*	鲜贝
shrimp	*xia ren*	虾仁
beancurd	*doufu*	豆腐
beancurd, shreds	*gan si*	干丝
beancurd, fried	*zha doufu*	炸豆腐
eggs	*ji dan*	鸡蛋

Seasonings	*Zuoliao*	酌料
spicy	*la*	辣
mild	*dan*	淡
sweet & sour	*tiansuan wei*	甜酸味
chili sauce	*lajiaojiang*	辣椒酱
fermented black beans	*doushi*	豆豉
garlic	*suantou*	蒜头
local style	*fengwei cai*	风味菜
sweet	*tian*	甜
sour	*suan*	酸
salty	*xian*	咸
spicy garlic sauce	*yuxiang*	鱼香
burnt chili sauce	*gongbao*	宫保

Side ingredients	*Fuliao*	付料
bamboo shoots	*zhu sun*	竹笋
bean shoots	*dou miao*	豆苗
beansprouts	*dou ya*	豆芽
bitter melon	*ku gua*	苦瓜
cabbage	*gaoli cai*	高丽菜
cashews	*yaoguo*	腰果
chili peppers	*la jiao*	辣椒
chinese broccoli	*gailan*	芥蓝
cucumbers	*huang gua*	黄瓜
eggplants	*qie zi*	茄子
garlic stalks	*suan tai*	蒜台
ginger	*jiang*	姜
green peppers	*qing jiao*	青椒
green vegetables	*qing cai*	青菜
leeks	*da suan*	大蒜
longbeans	*dou jiao*	豆角
mushrooms	*mao gu*	蘑菇
napa cabbage	*bai cai*	白菜
peanuts	*huasheng*	花生
potatoes	*tu dou*	土豆
scallions	*cong*	葱
spinach	*bo cai*	菠菜
string beans	*si ji dou*	四季豆
sweet potatoes	*digua*	地瓜
tomatoes	*xi hong shi*	西红柿
turnips	*luobo*	萝卜
water spinach	*kong xin cai*	空心菜
yellow garlic chives	*jiu huang*	韭黄
yellow onions	*yang cong*	洋葱

Soups *Tang* 汤

hot & sour soup | *suanla tang* | 酸辣汤
eggflower soup | *danhua tang* | 蛋花汤
beancurd soup | *doufu tang* | 豆腐汤
Sichuan pork soup | *zhacairousitang* | 榨菜肉丝汤
snow cabbage & pork | *xuecairousi tang* | 雪菜肉丝汤
mushu soup | *mushu tang* | 木须汤

Cold mixes *Lung cai* 冷菜

beef with vinegar | *lu niu rou* | 卤牛肉
mixed cucumbers | *liangban huang gua* | 凉伴黄瓜
mixed eggplant | *liangban qiezi* | 凉伴茄子
fava beans | *mayou chandou* | 麻油蚕豆
anise peanuts | *lu huasheng* | 卤花生
fried peanuts | *zha huasheng* | 炸花生
sugar mixed tomatoes | *tangban xihongshi* | 糖伴西红柿
boiled shrimp | *zhu xiaren* | 煮虾仁
tofu noodles | *liangban gansi* | 凉伴干丝
peastarch noodles | *liangban fenpi* | 凉伴粉皮
pickled cabbage | *pao cai* | 泡菜

Egg dishes *Jidan cai* 鸡蛋菜

eggs with garlic chives | *jiuhuang chao dan* | 韭黄炒蛋
mushu pork | *mushu rou* | 木须肉
eggs with tomatoes | *fanqie chao dan* | 番茄炒蛋
omelette | *hong dan* | 烘蛋
fried eggs | *he bao dan* | 荷包蛋

Noodles *Mian* 面

pork chop noodles | *paigu mian* | 排骨面
chicken leg noodles | *jitui mian* | 鸡腿面
snow cabbage noodles | *xue cai rousi mian* | 雪菜肉丝面
Sichuan pork noodles | *zhacai rousi mian* | 榨菜肉丝面
beef noodles | *niurou mian* | 牛肉面
sesame noodles | *dan dan mian* | 单单面
mala noodles | *mala liang mian* | 麻辣凉面
meat sauce noodles | *zhajiang mian* | 炸酱面
fried noodles | *chao mian* | 炒面
soup noodles | *tang mian* | 汤面

Starchy foods   *Zhushi*   主食

North China

noodles, soupy	*tang mian*	汤面
noodles, fried	*chao mian*	炒面
noodles, sauced	*zhajiang mian*	炸酱面
noodles, hand-pulled	*shoulamian*	手拉面
crepes	*jianbing*	煎饼
flatbread	*shaobing*	烧饼
filled flatbread	*huoshao*	火烧
fried flatbread shreds	*chaobing*	炒饼
meat dumplings	*shuijiao*	水饺
thin pancakes	*bobing*	薄饼

South China & Taiwan

rice, plain	*fan*	饭
rice, fried	*chao fan*	炒饭
barbeque pork buns	*chashao bao*	叉烧包
egg crepes	*danbing*	蛋饼
wonton	*hundun*	馄饨
rice porridge	*xi fan*	稀饭
rice noodles	*mifen*	米粉
wide rice noodles	*hefen*	河粉
rice noodle rolls	*chongfen*	肠粉

Beverages   *Yinliao*   饮料

coffee	*kafei*	咖啡
black tea	*hong cha*	红茶
green tea	*lu cha*	绿茶
milk tea	*naicha*	奶茶
iced tea	*bing hong cha*	冰红茶
fruit juice	*shuiguo zhi*	水果汁
haw juice	*shanzha zhi*	山楂汁
beer	*pijiu*	啤酒
wine, rice	*huang jiu*	黄酒
wine, grape	*putao jiu*	葡萄酒
distilled spirits	*bai jiu*	白酒
soda	*qi shui*	汽水
cola	*kele*	可乐
boiled water	*kai shui*	开水

Breakfast foods	*Zaodian*	早点
wonton in soup	*hundun tang*	馄饨汤
crepes	*jianbing*	煎饼
egg crepes	*danbing*	蛋饼
rice porridge	*xifan*	稀饭
pickles for porridge	*xian cai*	咸菜
pork buns	*rou bao*	肉饱
pan fried dumplings	*sheng jian bao*	生煎饱
savory soy milk	*xian doujiang*	咸豆浆
sweet soy milk	*tian doujiang*	甜豆浆
fried doughsticks	*youtiao*	油条
baked biscuits	*shaobing*	烧饼
rice noodle rolls	*chongfen*	肠粉
sesame noodles	*majiang mian*	麻酱面
scallion oil cake	*congyoubing*	葱油饼

Ices	*Bing*	冰
fruit ice	*shuiguo bing*	水果冰
four fruit ice	*siguo bing*	四果冰
pudding ice	*bu ding bing*	布丁冰
ice cream	*bingqiling*	冰淇淋

Lodging

22. We'd like a room for ( ) people.
Women yao yijian ( ) ren fang.
我们要一间( )人房。

23. We want a bed for each person.
Women yao meige ren yige chuangwei.
我们要每个人一个床位。

24. We want the whole room to ourself, not together with others.
Women yao zhu baofang, buyao gen bieren tongzhu.
我们要住包房，不要跟别人同住。

25. We'll take any room you have, **regardless of quality.**
    Ruguo meiyou haoyidiande fangjian, putongde ye keyi.
    如果没有好一点的房间，普通的也可以。

26. We want to stay for (   ) nights.
    Women yao zhu (   ) wanshang.
    我们要住( )晚上。

27. What is the price per night?
    Zhege fangjian yige wanshang duoshao qian?
    这个房间一个晚上多少钱？

28. Please write down our total bill in advance.
    Qing shixian xiexialai zong jiage.
    请事先写下来总价格。

29. Do you have anything a little better?
    Youmeiyou haoyixie de fangjian?
    有没有好一些的房间？

30. Do you have any cheaper rooms?
    Youmeiyou bijiao pianyide fangjian?
    有没有比较便宜的房间？

31. Can you give us a cheaper price?
    Nengbuneng suan pianyi yidian?
    能不能算便宜一点？

32. Is it OK to camp here?
    Women xiang zai zheli luying, xingbuxing?
    我们想在这里露营，行不行？

33. Do you have a city tourist map for sale?
    Zheli youmeiyou mai shiquditu?
    这里有没有卖市区地图？

34. The luggage isn't easily removed from the bikes. We need to take our bikes to our room, OK?
Zhege xingli burongyi cong dancheshang chaixialai. Women yao ba danche dai dao fang li zai chai, xingma?
这个行李不容易从单车上拆下来，我们要把单车带到房里再拆，行吗？

35. Where shall we store our bikes?
Chezi yinggai fang zai nali?
车子应该放在那里？

36. What time does the hot water come on?
Ji dian zhong you re shui xi zao?
几点钟有热水洗澡？

37. Please get me some toilet paper, OK?
Qing gei wo yixie weishengzhi, hao ma?
请给我一些卫生纸，好吗？

38. We need another thermos of boiled water.
Qing zai gei women yiping re kaishui.
请再给我们一瓶热开水。

39. Please refund our room deposit.
Qing ba yajin huan gei women.
请把押金还给我们。

40 Can we make an international direct dial phone call from here?
Zai zheli nengbuneng zhibo guoji dianhua?
在这里能不能直拨国际电话？

41. Since there are no rooms here, will you help us find a room in another hotel?
Jiran zheli meiyou fangjian, nengbuneng bang women lingwai zhao yige difang?
既然这里没有房间，能不能帮我们另外找一个地方？

42. Please call them and ask if they have rooms available. Thanks!
Qing bang women dayigedianhua, kankan tamen youmeiyou kungde fangjian. Xiexie ni!
请帮我们打一个电话，看看他们有没有空的房间。谢谢您！

43. How do we get there from here? Please draw us a map.
Cong zheli dao nali zemme zou? Qing gei women hua yige ditu.
从这里到那里怎么走？请给我们画一个地图。

hotel	*fandian*	饭店
guesthouse	*binguan*	宾馆
inn	*luguan*	旅馆
hostel	*zhaodaisuo*	招待所
room with bath	*biaojunfang*	标准房
bathroom	*weishengjian*	卫生间
dormitory	*sushe*	宿舍
restaurant	*canting, canguan*	餐厅，餐馆
winehouse	*jiujia*	酒家
men's	*nande*	男的
women's	*nude*	女的

Dealing with the Gong An

44. We'll be leaving tomorrow.
Women mingtian jiu likai zheli.
我们明天就离开这里。

45. We are going to (　　) and didn't know this area was closed.
Women benlai yao qu (　　), buzhidao zheli bushi kaifa diqu.
我们本来要去(　　)不知道这里不是开发地区。

46. Can you suggest the best route out?
Qing gaosu women likai zheli yao zou naitiao lu zui hao.
请告诉我们离开这里要走那条路最好？

47. We'll stay inside the hotel compound if that's necessary.
Women keyi liu zai luguan, buyao chuqu.
我们可以留在旅馆，不要出去。

Changing Money

48. Can you change some currency for us?
Ni nengbuneng gei women huan yixie qian?
你能不能给我们换些钱？

49. Please write how much RMB you will exchange for US$ 100.
Meijin yibai kuai huan duoshao renminbi? Qing ni xiexialai.
美金一百块换多少人民币？请你写下来。

50. I want to count it myself before giving you my cash.
Women xian suan RMB cai ba meijin gei ni.
我们先算人民币才把美金给你。

Transportation

51. Where can we buy ferry tickets?
Yinggai qu nali mai chuanpiao?
应该去那里卖船票？

52. We want ( ) first class boat tickets to ( ).
Women yao mai ( ) zhang dao ( ) de yideng chuanpiao.
我们要卖( )张到( )的一等船票。

53. How much per ticket?
Mei zhang chuanpiao duoshao qian?
每张船票多少钱？

54. What is the charge per bike for shipping?
Meiliang danche de yunfei yao duoshao?
每辆单车的运费要多少？

55. Can you upgrade our tickets to a better class of cabin?
Nengbuneng bu piao huan yige hao yi dian de chuancang?
能不能补票换一个好一点的船舱？

Purchases

56. I need to make some copies. Is there a copy service here?
Women xuyao yingyin. Zheli youmeiyou yingyin fuwu?
我们需要影印。这里有没有影印服务？

57. How much for a haircut?
Jian toufa yao duoshao qian?
剪头发要多少钱？

58. I want to buy that. Please write down the price.
Wo yao mai nage. Qing xiexialai duoshao qian.
我要买那个。请写下来多少钱。

Everyday Items

shampoo	*xifajing*	洗发精
soap	*feizao*	肥皂
laundry soap	*xiyifen*	洗衣粉
toothpaste	*yagao*	牙膏
instant noodles	*paomian*	泡面
instant coffee	*surong kafei*	速溶咖啡
milk powder	*niunai fen*	牛奶粉
sugar	*tang*	糖
tea leaves	*cha ye*	茶叶
towel	*maojing*	毛巾
rain cape	*yu yi*	雨衣
toilet paper	*weishengzhi*	卫生纸
kerosene	*meiyu*	煤油
unleaded gas	*wuqianqiyu*	无铅汽油

Directions

59. Please view this map. What is our current location?
Qing kankan zhezhang ditu. Women xianzai de didian zai nali?
请看看这张地图，我们现在的地点在那里？

60. Which direction is it to (   )?
Qu (   ) yinggai zou shenme fangxiang?
去(   )应该走什么方向？

61. Which way to the Beijing Shoudu airport?
    Dao Beijing Shoudu jichang yinggai zemme zou?
    到北京首都机场应该怎么走？

62. We're hungry. Can you take us to a nearby restaurant?
    Women yao chi fan. Nengbuneng dai women qu yige canting?
    我们要去吃饭，能不能带我们去一个餐厅？

62. We're looking for lodging. Could you point out a nearby inn?
    Women xuyao zhusu de difang. Zhe fujin youmeiyou luguan?
    我们需要住宿的地方。这附近有没有旅馆？

63. Please direct me to a night market for street food.
    Qing nin gaosu wo, zheli de yeshichang zai nali? Zemme qu?
    请您告诉我，这里的夜市场在那里？怎么去？

64. Where's the nearest toilet?
    Zui jin de cesuo zai nali?
    最近的厕所在那里？

65. Write your address clearly and I'll send you a photograph.
    Qing ba nide dizhi qingchude xiexialai, wo hui ji zhaopian gei ni.
    请把你的地址清楚地写下来，我会寄照片给你。

66. Please write clearly the answer to this question.
    Wo ganggang wen ni de wenti, qing ni ba daan qingchude xiexialai.
    我刚刚问你的问题，请把答案清楚的写下来。

Geographic terms

east	*dong*	东
south	*nan*	南
west	*xi*	西
north	*bei*	北
road	*lu, jie, dao*	路，街，道
intersection	*lukou*	路口
expressway	*gaosu gonglu*	高速公路
slow lane	*manchedao*	慢车道

bus station	*qiche zhan*	汽车站
train station	*huoche zhan*	火车站
city	*shi*	市
township	*zhen*	镇
village	*cun, zhuang*	村，庄
country village area	*xiang*	乡
county	*xian*	县
province	*sheng*	省
lake	*hu*	湖
mountain	*shan*	山
river	*he*	河
creek	*xi*	溪
bridge	*qiao*	桥
atlas by province	*fensheng gonglu dituci*	分省公路地图册
map of Guangdong	*Guangdong sheng ditu*	广东省地图
map of Jiangsu	*Jiangsu sheng ditu*	江苏省地图
map of Zhejiang	*Zhejiang sheng ditu*	浙江省地图
map of Shandong	*Shandong sheng ditu*	山东省地图
map of Hebei	*Hebei sheng ditu*	河北省地图
map of Beijing	*Beijing shi ditu*	北京市地图
map of Taiwan	*Taiwan ditu*	台湾地图

Have a good journey!
Yi lu ping an!

一路平安

SIGNS

餐馆
Restaurant

旅馆
Inn

公厕
Public Restrooms

饭店
Hotel

男
Men

女
Women

宾馆
Guesthouse

停吃住
Stop, Eat, Sleep

餐厅
Dining Hall

INDEX

I

inns 48, 50

J

Jiangsu Province 158
Jiaozhou 196
Jingan 133, 136
Jinghai 227, 229

K

Kai Tak Airport 120, 123
Kaiping 139, 142
Keelung 67
Kenting 88, 101
Kenting National Park 104
Kinshan 60, 61, 66
Kowloon 121
Kukuan 77
Kunshan 164, 168

L

Langfang 229, 234
language 51–52
Lantau Island 120, 123
laundry service 35
Lishan 77
Liukuei 107
lodging 50
lost, what to do when 54
luggage 31–32
lunch 44, 47

M

Macao 15–16, 128, 131, 135
Macao Ferry 129
mail 22–23
maintenance, bicycle 32–33
map legend 56
maps 21–22
Mazhan 201
Ming Tombs 239, 246
money 36–39
Muslim food 224

N

navigation tools 30–31, 53–54
Ningbo 158, 160, 190, 192

O

Oluanpi 101

P

panniers 31
passports 18, 51
Pearl River Delta 128, 130
People's Republic of China 17–18
phraseguide 52
Pingtung 88, 102, 105
police 40–41
political subdivisions 55
pronunciation, Chinese 52
Purple Sand First Teapot Factory 177

Q

Qingdao 193, 195
Qingyun 222
Qixingyan 144, 146
Qixingyan Park 128

R

rain gear 33
repairs, bicycle 32
research, travel 19–21
road conditions 41–42
route log legend 56
route logs 53

S

safety, traffic 41–42
security, personal 39–40
Shandong 193, 213
Shanghai 158, 163
Shanghai Hongqiao Airpor 162
Shaoxing 160, 184, 188
signs, road 53, 55

About the Author

After two years of Chinese language study at the University of California at Santa Cruz, Roger Grigsby lived in Taiwan for a year, where he met his future wife, April Shen, and got hooked on Chinese food. In 1979 he started the O'mei Restaurant in Santa Cruz, and has been serving Sichuan-style Chinese cuisine to the community ever since.

When Grigsby purchased an Alex Moulton bicycle in 1988 he had no bicycle touring experience. He wanted to explore his old stomping grounds around Taipei, and needed a cycling guidebook for the area. When he found that there weren't any such guides available, it was obvious that something had to be done to correct the situation! More than five years and 8,000 touring miles in the Orient went into producing *China by Bike*.

Grigsby continues to do at least one long cycle tour each year.

THE MOUNTAINEERS, founded in 1906, is a nonprofit outdoor activity and conservation club, whose mission is "to explore, study, preserve, and enjoy the natural beauty of the outdoors...." Based in Seattle, Washington, the club is now the third-largest such organization in the United States, with 14,000 members and four branches throughout Washington State.

The Mountaineers sponsors both classes and year-round outdoor activities in the Pacific Northwest, which include hiking, mountain climbing, ski-touring, snowshoeing, bicycling, camping, kayaking and canoeing, nature study, sailing, and adventure travel. The club's conservation division supports environmental causes through educational activities, sponsoring legislation, and presenting informational programs. All club activities are led by skilled, experienced volunteers, who are dedicated to promoting safe and responsible enjoyment and preservation of the outdoors.

The Mountaineers Books, an active, nonprofit publishing program of the club, produces guidebooks, instructional texts, historical works, natural history guides, and works on environmental conservation. All books produced by The Mountaineers are aimed at fulfilling the club's mission.

If you would like to participate in these organized outdoor activities or the club's programs, consider a membership in The Mountaineers. For information and an application, write or call The Mountaineers, Club Headquarters, 300 Third Avenue West, Seattle, Washington 98119; (206) 284-6310.

Send or call for our catalog of more than 300 outdoor books:
The Mountaineers Books
1011 SW Klickitat Way, Suite 107
Seattle, WA 98134
1(800)553-4453